HEAD HUNTERS

I0895444

JAZZ PERSPECTIVES

Lewis Porter, Series General Editor

Open the Door: The Life and Music of Betty Carter
By William R. Bauer

Jazz Journeys to Japan: The Heart Within
By William Minor

Four Jazz Lives By A. B. Spellman

Head Hunters: *The Making of Jazz's First Platinum Album*
By Steven F. Pond

Lester Young By Lewis Porter

OTHER BOOKS OF INTEREST

Before Motown: A History of Jazz in Detroit 1920–1960
By Lars Bjorn with Jim Gallert

John Coltrane: His Life and Music
By Lewis Porter

Charlie Parker: His Music and Life
By Carl Woideck

The Song of the Hawk:
The Life and Recordings of Coleman Hawkins
By John Chilton

Rhythm Man: Fifty Years in Jazz
By Steve Jordan with Tom Scanlan

Let the Good Times Roll:
The Story of Louis Jordan and His Music
By John Chilton

Twenty Years on Wheels
By Andy Kirk as Told to Amy Lee

HEAD HUNTERS

The Making of Jazz's First Platinum Album

Steven F. Pond

University of Michigan Press
Ann Arbor

First paperback edition 2010
Copyright © by the University of Michigan 2005
All rights reserved
Published in the United States of America by the
University of Michigan Press
Manufactured in the United States of America
∞ Printed on acid-free paper

2013 2012 2011 2010 5 4 3 2

No part of this publication may be reproduced,
stored in a retrieval system, or transmitted in any form
or by any means, electronic, mechanical, or otherwise,
without the written permission of the publisher.

A CIP catalog record for this book is available from the British Library.

Library of Congress Cataloging-in-Publication Data

Pond, Steven F., 1951–
Head hunters : the making of jazz's first platinum album /
Steven F. Pond.
p. cm. — (Jazz perspectives)
Includes bibliographical references (p.) and discography (p.).
ISBN-13: 978-0-472-11417-7 (cloth : alk. paper)
ISBN-10: 0-472-11417-4 (cloth : alk. paper)
1. Hancock, Herbie, 1940– Head hunters. 2. Jazz-rock (Music)—
United States—History and criticism. I. Title.
II. Series: Jazz perspectives (Ann Arbor, Mich.)

ML417.H23P66 2005
781.65'7—dc22 2005014482

ISBN 978-0-472-03448-2

For Susan, Rachel, Heather, and Mackenzie,
with all my love.

Contents

Preface

"Should you be talking, really, about 'fusion'? Isn't it really 'fusing'?" This is the point that Olly Wilson raised with me some years ago as we discussed how to categorize the music that *Head Hunters* "belongs" to. Although it isn't possible to avoid using *some* noun to describe the music (I call it *fusion jazz*), Wilson did steer me away from restricting my research to a genre (or better put, a construction) and instead encouraged me to concentrate on the activity behind it. At its most basic level, this book is about the various kinds of fusing activity that resulted in *Head Hunters*. Beyond the topic of the album, or even of fusion jazz, this book addresses the way we think about music-making, musical reception, and jazz historiography. Jazz (and, I think, music in general) is largely collaborative and happens at the nexus of a host of interactions, between musicians on the stage or in the studio. Nuances of performance, a nod across the stage, a sudden breath taken by the bassist, a surprising turn of phrase that elicits a response, or just knowing your bandmates' style so well that you can anticipate their musical moves—these important parts of jazz elude capture on the page. Feeding into these moments of musical expression are the equipment with which musicians play and record players' relationships with promoters and labels, their affections, and their politics. The more we know about who the musicians are—how they come to be playing together; what skills, personal quirks, philosophies, tastes, friendships, education, childhoods, repertoire knowledge, and other backgrounds they bring to the project; and how these backgrounds intersect with our own array—the better we can understand the notes we hear.

The body of literature on fusion jazz is frustratingly small, especially considering the impact—musical, social, and industrial—of groups and artists such as Return To Forever, Weather Report, Lifetime, the Mahavishnu Orchestra, Stanley Clarke, Jean-Luc Ponty, George Duke, Jack DeJohnette, Larry Coryell, and Herbie Hancock. Stuart Nicholson's groundbreaking history, *Jazz-Rock*, adds a wealth of background information and identifies significant trends, and Julie Coryell and Laura Friedman's book of short interviews, *Jazz-Rock Fusion: The People, The Music*, allows the music's story to be told by a spectrum of musicians in their own words.[1] Valuable as these resources are, they also point out the need for additional, focused studies.

In working on this book, I bumped into the deep reservations and indecision that some in the jazz community hold about discussing fusion whatsoever. The controversy surrounding this music, and people's discomfort at dealing with the commercial aspects of any music, became one of the most tempting aspects of *Head Hunters* to explore. The album's conspicuous success brings this discomfort into sharp focus. Released on October 13, 1973, *Head Hunters* debuted on the *Billboard* Top 200 chart on January 12, 1974. Another leading chart, the *Cash Box* Album Top 175 chart, debuted the *Head Hunters* album on January 26, 1974; the album stayed on that list for thirty-five weeks, peaking at number 10.

In another big-picture measure of consumer popularity, the Recording Industry Association of America (RIAA) certifies record sales and bestows gold and platinum awards to recordings that post sales of five hundred thousand and one million units, respectively.[2] The association certified the album as gold on April 23, 1974; twelve years later, *Head Hunters* went platinum, on December 21, 1986.[3] By way of comparison, Miles Davis's *Bitches Brew* boasted three hundred thousand unit sales during its first year.

The single "Chameleon" appeared on the *Billboard* Top R&B Singles chart on February 23, 1974, rising to number 18 during its sixteen-week run. It debuted on the *Billboard* Hot 100 chart on March 23, climbing to number 42 over its eleven-week chart life.[4] "Chameleon," its sales tracked separately from the album, was never certified for an award by the RIAA. *Billboard* chart researcher Joel Whitburn rates Hancock as the 251st best-selling album artist of all time (regardless of music category), largely on the strength of *Head Hunters* (forty-seven weeks on the Top 500 chart) and 1983's *Future Shock* (sixty-two weeks on the chart).[5]

Again, to put these figures into perspective, Miles Davis's sales blockbuster *Bitches Brew*, released in early 1970, also earned a gold record—but not until six years after its release, on May 13, 1976. And Davis's 1959 *Kind of Blue* (now the overall record holder in jazz sales) achieved gold status on October 8, 1993, going on to multiplatinum status (three million units) on January 16, 1997. *Kind of Blue*'s gold status, then, was reached after thirty-four years, a mark *Head Hunters* achieved in less than six months. Sales statistics only tell a fraction of the story, but in many ways they stimulate and challenge our thought processes about how we "bag" the music, by what measure and why.

Two notable bits of album trivia should be covered at this point. First, authors, discographers, the musicians, and virtually everyone else connected directly to the album refer to it as *Headhunters*. The album's official title, though, is *Head Hunters*. The two-word title apparently originated in Columbia Records' art department.[6] The subtle spacing between "Head" and "Hunters" on the album cover somehow translated to the two-word title when the album was released. Subsequently the musicians released several albums under the name "the Headhunters"—with and without Hancock. For clarity, I refer to the 1973 album as *Head Hunters* and to the group—whose name remained unambiguous—as the Headhunters. Second, although the exact recording and mixing dates are unknown for the album, David Rubinson, its producer, told me that the recording took a single week; Herbie Hancock recalls this as happening in late August or early September 1973.

This book exists, first, to tell the story of the musicians and how they found themselves in the studio, producing an album of landmark importance. Whenever possible, their words speak instead of mine. Always, in writing the book, I have kept four kinds of readers in mind: jazz fans, jazz aficionados, scholars from a range of disciplines, and not least the musicians and other people who figure so prominently in the album's history. None of this would have been possible without the story's central figures. I have tried to make it possible to read the book without looking at the endnotes; however, explanations of terms or background that would require too long a digression in the text have been placed in the notes. Likewise, I have tried to keep the cultural studies and music technical jargon to a minimum.

Numerous people helped me to bring this project forward. First and foremost, my deepest thanks go to Herbie Hancock, Fred Catero, Patrick Gleeson, Bob James, Bruce Lundvall, Bennie Maupin, David Rubinson, Vernon Slaughter, and Bill Summers for their insights, as well as their generosity of time and spirit in consenting to be interviewed, helping clarify points along the way, and connecting up missing links. Also, the mentorship and support of Ben Brinner, Jocelyne Guilbault, C. K. Ladzekpo, Bonnie Wade, and particularly Olly Wilson, all at the University of California, Berkeley, will never be forgotten. All of my Cornell University colleagues have been helpful and supportive in many ways. I would like especially to thank Lenore Coral, Becky Harris-Warrick, Marty Hatch, Judith Peraino, Nick Salvatore, Mark Scatterday, James Webster, and Neal Zaslaw for many stimulating conversations, for generously sharing their ideas, and for their nuts-and-bolts administrative support. Mark DeWitt, Danielle Fosler-Lussier, Travis Jackson, Beth Levy, and Steven Swayne have all contributed valuable feedback to this work at various stages. I would also like to thank my seminar students for their many contributions of perspective, particularly Bethany Collier, Steve Curtis, Lisa Feder, Yotam Haber, and Nick Wille. Thanks also go to my colleagues in the Society for Ethnomusicology and the International Association for the Study of Popular Music, who heard early versions of my work and whose lively discussions added much to it, as well as to Cornell's music department and its Africana Studies program, where portions of this work were discussed in colloquia.

Finally, my editors at the University of Michigan Press—Lewis Porter, the series editor, and Chris Hebert—have been patient, perceptive, and exacting, much to the book's benefit. Nor could I have embarked on, much less completed, this work without the support of my extended family, in particular my parents and parents-in-law, William and Eloise Pond and Roland and Virginia Evans; my daughters, Rachel and Heather, and their spouses, Isaac Camero and Steve Lacey; and my son, Mackenzie, who tolerated this rather large wrinkle rolling through our family lives. Luckily, my grandchildren, Lorenzo and Naomi, were beacons of joy but had to endure little of my preoccupation. Most of all, I thank my wife, Susan, whose contribution cannot begin to be calculated.

CHAPTER 1

Fusion Jazz and the HEAD HUNTERS Project

Did Herbie Hancock need the money? When Mongo Santamaria covered Hancock's modest hit "Watermelon Man" in 1963, Santamaria earned a gold record, selling over five hundred thousand copies, a rarity in jazz. The song's wild popularity spawned more than two hundred cover versions. Hancock's composer royalties blossomed, to say the least.

Was he chasing fame? By the time he joined the great Miles Davis quintet of the mid-sixties, Herbie Hancock already carried enfant terrible status in the jazz world. At the time of his departure from the group as a regular member in 1968, critics and readers' polls alike were pegging Hancock in the topmost ranks of the jazz pantheon. Over the next few years, his reputation as an avant-garde experimentalist also grew.

Hancock had royalties and jazz credentials in his pocket. But neither guaranteed audiences or ticket sales at a time when jazz audiences of all stripes were shrinking. Then in November 1973, he released *Head Hunters*, a recording that would gain acclaim, at least until the decade's end, as the best-selling jazz album of all time and paradoxically be castigated as a musical sellout, not jazz at all.[1]

During his forty-plus-year career, the jazz press, musicians, and not least Miles Davis himself have lionized Hancock.[2] He has held influential roles in multiple jazz streams. First gaining prominence playing soul jazz in the early sixties, his modal excursions in Davis's quintet placed him as one of jazz's top pianists by the decade's end. Hancock's early post-Davis experiments with his avant-garde Mwandishi group have recently been rediscovered by a new generation of jazz students.[3] And the neo-bebop movement that has dominated jazz since the eighties owes some of its early impetus to Hancock's mid-seventies reunion group, V.S.O.P. Yet throughout these years, he drew fire for veering periodically from the true jazz path. An early digression, *Fat Albert Rotunda* (1969), was excused as a big band, R&B romp, a lighthearted score for Bill Cosby's cartoon character. The biggest jolt, Hancock's hip-hop song "Rockit" (*Future Shock*, 1983), one of the first songs by a black artist to get major MTV exposure, left Hancock's jazz purist audience stunned and irate. If "Rockit" marked Hancock's resolute departure from jazz, purists saw *Head Hunters* as the fork in the road, the spot where Hancock strayed. *Head Hunters*, not the modal *Maiden Voyage* (1965), nor the avant-garde *Mwandishi* (1971), nor even any of the albums recorded with the Davis quintets, brought Hancock the most visibility, financial rewards, and assuredly, controversy.

Critical reception was and remains sharply divided. *Head Hunters'* popularity signaled either a jazz victory, staking a claim to new territory, or a jazz catastrophe. For some, it marked a serious downward slide for jazz aesthetics, a tailspin precipitated by fusion jazz's fixation on commercial success.[4] For denigrators of the album and the genre, marketing stayed in the foreground, a prime motivation behind the music and, thus, the source of its shame. Fusion lovers, on the other hand, seemed carefully to avoid stepping in the mud of commercialism. For them, fusion jazz was about art and jaw-dropping virtuosity, not sales figures. These rifts have only deepened with time.

Which view of Hancock and *Head Hunters*—art driven or commerce compromised—carries the greater truth? Can art be considered separately from commerce? The *Head Hunters* controversy highlights a larger ellipse in jazz histories. Generally, chops have been analyzed and stories told with slender consideration of the market.[5] When commerce is mentioned at all, it is often with distaste and circumspection. In reality, however, fusion jazz, and jazz generally, operates within an artistic apparatus *and* a commercial one, shaped and channeled by other realms of influence and interchange as well.

Contesting the Borders of Jazz

Was fusion jazz the "path of the sellout" or a shining new direction in jazz history?[6] These fiercely conflicting attitudes about fusion jazz show up in a variety of ill-fitting, idiosyncratic labels for the music. The fight over what music fits within these labels—even which labels to use—is agitated by a long history of dispute over the definition of jazz itself.

When the subject of fusion arises, whether in the popular press, scholarly literature, or insider conversations, reliable combinations of names and albums pop up: Miles Davis's *Bitches Brew*, *Birds of Fire* by the Mahavishnu Orchestra, Weather Report's *I Sing the Body Electric*, Return to Forever's *Hymn of the Seventh Galaxy*, and Herbie Hancock's *Head Hunters*, all of which were released in the first three years of the seventies.[7] These albums do more than occupy space within the same genre; they act as a shorthand reference to describe its core. Why then do they sound so different from each other? Why do they use largely different instrumentation, derive from different musical influences, and appeal to different audiences? If the *core* is so hard to nail down stylistically, how tenuously must the genre's outer reaches relate to this core and to each other?

The musical factors for grouping these albums together seem slippery. What besides these factors may have motivated disparate observers to construct or perpetuate this grouping? Are internal musical features the only criteria, or even the best criteria, to use in judging genre membership? Beyond the music, were there other, extramusical reasons to cluster these albums together, such as their markets or means of production?

Answers may lie not in what draws the albums together musically but in *why* and *by whom* they are set apart, collectively, from the rest of jazz. For example, jazz historian Grover Sales describes the birth of "jazz-rock fusion," saying: "Some bored rock artists had been gravitating toward jazz, while some jazz players dallied with rock to recapture their dwindling audience."[8] He thus dismisses jazz-rock fusion as a marriage of convenience, a Faustian bargain for market share by jazz artists, who seem to have been poor but not bored. Yet even if denigrating the music, Sales does not altogether sever it from jazz. Others do.

"Whatever it is, it ain't jazz," is more than a street characterization. Wynton Marsalis, director of Jazz at the Lincoln Center for the Performing Arts, executive advisor for the Ken Burns *Jazz* project, and for many the public face of jazz, has become a prominent spokesperson for this point of view.[9] In his book *Sweet Swing Blues on the Road*, Marsalis answers a fictional interviewer posing questions on what jazz is and who gets to say so. Jazz, to Marsalis, is defined nightly on the bandstand by "real jazz musicians, who can swing and play some blues."[10] He pointedly excludes avant-gardists Anthony Braxton, Cecil Taylor, and the Art Ensemble of Chicago (A.E.C.), as well as fusion jazz players like Steve Coleman, David Sanborn, and Miles Davis, pointing to statements by them that, as he tells it, "they don't play jazz and don't want to. It's the critics who insist that their music is jazz."[11]

But the book's fictitious interviewer cannot point out that Marsalis's jazz sine qua non, to "swing and play some blues," is not universally accepted. Marsalis misrepresents the contexts of these musicians' statements. Braxton, members of the A.E.C., and Davis have all argued forcefully that the word *jazz* is not a standard they seek to measure themselves against but is instead a critical category imposed from outside the musician's perspective.[12] On this point at least, they agree with Marsalis: it's the critics, rather than these musicians, who insist that their music is jazz. Where they disagree is regarding the amount of reverence and fixity awarded the term. To these musicians, jazz as a category confines them to a second-tier artistic status, too pretentious to be popularly relevant but too populist for the European elite. The problem, to them, is that restricting themselves to "jazz" not only confines them stylistically but also exposes their music to the charge of being *merely* jazz, described as such because of their music's focus on improvisation, and therefore not easily analyzable in ways acceptable to the art-music academy.

Positioning jazz in an elite musical tier is certainly central to the add-on tag "America's classical music," a characterization that has gathered momentum, particularly since the fifties. Jazz pianist, composer, and educator Billy Taylor, whose early and sustained advocacy of the term links him closely with it, articulates why jazz partisans guard this version of jazz identity so religiously. "Jazz is America's classical music," he writes, "yet many Americans have been consistent in their bias against it." Taylor points with pride to the idea that African Americans "producing music which expressed themselves . . . created a *classical* music—an authentic *American* music which articulated uniquely American feelings and thoughts, which eventually came to transcend ethnic boundaries."[13] Jazz historian Grover Sales, in his popular book *Jazz: America's Classical Music*, develops the term as a major theme, as do Ken Burns and Wynton Marsalis.[14] Nevertheless, Taylor knows all too well that jazz sits a rung lower on the social-status ladder than its European counterpart. The values he packs into this label—American cultural nationalism, high-art identification, the black tradition from which jazz springs, and the importance of the inclusion of jazz in higher education—have only partially penetrated the mainstream. The push toward mainstream recognition for African Americans' high-art accomplishments by means of such a term, however, has had an unintended side effect: consideration for inclusion is too often restricted to those accomplishments that fit comfortably within a prepackaged understanding of what "high art" or "classical" means.

True, jazz has made it into the academy, but with qualifications. There is an increased presence of jazz greats on campus; Max Roach, Anthony Braxton, Kenny Burrell, and David Baker come to mind. But the overwhelming majority of these musicians enter the academy through a side door, as instructors or artists-in-residence. Combined with the persistent shortage of jazz musicians pursuing doctoral degrees, the sine qua non for professorial status, jazz musicians in the academy occupy a shadowy rank. Yet university music departments and music schools that offer courses on jazz keep largely to degree paths in performance and music education (i.e., they mostly offer master of musical arts or master of musical education degree programs). Despite the enthusiastic inclusion of jazz performance curricula at the undergraduate level, jazz history and culture are seldom taught beyond a survey course, the jazz equivalent to Music Appreciation. Jazz theory education, when offered, has traditionally mirrored the Western kind, with much attention placed on harmony and melody and little enough, for example, on the role of expressive timbres.[15] Even if casting jazz as America's classical music presents it at the topmost tier of African American traditions and provides a space for American cultural nationalism, jazz still encounters a glass ceiling, keeping it from true parity with European elite tradition. Demonstrating the depth of this separation, Sales recalls Leonard Bernstein's well-meaning but patronizing statement that "serious music [*sic*] in America today would have a different complexion and direction were it not for the profound influence upon it of jazz."[16]

Considering these glass ceilings, defensive postures in jazz literature are understandable, and even more understandable is the attempt to keep at arm's length anything that disrupts jazz's association with artistic seriousness. Marsalis, Sales, and others group *Head Hunters* away from jazz and together with other albums heavily marketed to an expanded audience that includes more white, middle-class pop listeners and youth generally; in doing so, they promote the same kind of distance between what they characterize as jazz's core and fusion that classical music partisans have maintained between their music and jazz. My point is not to focus on the specifics of Marsalis's "swing and play some blues" limitation, or on Sales's dismissal of jazz-rock, but on the subtext of exclusivity and the fear of taint implied in their arguments. Anxieties over contamination (by unconventional musical features? popularity? marketing? interloping ethnicities? nationality?) ignore the musical facts. Jazz, in reality, is music not of exclusion but of expansion, engaging many historical and cultural intersections. The tension between jazz musicians' attraction to kaleidoscopic stylistic interactions and an ongoing battle for jazz's cultural ownership takes place across four main fields: ethnicity, region, class, and generation.

From its earliest days forward, jazz has represented an engagement between African and European aesthetic orientations, naturally weighted to African Americans as originators of the engagement. Answering the question of "how closely jazz [is] bound up with the experience of African Americans," Wynton Marsalis aptly answers: "It's inseparable—in its inception. They created it."[17] Racist resistance to jazz early on has eventually given way to acceptance, popularization, adoption, and finally internalization by mainstream whites, in waves of enthusiasm since the 1920s. To many black jazz musicians, these enthusiasms, these aesthetic internalizations, result in cultural and economic appropriation, the love that kills.[18]

In response, black musicians periodically have forcefully reasserted jazz's black pedigree—seen, for example, in the racial politics surrounding bebop in the forties, hard bop in the fifties, and avant-garde jazz in the sixties—discomfiting many of its non-black, and even non-American, musicians and fans.[19] Jazz's steadily whitening audience and the legions of non-black students in the nation's college jazz programs heighten this defensiveness. Non-black musicians and aficionados, not wanting to see themselves as stealing another's cultural tradition, nonetheless assert a sense of ownership over their own creative output.[20] Musicians who cry foul over Crow Jim, or reverse discrimination, likely have so thoroughly internalized jazz's African-based engagement with European music that they *can* think of it as beyond race. But to African American musicians, the tradition remains African American, no matter who plays the music.

Complicating this picture further, African diasporic influences range beyond a strictly U.S. regional framework. The "Spanish tinge" described by Jelly Roll Morton, and rechristened the "Latin tinge" by John Storm Roberts, is more than a veneer.[21] Despite the small attention paid to the Latin influence in jazz, it has permeated the music since its ragtime beginnings, a fact that points up a diasporic connection in jazz generally. Also an engagement between European- and African-based aesthetics, the Latin tinge in jazz incorporates one European-African engagement into another, through the lens of Afro-Caribbean people who have made their own, regional set of adjustments. All of these aesthetic engagements act in musical and cultural intersection.

Jazz's contested ethnicity is complicated by its class ambiguity. Jazz lore celebrates the fact that the music produced by America's most downtrodden underclass proved resilient enough to become hugely influential across the globe by the end of the twentieth century. This celebratory posture masks defensiveness over jazz's social position. Ever since New York socialites trooped over to Harlem's nightclubs in the twenties, jazz has maintained a mutually uneasy attraction with America's elite class. Grover Sales, saying that neither the public nor the musical establishment could take completely seriously a music associated with hedonism—"How could you be 'serious' and have such a screaming good time?"—goes on to proclaim jazz's eventual elevation ("America's classical music").[22] Yet in the United States, jazz faces long-term, unresolved issues of race and class. Class ambivalence shows up in the kinds and locations of jazz venues, the spotty public funding for jazz musicians, and the demographic extremes of its audience.[23] The resolute procession to respectability that Sales suggests underplays the complexity of the journey and the elusiveness of the destination.

Generational conflict also plays a crucial role in jazz's—and fusion jazz's—identity. Bernard Gendron investigates a recurring generational struggle, as of the forties, through two propaganda wars between modernism and revivalism, the first between proponents of swing ("modernists") and proponents of the New Orleans–style jazz of the twenties (revivalists, or "moldy figs"): "These purists [revivalists, ca. 1942] were driven not only by nostalgia but by revulsion toward the swing music industry, which by shamelessly pandering to the mass markets had in their eyes forsaken the principles of 'true' jazz."[24] A second war emerged shortly thereafter: "By 1946 . . . modernism was now being represented by the bebop school . . . while swing music suddenly found itself . . . on the side of the traditional and the tried-and-true."[25]

Bebop dripped youthful exuberance. Key musicians, Dizzy Gillespie, Charlie Parker, Miles Davis, and Howard McGhee among them, turned the jazz world on its ear while they were in their early twenties. By the fifties, a new war of words had broken out. Bebop, by now slightly long in the tooth, splintered into factions. (Mis)categorized according to geography—"West Coast" cool jazz, as opposed to "East Coast" hard bop—the contestation, at least on the surface, pitted a perceived (white) classicization in jazz against a rootedness in African American expressivity.[26] However, the audience had aged along with the music. The cool and hard warriors hadn't considered American youth, a large portion of whom were not unequivocally committed jazz fans. Taken together, cool and hard bop fans were far less numerous than the jazz audience had been during the earlier battles.

Jonathan Kamin describes how a rising postwar youth culture complicated the hard bop–cool propaganda exchange. Some of these young fans (black *and* white) began to bracket off both cool and hard bop as mannered and irrelevant. As they drifted toward rhythm-and-blues and, soon enough, rock 'n' roll, the older combatants found themselves allied generationally: "Thus rock 'n' roll received criticism from many of the same quarters that saw in jazz a threat to traditional culture thirty-five years earlier. . . . Great pains were taken to differentiate jazz from rock 'n' roll and to disclaim any relationship."[27] Where jazz as a whole had been decried earlier in establishment corners as overly sensual and anti-intellectual, rock 'n' roll now emerged as its replacement in venality.

By the 1960s, jazz had begun to smart from several wounds. With audience segments turning away, many jazz partisans cried out for the kind of legitimacy and support conferred to classical music (e.g., public funding, inclusion in university curricula, and a shift to noncommercial radio), receiving what could only be called a half-felt embrace. Some jazz musicians began to experiment with popular music but failed to gain a foothold alongside their youthful competition, losing credibility with their jazz audiences into the bargain. The lucky few who connected with a pop audience—rarely a rock audience, until Miles Davis broke out with *Bitches Brew*—were seen as anomalies.

The sources of various contestations over jazz definition—generational marking, ethnic and American nationalism, class aspirations and conflict, and access to the academy—share one piece of common ground: characterizing jazz as a high-art music, distinct from any other. Jazz the definition, like jazz the music, has changed over time, responsive to and exploring incessantly moving musical and social environments. Musicians, the audience, critics, historians, the industry, all contrive their views, drawn from an ever-building history of changing musical trends, social settings, political goals, and personal preferences. Stuart Nicholson identifies the tendency toward the subjective in contriving these definitions, saying that "if it had this, this, and this, it was jazz, but if it had that, it wasn't. Usually, whoever was doing the defining put themselves at the center of the action."[28]

Mark Gridley, Robert Maxham, and Robert Hoff illustrate the traps of exclusion in the struggle to find an uncontested definition of jazz. They list three approaches to defining jazz, each with some claim to merit and each skewed from the perspective of the other two approaches. These include (1) a *strict* definition of jazz as improvised music that swings ("in a jazz sense"), has blues feeling, and is improvisational; (2) a *family resemblances* definition, after Wittgenstein, in which the presence of any of a variety of traits previously associated with jazz needs to be present; and (3) a *jazzness* definition, in which the listener evaluates the presence of jazz traits (as per the family resemblances approach), weighing the aggregate evidence as jazzlike or not. Each analytic framework leads to different conclusions. For jazz scholars, they write, the most useful definition is the "strict definition," because "its simplicity allows us to determine what is not jazz, though it excludes much music that the public ordinarily calls jazz." They point to exclusions such as some concert pieces by Duke Ellington and Stan Kenton whose tight arrangements feature "little, if any" improvisation, as well as improvised music that doesn't swing, like Johnny Hodges's solo in Ellington's "Come Sunday" section of *Black, Brown, and Beige*.[29] Not jazz? If such core jazz performers and pieces don't fit the definition, perhaps the problem is with the definition.

By the time of *Head Hunters*, the jazz message already had a twenty-five-year history of sanctification. The confusing intersection of racial politics, notions of high art, and American egalitarianism had become the basis for rupture in the various definitions of jazz. Everybody was a little bit right, but limitations abounded. Small wonder the marriage of jazz with youth-oriented popular music set jazz conservatives struggling to give it a name that kept it at arm's length from jazz "proper."

JAZZ-ROCK, FUSION, or FUSION JAZZ: What's in a Name?

The struggle to name the music engaged participants from the inside of fusion jazz, as well. Patrick Gleeson, synthesizer keyboardist with Hancock's Mwandishi group immediately preceding *Head Hunters*, objected in the early seventies to the term *jazz-rock*, saying that members of Hancock's septet, as well as the Mahavishnu Orchestra, Weather Report, and Return To Forever, preferred *fusion* as a general term.[30] Gleeson used emblematic performers to define the genre. Even here, he pointed out, the very center of the musical movement was difficult to nail down:

> If you really want to talk about what is *fusion*, you could (not necessarily have to) narrow it to Mahavishnu Orchestra and Tony Williams's

> Lifetime. That would be the essence of the whole thing. And the farther you get from that, the more dubious the relation between the music and the term *fusion*, or the broader you have to define *fusion*. . . . And then the term *jazz-rock* to me, on further reflection: if you wanted again to narrow it down to just the essence, you would start with Blood, Sweat, and Tears. . . . And this still leaves out two components. One is the whole Bob James thing with [independent label Creed Taylor, International]. . . . And that still leaves out, to me, almost the very center. *Because we still don't have a precise name for what Herbie was doing and what Miles [Davis] was doing.* And I think that there, you don't call it—you don't put the "jazz" first, because that implies that really the nomination is rock and the kind of rock it is is *jazz-rock*. I think what this is is *funk-jazz*.[31]

Since the late sixties, musicians, marketers, industry observers, and fans have all ventured to label the category in which *Head Hunters* belongs.[32] This is no casual matter. Despite the fact that fusion jazz commands only a tiny segment of the scholarly literature on jazz published over the past decade or so, historical treatments of this music generate a surprising amount of heat.[33] *Jazz-rock*, *fusion*, *jazz fusion*, *fusion jazz*, *jazz-rock fusion*, and *jazz/rock fusion* have all been claimed, often vehemently, to denote the same music, and the terms have important semantic differences.[34] The critical and historical discourse surrounding fusion jazz addresses a confusing blend of formal characteristics, claims of authority and authenticity by and about performers, and assessments of commerce's impact. The lack of agreement about precisely what to call this music reveals more than a simple confusion of terms. Each term suggests a strategic, as well as musical, point of reference. Underlying these naming strategies is a hierarchical message in which the term, *jazz-rock* (or *fusion*), tags the music as both different from (read: less than) jazz and different from (more than) rock.[35] Just as there is a common effort to distance jazz from fusion, there is a simultaneous and historically precedented move to distance both categories from rock, at least that part of "rock" considered inseparable from "pop."[36] If fusion cannot legitimately be separated from jazz but also cannot be separated from rock, then the distance from rock so deeply desired by many in the jazz world could be called into question. In curious contrast, musicians, critics, historians, music industry people, and audience members alike at times have placed hard bop, bebop, cool, swing, Cubop, and Dixieland all under the jazz umbrella.[37]

Bob James, one of the "jazz-rock" performers mentioned by Gleeson, was himself attracted to the term *fusion* in the seventies (as opposed to *jazz-rock*), meaning a musical process: "fusion, to me, is such a simple word; it means fusing different things together." All the same, James was quick to distance his music from that of other musicians Gleeson talked about. To him, fusion meant his own classical and R&B-inflected jazz, as opposed to the "the kind of progressive, note-y, adventurous music that John McLaughlin was making, amongst a lot of other people." Talking in 1996, James pointed to an interview fifteen years earlier that had turned to the naming dilemma: "We couldn't think of a name to call it then. We couldn't decide whether it was jazz or not. . . . Hopefully, one of these years, somebody's going to figure out what to call it."[38] The fact that Gleeson and James cite "fusion" as a way to distance themselves from, well, each other is not as self-canceling as it may seem. Both use the term as a way to describe what they are doing, that is, creating a new music by joining elements of jazz with elements from other styles, as a process. They also apply a secondary meaning to the term *fusion*: their own, specific results from that process.

James Lincoln Collier emphasizes musical product in his choice of a hybrid label, jazz-rock.[39] In his 1986 article on jazz history for the *New Grove Dictionary of Jazz*, Collier begins by describing jazz's blending with rock as a practice, a mode of expression. He soon moves beyond practice, bracketing off jazz-rock from both its parents. Further, the parent terms, *jazz* and *rock*, carry their own conflicting, multivalent meanings. Because Collier, given his confined topic, leaves these parents unexamined, the definition leaves lingering questions.[40]

Among these complicating questions is the contemporaneous reimagining of rock as an art form distinct from pop, in the aftermath of the Beatles' *Sgt. Pepper's Lonely Hearts Club Band*. Rock historian Reebee Garofalo writes: "As the counterculture and the social movements that accompanied it deteriorated in the early seventies, rock increasingly found refuge in its newly acquired status as art. If rock-as-counterculture had existed outside market relations, then rock-as-art hovered above them. This was, of course, *a hopelessly contradictory belief*, but it echoed the anti-commercialism of the period and made musicians central to the creative process."[41] The contradiction is that a growing number of rock musicians in the seventies sought to redefine themselves as artists (rock-as-art), despite the impossibility of ignoring the role of the music industry (rock-as-art's opposite, or rock-as-pop). However, few songs in jazz, rock, or pop are stylistically singular. Is the Righteous Brothers' recording of "You've Lost That Lovin' Feelin'" a Tin Pan Alley pop song, rock, or soul? The most distinguishing feature in the final analysis of rock versus pop may be a recording's relationship to the music industry and, pointedly, who its audience is assumed to be, mainstream or aficionado.[42]

Reconfigured as art, rock seemed to threaten jazz musicians' artistic turf, adding insult to an earlier injury. In the fifties, Jonathan Kamin points out, "jazz had only recently become respectable as 'America's only native art form,' and people in the jazz world were guarding their new-found respectability jealously."[43] Rock 'n' roll had already taken audiences from jazz musicians, as well as from R&B artists.[44] Jazz-rock seemed positioned to produce a new round of cultural appropriation on top of the commercial one.

Stanley Crouch, savaging Miles Davis's *Bitches Brew* as "the path of the sellout," considers the album little more than a commercial endeavor, launching "jazz-rock, with its multiple keyboards, electronic guitars, static beats, and clutter." Crouch points to rock's stylistic markers without distinguishing between rock's commercial and artistic aspirations. To Crouch, rock *is* pop; the entire genre, with Davis in the forefront, is "rapaciously commercial."[45]

Stuart Nicholson, whose *Jazz-Rock: A History* stands as the only authoritative study on the music to date, opts for the term *jazz-rock* and, in so doing, attempts to make a distinction between artistically elevated ("jazz-rock") and commercially motivated ("fusion") music. "I have stuck to the old-fashioned term *jazz-rock*," he writes, "because . . . I wanted to make a distinction between it and *fusion* (and its latter-day equivalents, variously marketed as *smooth jazz, quiet storm, lite-jazz, hot tub jazz*, or *yuppie jazz*)."[46] Similarly, Grover Sales, in *Jazz: America's Classical Music*, distinguishes between "jazz-rock fusion" and "crossover," by which he means jazz musicians "who have 'crossed over' into the more lucrative area of pop-soul."[47]

Crouch, Sales, and Nicholson all seek to protect the good name of jazz from the malign influences of rock-as-pop and the music industry's commercial machinery. However, Garofalo's comment—that rock-as-art's attempt in the seventies to rise above the means of its production and dissemination was "hopelessly contradictory"—is true for jazz as well, especially for a jazz style making extensive use of recording technology. Nicholson's rationale for naming establishes an ideological demarcation more than a stylistic one.[48]

Concern about commercial success, on its own, does not completely explain the impetus behind these anti-fusion postures. Rock 'n' roll's simultaneous appropriation of rhythm-and-blues and displacement of some post-bebop jazz in the fifties left deep wounds that fusion jazz reopened. If jazz is black music, as Amiri Baraka, Scott DeVeaux, Richard Crawford, and a host of others assert, then fusion jazz, with its ethnically diverse personnel distribution and audience demographics, and in particular its comfortable fraternization with rock music, seemed to some a watering down of a black musical tradition.[49]

In conversation, Patrick Gleeson stressed the racial politics involved in identifying fusion but saw racial identities arrayed along a continuum. While core groups, dominated by Miles Davis alumni, like Weather Report, Return To Forever, the Mahavishnu Orchestra, Lifetime, and Herbie Hancock's Mwandishi and Headhunters groups, played "fusion," other groups played "white" music in varying degrees. The categorization ranged along racial lines. Gleeson pointed out the interracial makeup of the core bands and their ideologies that stressed jazz's African American connections. Of these, Gleeson and other Mwandishi band members considered Hancock's music the most strongly black-identified: "funk-jazz."

Gleeson, who is white, also felt, along with his black band members, a shared sense of Otherness. They saw themselves, in their artistic aspirations, opposed to mainstream ideals and to mainstream inattention toward black cultural authenticity. Mwandishi drummer Jabali Billy Hart called Gleeson after hearing a mainstream group play a "watered-down" version of rock-influenced jazz, saying, "They got your shit, man." Gleeson's synthesizer sounds now had been appropriated for mainstream use.[50] Echoing this concern but using a different term, *Head Hunters* producer David Rubinson described "jazz fusion" as industry code: "Jazz fusion meant 'white people.' 'Oh, this band has some white people in it.' . . . It meant white people playing black music."[51] Agreeing, Gleeson told me:

> The interesting thing is that fusion in both of these groups [Tony Williams's Lifetime and the Mahavishnu Orchestra] also is interracial. Which is of no small significance, because at the time, there were two completely different [musical] backgrounds. I mean, Jack Bruce [ex-member of the British supergroup Cream, then playing with Lifetime] had a completely different background obviously than Tony. And Mahavishnu [John McLaughlin] of course was like I was with Herbie [in the Mwandishi group].[52]

Besides these musicians, many critics, educators, and scholars express concern over jazz-rock's effect on jazz's black identity. Stanley Crouch, for example, describes Miles Davis's defection to fusion jazz as racial betrayal and renegadism. Calling his effect on the music scene "pernicious," Crouch equates Davis's fusion jazz with minstrel images of Zip Coon and Jasper Jack.[53] Jazz educator Mark Gridley, defining a cluster of labels—jazz, rock, funk, and jazz-rock—connects Davis, Hancock, and McLaughlin as key performers in the industry-termed "jazz-rock" but says that funk, not rock, "attracted a number of jazz musicians during the seventies. Therefore, the *jazz-rock* label itself is not appropriate for the music which it identifies," which instead "would more accurately be termed *jazz-funk* or *jazz-R&B fusion*."[54] Although ignoring the obvious rock connections that do exist, Gridley does correctly challenge the assumption that rock is the only music that has some kind of relationship with jazz. But funk is only one of *many* streams involved in this music. If Gridley's disagreement with the term is that it omits a major component, his proposal of "jazz-funk" suffers from the same arbitrariness, a reminder of the limitation of his "strict" approach to defining jazz.[55]

Gridley's foregrounding of funk in his definition of fusion is one way of grappling with musical and social intersections, as is Rubinson's pointing to fusion as an industry code word for the inclusion of white musicians. For Crouch, Davis betrays the dignity of "Afro-American culture itself," a critique that resonates with the embrace of high-art culture during the Negro Renaissance.[56] But fusion jazz musicians, Davis included, with their tendency to blend disparate music styles, are quite likely to cross *any* line.

The energy and ink critics have spent on coming up with a name for this music illustrate a complex set of problems in seeing beyond the packaging-by-terms to the music inside. In the rush to define fusion jazz out of the jazz picture, a confusing proliferation of names resulted, many of them self-canceling. (Figs. 1–3 recap the variety of definitions for "jazz-rock," "fusion," and related labels.)

The diversity of the streams being fused, their unconventional blending, and their kaleidoscopic constituencies combined to blur the

Gridley	A misnomer for the syncretic blending of funk and jazz; should be called *jazz-funk*
Nicholson	An artistic combination of jazz and rock (as opposed to fusion)
Collier	A syncretic blend of jazz and rock
Gleeson	An adaptation of big band format, foregrounding (white) rock (exemplified by Blood, Sweat, and Tears)
Crouch	Commercially motivated music; the "path of the sellout"

FIG. 1. *Jazz rock* as a term.

Nicholson	A commercialized combination of jazz and rock (as opposed to jazz-rock)
Gleeson	The most progressive combination of jazz and other styles, exemplified by the Mahavishnu Orchestra and Lifetime
James	A combination of jazz with classical and other genres; the act of fusing styles together (excludes the Mahavishnu Orchestra)

FIG. 2. *Fusion* as a term.

Jazz-funk (Gridley)	A preferred name for blending funk and jazz (the term does not account for other streams)
Jazz-R&B fusion (Gridley)	A second preferred name for blending funk and jazz (ostensibly an expandable term to allow for other R&B based music styles)
funk-jazz (Gleeson)	Funk-influenced jazz
jazz fusion (Rubinson)	Black music played (inauthentically) by white people

FIG. 3. Terms that underscore racial issues.

music's identity. With the disquieting intersection of jazz and popular music in the seventies, the fears outlined by Kamin still loomed large. These included fears that a white mainstream would appropriate a black musical form; that jazz musicians would lose their market because of this appropriation; that jazz would lose its hard-won respectability; and that black jazz musicians would lose control over how to define, present, and evaluate jazz as *their own*. All of this fueled efforts in the jazz community to distance jazz from rock.

In this book, I use the term *fusion jazz*. The consistent parent is jazz, at least as an identity; the most widely accepted terms all assume some modification of "jazz." And, certainly, no commentator agonizes over whether the music has enough "rock" content; the issue for those engaged in the dispute was and remains: is it *jazz*?

Jazz, throughout its history and no matter which trend or style, engages both tradition and innovation. Rather than a separate stream, fusion jazz of the early seventies can be seen as one of these engagements. It was a *way* of doing jazz, focused on several criteria: musical processes (melody, harmony, improvisation, and the piece's formal plan); instrumentation and timbre; personnel (from musicians to arrangers to producers and engineers); and the collective relationship of all these with the state of production and recording technologies.

Of these, timbre and personnel bear emphasis here. The inclusion of amplified and synthesized instruments, as well as non-Western instruments and other instruments not normal to jazz, went well beyond simply making sounds loud, distorted, or unexpected. The point was to experiment with expanded, expressive timbral possibilities. Just as instrumentation increased the range of sound in fusion jazz projects, lead jazz musicians in the initial movement sought to push back stylistic confines by linking with a pastiche of other players. They brought with them not only their jazz-oriented sensibilities but also their historical identities as jazzmen.[57] Tony Williams, Chick Corea, Wayne Shorter, and Herbie Hancock are clear examples of this, through their association with Miles Davis, as is Joe Zawinul, in his work with both Davis and Cannonball Adderley.[58] This was the heart of the controversy: they seemed to be defectors from jazz to rock. From the perspective of these jazz performers, playing with funk- and rock-based musicians provided an exhilarating orientation to groove and offered opportunities to explore new improvisational and compositional territory. From the perspective of the funk and rock musicians, it did likewise; jazz techniques expanded their own chops.

Beyond these criteria, a host of other factors influenced the music, including the broadcasters and marketers whose efforts helped make the recording infrastructure possible, the audiences who found meaning in the sounds, the personal histories and tastes of the players, their musical and personal interactions, and the social climate of the times. *Head Hunters* resulted from its unique intersections within this "web of affiliations."[59]

Selling and Selling Out

Connections between the music and marketing loom over any discussion of fusion jazz. The joining of R&B- and rock-based production and marketing teams with jazz-oriented players clearly figured in the success of the *Head Hunters* album, as well as of fusion jazz generally in the early seventies. Despite grudging admiration for its merchandising effectiveness, musicians, critics, and historians alike routinely vilified marketing's impact on the music, claiming that sales, not art, now motivated the musicians. The fact is, though, that music, especially recorded music, has always depended on a distribution and sales apparatus. Acknowledging the influence of the marketplace on music is as uncomfortable for those who would promote jazz as art as it has been for historical musicologists interested in the work of such masters as Mozart and Haydn.[60]

Efforts to distance "artistic" albums from "commercial" ones as separate genres of music—a good and an evil twin—illustrate the level of ideology attached to something as seemingly straightforward as defining a genre. As Gary Carner, seconding a point made by Scott DeVeaux, has argued, the history of jazz writing is marked by a "near century-old eagerness to advance the music's respectability. In order to make jazz cohere as one majestic entity, jazz writers have habitually canonized their heroes, purchasing for their favorites a seat on the 'jazz tradition' train in which each conflicting style is assigned its evolutionary place no matter how different or wide-ranging."[61] It follows that writers on fusion jazz would exclude certain artists, and albums by those artists, as so tainted by commercialism that they cannot belong to the same genre as the art music ones.[62] But criticism and categorization should be separate matters: Mozart and Haydn may hold justifiably high prestige for their classical works, but this does not disqualify less favored composers from being classical, and it certainly does not exclude these lesser lights or stylistic variations from membership in the Western art-music tradition generally. Similarly, bifurcating fusion jazz may be useful in polemicizing one's preference for a certain type of album within the genre, but it does little to illuminate the process of fusing.

Classification rhetoric permeates the marketing apparatus, as well. The music industry attempts to place this highly eclectic array of music and musicians into a single marketing framework. For the music industry, the function of genre naming is predictive: the idea is to suggest to audiences of *this* album that they might also enjoy *these others*. Therefore, the category "fusion jazz," under whatever name, represents to the music industry a collection of products grouped together by potential customer and not necessarily by similarities in their sounds.[63]

Nicholson, Crouch, Gridley, and other observers—whether they are attracted or repelled—seem to weigh commercial success whenever they encounter fusion jazz almost as if assaying artistic worth in inverse relation to record sales. *Head Hunters* enjoyed huge commercial success, having sold over 750,000 copies six months after its release. Judging by the inverse sales-to-art principle, this alone should disqualify it as high art. Yet musicians, audiences, and commentators on fusion consistently include *Head Hunters* in best-of lists. The answer to the question, "Is *Head Hunters* an example of fusion-the-prostitute or fusion-the-artist?" is that *any* musical endeavor sold to a mass audience may or may not be artistically expressive but, in the fullest consideration, is also commercially influenced.

Grover Sales, in his chapter "Jazz Today," reports that Freddie Hubbard, who in 1960 had been "a cohort of Ornette Coleman and Eric Dolphy before his defection [*sic*], made this revealing comment to impresario Norman Granz: 'I want to get back to playing some real jazz and not this shit [i.e., "crossover"] I'm into now.' "[64] For Sales to use Hubbard's association with Coleman and Dolphy as representing "real jazz" is strange, since the free jazz they played together was as famously castigated as anti-jazz in 1960 as fusion jazz was in 1973. Hubbard, in fact, may have been expressing frustration with industry-generated pressure to create hits. His marketability was flagging at the time, and he likely recognized a professional need for redirection. However, Sales seizes on the quote to demonstrate a jazz icon repenting his departure from the true path.

There is no provision in this point of view for any shortcomings in the jazz tradition or for shifts prompted by catholicity of taste. Comments by musicians such as Miles Davis, Herbie Hancock, Chick Corea, and Joe Zawinul portray a desire to expand beyond confining notions of tradition.[65] When I asked Hancock if his modal jazz reunion with members of the Miles Davis group in the late seventies (V.S.O.P.) represented a turning away from fusion jazz, he responded:

> Not at all. I mean, neither was doing the *Head Hunters* thing a move away from doing acoustic stuff. . . . People have a tendency to think that whatever you're doing means that you won't be doing what you were before, [ever again]. . . . I think that our society kind of supports the idea that you can only do one thing. And the fact of the matter is human

> beings can do many things. But in most cases, we never get to find that out. Because if we find one thing that we can do, we have a tendency to rest on our laurels. And enter a holding pattern there, because it's safe.[66]

Head Hunters producer David Rubinson put it bluntly:

> So what happened with all these critics was that they confused making money with the *desire* to make money. In other words, they'd say, "Jesus, this record was successful, he made a lot of money. That must have been his motivation." And that's completely backwards. The motivation was to make the music that they wanted. And the fact that it sold was a side effect. Herbie woke up one morning and had a hit record; he had no idea. That's why I said, "What did Beethoven say when you told him his middle quartets weren't as good as the other quartets? He didn't *know* they were the middle quartets." And the same thing with Herbie. He had no idea of "Let's make some records. Are they going to sell?"[67]

Rubinson's comment, while heated, does address the *perception* of selling out. It is possible that Hancock could have been oblivious to the presence of the market as he created his music, but not likely. However, Hancock defends the artist's right to explore musically, even in so-called commercial realms, without apology. He articulates this point in response to a charge of selling out by Wynton Marsalis in a shared interview. Hancock says that he would respect Gauguin drawing a comic book if, by doing so, he tried "to make something happen with the cartoon" artistically and to "learn from dealing with a medium that's more popular than the one he was accustomed to."[68] Throughout his eclectic career, Hancock has shown a willingness to expand beyond the confines of expected musical roles, asserting immunity from control by critical camps.

In 1976, George Wein, impresario of the Newport Jazz Festival, produced a retrospective concert of Hancock's career. Hancock performed with three groups, representing different periods in his career: his current Headhunters group; the avant-garde septet that played on the post-Davis albums (the Mwandishi group); and the re-formed Davis quintet, with Hubbard in the Davis role (V.S.O.P.). The success of the concert led to the formation of a V.S.O.P. tour the next year, which played to one hundred thousand fans over three months.[69] Hancock's name recognition, largely through *Head Hunters*, helped fill seats and added energy (as well as ticket and record sales) to a fledgling neo-bop revival movement, which would eventually be spearheaded by Wynton Marsalis. Marsalis, by the way, playing in the group's second tour in 1981, gained important exposure as a virtuoso on the rise. The popularity of the neo-bop movement seems, in retrospect, a reaction against fusion jazz, and Hancock logically could have followed the new winds of popularity. But he stayed active in post-bebop as well as fusion (and, with 1983's *Future Shock*, R&B). Further, he pointed out that acoustic jazz, although not as popular as fusion jazz in the seventies, had never died: "It just wasn't getting the recognition that this new form [i.e., fusion jazz] was getting, because the new form related a little more easily to the most popular form of music at that time, which was rock 'n' roll."[70]

Musically, Hancock saw connections among these periods in his career. He had used the straight-eighth (as opposed to swing) rhythmic orientation, dominating much of fusion jazz, as early as "Watermelon Man" (1962) and continued to do so with "Cantaloupe Island" (1964), "Maiden Voyage" (1965), and "Speak Like a Child" (1968).[71] All of these foreshadowed his treatment of rhythm in *Head Hunters*. Also evident in these songs is the combining of these straight-eighth rhythms with modal melodies and extremely slow harmonic rhythm.[72] Seen in the long historical view of his earlier recordings, *Head Hunters* is as much a continuation of earlier lines of development as it is a break from them.

David Rubinson underscored this when I interviewed him. Speaking of *Head Hunters*, he said: "That goes back to [the original recording of] 'Watermelon Man.' That's the whole genre. That's [hard bop drummer] Grady Tate and all the old guys down at Rudy Van Gelder's."[73] Likewise, Bill Summers, percussionist on the *Head Hunters* album and Hancock sideman for the next ten years, laid the album's beginnings generally with the funky jazz style of hard bop in the late fifties and early sixties and specifically with Hancock's 1962 hit "Watermelon Man."[74]

For Summers, Rubinson, and not least Hancock himself, *Head Hunters* was a continuation not only of Hancock's own earlier ideas but also of precedents set by other hard bop players. With the emphatic incorporation of elements from rock, soul, gospel, "classical," avant-garde, and non-Western musics, fusion jazz generally (and *Head Hunters* in particular) may seem to be veering away from the "jazz tradition train" track.[75] But from the point of view of musicians playing this music, some of whom—Hancock, Summers, and Gleeson—are quoted in this book, as well as production figures such as Rubinson, the fusion trajectory is part of jazz, not tangential to it.

"Before the Music Got Separated"

The purist resistance to fusion may seem to invite a modernist defense, in which fusion jazz players would rejoin that they retain the "spirit" of jazz, expanding musical boundaries and enhancing improvisation in an "evolutionary" progression.[76] Some fusionists do make such an argument. Musicians' responses to the revivalists, however, just like musical styles, often elude easy classification. Many fusion jazz musicians are undecided or unconcerned about what to call their music. David Rubinson told me that Herbie Hancock never used the term *fusion* or any other such term.[77] When I asked *Head Hunters'* bassist, Paul Jackson, what to call the album's genre, his wife relayed this e-mail message: "As to your question of how Paul's music was called in the seventies, and whether the term makes any difference, Paul said no, it does not make any difference and he does not know how it was called. He suggested you make up new terminology."[78] When musicians aren't attached to labeling their music, who is? To Rubinson, the answer is "the critics and record companies, to sell it or label it."[79] Labeling the music, even broadly as jazz or pop, helps bring listeners and musicians together in the marketplace and suggests a vocabulary and context in which to talk about individual recordings. But labeling hardens constructions and canons within a genre, cementing the concept, by historians and journalists, of jazz as "one majestic entity" (to invoke Scott DeVeaux's image) and allowing the music industry to assert and retain power over production and marketing of jazz recordings.[80]

Jazz categories have not always been cast in such rigid, canonical terms. David Rosenthal, meditating on the hard bop scene in the first half of the sixties, describes the connectedness of musicians we now place in separate camps: "I can recall those glorious jukeboxes where Jimmy Smith, Miles Davis, and Cannonball Adderley rubbed shoulders with Martha Reeves, the Impressions, Muddy Waters, and Howlin' Wolf. . . . All this occurred before, as Andrew Hill put it, *the music got separated.*"[81] The jukebox's musical eclecticism existed in a socially framed venue, the café or club in which it sat. Rosenthal's reminiscence highlights how consumers, critics, record shops, jukeboxes, clubs, and record labels combine to play a role in defining and contextualizing commercially released music of any stripe and how sorting the music into this or that bin may reveal the sorter's interests as much as, or even more than, immanent features in the music.

Despite Rosenthal's cozy recollection, the music began to be separated long ago, though the parsing of popular music categories has increased relatively recently. There was an industry-wide "race" music category as early as the twenties, but Billboard did not establish a "jazz" category until 1969.[82] Since the late 1940s, the industry, musicians, critical journalists, and jazz scholars periodically have sought to partition black musics, each vested party furthering specific goals. A lead naming goal for the music industry across all genres is control over targeted marketing systems. For the others, splitting larger categories ("race") into more focused ones is seen as an opportunity to increase recognition for each of those genres ("rhythm-and-blues," "gospel," etc.) and the artists who perform within them.[83]

Certainly, to leave broad swaths of musical styles as undifferentiated could risk confusion in sales and critical arenas. But to make a claim that genres, such as jazz—not to mention subgenres, such as fusion jazz—are identifiable merely in concrete, formalist terms is inaccurate, or at best incomplete. Combining those recordings from the jukebox into a single image, Rosenthal invokes an attitude of amicable elbow-rubbing, not sonic mush.[84] The seventies also saw an exchange of influence across a boundary between jazz and other popular musics, the vitality of which demonstrated a boundary permeable from both directions.

Commercialism in a Web of Affiliations

Many of the critics and historians who have relegated fusion jazz players to some separate realm from jazz have pointed to the siren call of money as enticing musicians away from higher artistic ground. The influence of the market is not to be denied, but it tells only part of the story. Fusion musicians, making greater use of electronic instrumentation and recording technology, made significant gains in their level of control over the means of production in the recording process. David Rubinson forcefully raised the importance of this point, saying that "record company execs were panicked because their power structure was disappearing and the critics were pissed off because they were losing control over it. So it was the threat of being left out; there was [the Headhunters group] who could eliminate the middleman, and they could make any sound they wanted. And getting control was really what it was about."[85] Fusion musicians' commercial success allowed them not only greater voice in the recording process but also greater decision-making power over their recordings' musical content. Generally speaking, commercial success encouraged record executives to trust musicians' judgment more and so to intercede less. It is important to keep in mind here that this newfound power over process and content did not totally liberate fusion jazz musicians from either artistic or commercial considerations. But defining musicians or recordings out of the genre on the basis of their commercial "excesses" leads to misconceptions about creative freedom and the degree of jazz's immunity to commercial/financial influence. All professional musicians play their music and at the same time ply their trade. In fact, commercial concerns are only part of a larger matrix within which any musician creates a (musical) identity.

Ethnomusicologist Mark Slobin addresses this larger matrix of influences, seconding Arjun Appadurai's nuanced view of (musical) subcultures, through a set of dimensions, or "—*scapes*": ethnoscapes, mediascapes, technoscapes, finanscapes, and ideoscapes. Embracing Appadurai's concept but grappling for terminology that avoids a landscape's static quality, Slobin briefly lands on sociologist Georg Simmel's "web of affiliations," an image that serves my analysis well. The metaphor of a web reinforces the notion that subcultural dimensions are interlinked, rather than discrete or hierarchical. And the metaphor further allows for a shifting viewpoint, from the subcultural to the interpersonal to the personal. Subsequent chapters sketch some of the many strands in the web of affiliations that held *Head Hunters*. As Appadurai says, "the warp of stabilities is everywhere shot through with the woof of human motion."[86]

Instead of the fixity and linearity of portraying jazz within a single, overarching narrative (what Carner, rephrasing DeVeaux, calls the "jazz tradition train"), this book follows a fluid approach. Analyses (music theory, history, cultural analysis), if focused on one or a few aspects of music-making, miss the mark. They shortchange music's multiple contexts: its planes of identity in intersection. If we highlight a single component of identity (say, being under contract to a particular jazz label, an example of Appadurai's *finanscape*), or even an entire dimension (the entirety of the *finanscape*), we must also take into consideration that these terms intersect other dimensions (e.g., local, regional, or transnational distribution). But as Slobin is quick to point out, none of these elements is easy, or even proper, to see in isolation: "My intent has been to give some sense of how looking at one variable introduces many others, elbowing any single factor and crowding the frame."[87]

Head Hunters demonstrates such a weblike intersection. As with any small-group music-making, the *Head Hunters* album, although led by Herbie Hancock, was recorded by several musicians, each with his own musical sensibilities informed by personal and musical backgrounds, status within the band, other concurrent projects, and so on.

As frequently happens in recorded music, the songs on the album were created through a combination of (1) written music charts composed prior to rehearsal and recording, (2) a playback-and-edit process during the rehearsal stage, and (3) improvisational interaction as the recording progressed. As also frequently happens in recorded music, the final form of the recording was influenced by the recording arts and sciences of the time, in a process that included the musicians as well as production personnel. Additionally, the album's aesthetic thrust incorporated several intersecting musical and cultural streams, including earlier and contemporary trends in jazz, R&B, funk, and rock, as well as traditional Central African, Afro-Brazilian and Afro-Cuban styles and avant-garde Western art music.

The creation of the album addressed youth culture in its multiple social and cultural contexts. These contexts included youth's problematic relationships with traditional authority, authenticity, and commercialism (especially in the face of co-optation by the music industry), as well as a deepening commitment to enhancing and valorizing black identity in the United States.[88] Although both Hancock and Bennie Maupin were over thirty at the time of the album's release, the rest of the group were in their mid-twenties. Maupin wrote melody fragments for "Chameleon" in response to the movements of young black dancers at the Wattstax soul music festival in Los Angeles. Hancock and other "young lion" alumni of Miles Davis's groups, like Chick Corea and Tony Williams, embraced new technologies, rock beats, and other signifiers of youthful opposition to an older order. Lastly, the album was produced by David Rubinson, a specialist in producing young, hip, black acts, such as Sly and the Family Stone and the Pointer Sisters, as well as San Francisco–scene groups, such as Moby Grape. (Rubinson later went on to become a partner with rock impresario Bill Graham.)

The intersection of all of these factors led to the production of *Head Hunters* as we know it. The process of touching on the desires of a large number of listeners well enough to motivate them to buy the album is more than simply a question of skill in bringing a work to market (*finanscape*). The presence of a market for the album assumes some shared sense of musical, political, class, and ethnic taste; the sales of an album on a massive scale (no matter how influential the marketing effort may be) reflect a position of leadership that appeals to this shared taste, achieving a sense of pointing the way: being ahead of, but also part of, the crowd.

Previous writing on fusion jazz errs too often by either avoiding or obsessing over the market's influence and misreading the music's relationship with commerce. To the charge of being overly concerned with the crowd (being "of" the crowd, as well as being ahead of it), Chick Corea weighed in two years before *Head Hunters*, casting the artistic role as both public and personal: "How high a goal can an artist set himself and get agreement on from people? That's a broad question and defines a very high purpose for the artist. For, as he gets agreement about his dream—when others find parts of themselves they align with his dream—the possibility of its realization becomes greater and greater."[89] The point, to Corea, is not *whether* artists must consider their audiences but *how* to lead them effectively, to invite them into the artist's expressive world. Corea acknowledges the truism that an audience cannot follow what they cannot fathom, while suggesting that the relationship is symbiotic, ultimately elevating artistic value through a shared sense of purpose.

Notions of art are tied to the times, predilections, and perceptions of the evaluators, both musicians and listeners. An earlier illustration of this is the "discovery" and rehabilitation of Bach's music by Felix Mendelssohn in the 1820s. The music had not changed in the interim from Bach's death some seventy-five years earlier, but standards of art had. Mendelssohn's reevaluation of Bach signaled yet another shift in standards, one that would allow for appreciation of Bach's convoluted harmonies, relative to the intervening classical composition style. Whether or not a piece is *art* is open to negotiation; the judgment is as tied to contemporary cultural understandings as to vogues in "objective" criteria.

For the moment, it might be useful to suspend the effort to include or exclude *Head Hunters* in the elusive and changeable genres of jazz or fusion jazz. The intricate web of affiliations that produced *Head Hunters* was one of a kind, as inevitably each confluence of people and contexts, past and present will be. Evaluating *Head Hunters* and fusion jazz in historical context requires both understanding the goals Herbie Hancock and others involved in the album wished to achieve and witnessing the process and results of their efforts, with a degree of independence from existing critical overlays.

Hancock: Musical Intentions

Although he had been prominent in the jazz scene for over a decade, in 1973 Herbie Hancock intended to produce a funk album. Why would someone of his position in the jazz world want to shift gears so completely? In a 1985 interview (shared with Wynton Marsalis), Hancock recalled the driving force behind the *Head Hunters* project:

> When I . . . started getting into jazz [in high school], I didn't want to hear anything but classical music and jazz. No R&B, nothing, until I heard James Brown's "Papa's Got a Brand New Bag" (1965). Later on, when I heard [Sly and the Family Stone's] "Thank You Falettin Me Be Mice Elf Agin" (1969), it just went to my core. I didn't know *what* [Sly] was doing. I mean, I heard the chorus but, how could he *think* of that? I was afraid that that was something I couldn't do. And here I am, I call myself a musician. It bothered me. Then at a certain point I decided to try my hand at funk, when I did *Head Hunters*. I was not trying to make a jazz record. And it came out sounding different from anything I could think of at the time.[90]

With *Head Hunters*, Hancock sought to put aside playing jazz as connoisseur music in favor of a decidedly more vernacular positioning. Hancock's producer, David Rubinson, explained this populist orientation to the press, saying Hancock planned to "try and communicate more directly with his audience—build intensity in his sets and try and turn the crowd on."[91] Hancock later told me: "The original goal was [that] I wanted to make a funk album that had nothing to do with jazz. But, you see, in the development, it kind of took on its own character, which was unique. Fortunately, I decided to pay attention to the way things were flowing and not just stick to what I originally had in mind."[92]

Hancock had been aware of the image of jazz as a "high art," particularly as this notion developed in the avant-garde scene of the late sixties and early seventies. His own work had been quite rarefied: his previous three albums (*Mwandishi*, 1970, issued 1971; *Crossings*, 1971; and *Sextant*, 1972) had incorporated avant-gardist notions of collectively improvising, deemphasizing tonal harmony in favor of sound "events," and using synthesized sounds.[93] He coupled these musical ideas with images of Africa on record jackets (such as *Crossings* and *Sextant*) and in song titles, such as "Sleeping Giant"and "Rain Dance," which refer to images of Africa and African life.[94] The Swahili name Mwandishi, which Hancock took during the period just before *Head Hunters*, underscores his loose involvement with the Black Arts movement, a political and philosophical movement that arose in the sixties, prominently in the Chicago, New York, Los Angeles, and St. Louis areas, and was exemplified in the organizational writings connected with the Association for the Advancement of Creative Musicians, the Black Artists Guild, the Last Poets, and others.[95] His explorations seem, on that basis, to have been doubly rarefied: intellectually based musical musings on a geopolitical Afrocentrism. With *Head Hunters*, Hancock sought to reconnect with his listeners. As *Down Beat* interviewer Eric Gaer reported shortly before the album was recorded, the music, of course, would still revolve around the artistry of Herbie Hancock. The changes, however, were intended to swing away from the existing attitude of "if the people dig it, O.K.—if they don't, so what."[96] It is clear that, with *Head Hunters*, Hancock chose funk, in part, as a point of shared cultural (African American) understanding that would enable this reconnection.

Regardless of this opening premise, funk was only a part of the result. *Head Hunters* slips as easily out of categories as into them. A mass of complications and contradictions (populist/artistic, artistically innovative/"rapaciously commercial," non-jazz funk/funk-jazz, Afro-centric/crossover), the album confounds the notion of jazz as an orderly current in myriad ways, troubling the waters and, in the resulting reflection, revealing its shifting, multiple surfaces.[97]

CHAPTER 2

"An African Thing"

Aesthetics and Identity in HEAD HUNTERS

> Following the lead established long ago by LeRoi Jones, I believe it is possible to approach the music as a *changing* rather than an unchanging same.
>
> —*Paul Gilroy*

> The common core of this Africanness consists of the way of doing something, not simply something that is done.
>
> —*Olly Wilson*

> It's really an African thing.
>
> —*Bill Summers,* Head Hunters *percussionist*

Take a look at the *Head Hunters* album cover; Africa returns our gaze. From a purplish, midnight blue background, the members of the Headhunters group look outward, sitting as if in a family portrait, each member's role represented by the instrument he holds in his hands. The shot, taken in black and white, is reproduced here in halftones ranging from cobalt to black. No white here. Harvey Mason and Bill Summers, the drummer and percussionist for the album, pose in front of Bennie Maupin, who holds a saxophone, and Paul Jackson Jr., holding a Fender bass. The gourd rattles cradled in Summers's hands and his Afro hairstyle make plain the music's roots.[1] If any doubt remains, the focal point of the photograph drives the connection home. In blazing yellow and orange tones, contrasting sharply with the background, we see Herbie Hancock, hands poised above a keyboard, his head replaced by an African ritual mask. This original album art also graces the CD reissue. On the reissue, the emblem in the top right corner, "Columbia Jazz, Contemporary Masters," reassures us that this is a jazz album, but it's difficult to know from the art. What we *do* know is that Africa is well represented.[2]

Closer consideration of the mask gives a secondary jolt. The eyes are radio knobs and the mouth a VU meter. Hancock playfully portrays a trickster god; even the mask is a trick. Clues come into focus: Hancock, one of the great jazz pianists, poises himself above a *synthesizer* keyboard. Now the Fender bass makes sense; if the music comes from Africa, the music technology delivering it comes through African American funk. Of course, analyzing the cover-art image only makes sense if Hancock had something material to do with it. Answering my question about the title *Head Hunters*, album producer David Rubinson tied it directly to the cover art, as Hancock and Paul Jackson's idea, which he helped realize in the photo session: "It was HH and Paul J [Jackson]. It was an obvious double entendre, which was then extended to triple and quadruple by the cover art. . . . HH named [the album]. I think with the strong complicity and major contribution of Paul J. This is definitely their kind of witticism. . . . I worked with the cover artist, who was a famous SF poster and comic artist [Victor Moscoso; the photo was shot by Waldo Bascom]. I explained the African-Technological concept."[3]

The album cover art continues an African visual trend in Herbie Hancock's preceding albums, a gradual but inexorable change begun a few years before. In contrast, the cover for Hancock's first album, *Takin' Off* (1962), features him as the genius at work, alert and sophisticated, framed by a suit, crisp shirt, tie, and conservatively styled hair.[4] The look typifies a significant visual vein for jazz musicians at the time. Onstage performance photos would show this sleek look morphed, the suit and tie now wilted from sweat, framing a face contorted with concentration, emphasizing the seriousness of the artistic endeavor. The suited look tapped into mainstream images of power and control; the accompanying respectability factor, a visual refutation of the stereotyped jazz bohemian, also fit neatly into the integrationist atmosphere of the Kennedy New Frontier era.

Changes in Hancock's musical direction by the early seventies began to make this older image obsolete for him. Hancock's two albums immediately before *Head Hunters* feature illustrations of traditional African characters: an old, wizened man (a shaman? a griot?) with young acolytes (*Crossings*) and ceremonial dancers (*Sextant*), each image set against a space-fantasy backdrop.[5] In contrast to the earlier necktied image or these more recent African/science-fantasy portrayals, *Head Hunters* proclaims a visual connection to Africa, but now the connection is diasporic and hybrid.[6]

Why use an altered ritual mask, a *play* on the visual representation of Africa? Is it merely imaging, a dollop of African sauce spooned onto American jazz for flavoring? Why choose Africa as the signifier for a funk-driven jazz album? Hancock had been deeply involved with small-group jazz since the early sixties, yet funk, growing out of soul, and rhythm-and-blues before that, spoke to a fundamental part of him:

> What is it about funk that attracted me in the first place? First of all, it was familiar, from the rhythm-and-blues part of my culture. You know, being African American, and living in a poor area of Chicago, it's kind of natural. But the reason I liked the music is not just because I happen to be African American. I mean, rhythm-and-blues is not the kind of music that only African Americans like. People all over the world like it. It's like the blues; the blues has an honesty, I think, that attracts people.[7]

Beyond its broad appeal and black populist message, funk turned out to be a gateway for Hancock to traverse between African and Western aesthetic traditions. Musically, Herbie Hancock had set out with the *Head Hunters* project to delve into his own funk associations. A fan of James Brown as well as Sly and the Family Stone, he pointedly wanted to engage funk's connection to hip and politically aware African American youth. A year after the album's release, he reflected: "I'm able to play the *plain funky truth*, which I really wasn't able to do before. . . . Sure, I'm getting a bigger white audience. But I'm also getting a big black audience, which I never had; the people I played to before were eighty to ninety percent white. I've finally been able to come out with some music the general black public can relate to."[8]

Hancock was able, with funk, to pursue "Africa" through African American music, investing his own music with the diasporic aesthetics absorbed by his generation. Funk musicians assumed a fundamental connection with Africanicity. Rickey Vincent, in his history of funk, articulates this, saying that understanding funk depends on "understand[ing] the evolutionary process of black (African) culture as it propagates throughout the world." "From the word and meaning of funk," he continues, "to the necessary process of communal music-making, dancing, worshiping, and truth-telling, Africans have provided Americans of all colors with vital aspects of their American cultural life."[9]

Culturally, politically, and musically, Africa was an important touchstone in the 1970s music scene. African sounds, images, and aesthetics wound themselves through *Head Hunters.* If the album's musicians brought an "African" sensibility to their music-making, what was that sensibility, how did it become manifest, and further, under what terms can it be conceptualized? Despite general agreement that there is *something* about African musical traditions that sets them apart from European ones and that this "something" turns up in African American music, nailing that difference is fraught with problems.

> I was involved in African music before I got to U.C. Berkeley. . . . I've always been attracted to drums. Even as a young person studying music. And any time I heard music that had Afro-Cuban drumming, like congas or anything that sounded like that, for some reason I was attracted to it.
>
> —*Bill Summers*

Summers's attraction to things African is just one among hundreds of moments of cultural recognition and response occurring past and present, back and forth, between Africa and the people of the diaspora. The "Africa" of aesthetics and tradition is far from a singular matter. Musicologist Kofi Agawu aptly challenges the existence of a simple, overarching African aesthetic in a continent with over two thousand languages, not counting dialects.[10] How can it be right or accurate, he argues, to collapse the cultural richness of African aesthetics and tradition into an overly simplified (essentialist) view? Yet an opposing, atomistic examination doesn't tell the whole story either. Paul Gilroy, anticipating Agawu by a decade, points out that anti-essentialist arguments similar to Agawu's, while rightly focusing on particular traditions and practices, tend not to account fully for large-scale trends that characterize the presence of Africa across the African diaspora.[11] In fact, the very notion of an African diaspora is tied to these threads of similarity, in approach and function if not necessarily in musical details, as it is also tied to particularity and divergence. It occurs in sometimes elusive qualities that make one notice things *African*.[12] Considering the extensive history of trade and exchange on the African continent and beyond, the fact that a particular group in Africa plays a particular instrument, melody, or rhythmic pattern does not conveniently seal its identity as *only* from that group. The labels "Western" or "European" share a similar inadequacy. European musical traditions, far from monolithic, carry cross-influences from other regions, societies, and times. Nonetheless, we can hear a Balkan folk song, a German lied, or an Italian tarantella and, though not familiar with the piece, or without more than a vague sense of its region, call it "European."

In solution, Gilroy invokes Amiri Baraka's elegantly expressive term "the changing same" to explain how significantly different-sounding music across the African diaspora still "works" in similar ways, reinforced through both shared aesthetics and recurring contact.[13] Bill Summers, mentioning both African and Afro-Cuban music in close succession, purposefully taps into this "changing same."

Many Africanist scholars, besides Gilroy, have noticed similarities across subcultures, both within the slave-exporting region and in the slaveholding areas in the Americas.[14] Ghanaian ethnomusicologist J. H. Kwabena Nketia, for example, points to distinct but remarkably similar musical, religious, and other cultural practices, calling these relationships "communities of taste."[15] Nketia points to the case of a traditional drummer, whose style is nonetheless different from his forebears and who assumes that his own style will disappear after him. Yet he is a traditionalist, a culture-bearer. He has internalized a set of playing conventions, ritual and social contexts, and ideals (what sounds pleasing) that he in turn passes on, stamped with his own personality. Tradition, in this sense, is realigned on a daily basis. It can be self-consciously inscribed, as traditionalism; however, it is always hybrid, changeable, and contingent on its context.[16] In a ritual setting, the extent of the lead drummer's changes are closely confined; he has more latitude in a social setting. He must navigate between his personal expressivity and the needs and expectations of the dancers and other musicians. Summers reiterates this: "Even the master drummer is playing, in many cases, the steps of the dancers. And he will signal changes that will not only change the rhythmic pattern of the fixed rhythm group but also maybe go into another dance. . . . But they're based upon many things other than the music itself: the liturgical function or the social function that's going on at that particular time. [And he plays] a series of rhythms that's traditionally used, to bring about a desired effect."[17]

Olly Wilson, composer and scholar of African American music, offers a way of seeing the diaspora's "changing same," describing a core of "African conceptual approaches to music making . . . the manifestations of which are infinite."[18] Wilson outlines these approaches, including tendencies toward call-and-response song structures, a percussive approach to music-making, a fluid speech-to-song continuum in melodies, a high density of musical events, the inclusion of environmental factors (especially incorporating physical body motion), rhythmic-metric contrast, and a "heterogeneous sound ideal."[19] The latter two—rhythmic-metric contrast and a heterogeneous sound ideal—are particularly important in *Head Hunters*, working in combination.

A traditional drum ensemble of the Anlo-Ewe people in coastal Ghana features a lead drummer and lead singer (Wilson calls these the *variable rhythmic* group), coordinating with a backdrop of ostinato lines played by a *fixed rhythmic* group of drums (in high-to-low pitch order: *kagan*, *kidi*, and *sogo*); bells (*gankogui*, the fundamental time-keeping instrument for the ensemble); beaded gourd rattles (*axatse*, also known in Afro-Cuban music as *shekere*); body percussion; and just about everyone present, singing responses to the leader's calls.[20] Each part contributes to the whole. The lines tend to be highly syncopated (displaying the rhythmic-metric contrast Wilson mentions). But what prevents the music from being a cacophonous jumble, or merely a densely packed wall of notes, is the fact that each of the instruments sounds strikingly different from its neighbors. The result is a matrix of sound in which the individuality of "voice" in its interlocking, charged relationship with the other voices—heterogeneity—gives the music variety and vitality;

such heterogeneity is a key element operating in *Head Hunters*. Demonstrating an example of "African conceptual approaches" in African American music, Wilson analyzes James Brown's "Super Bad."[21] Rather than focus on specific musical figures in common, Wilson is able to show that "Africa" reveals itself in the diaspora through the music's organization.

In addition to the shared aesthetics that Wilson identifies, the African diaspora appears in *Head Hunters* through Signifying(g), an African-based critical practice described by Henry Louis Gates Jr.[22] Gates, drawing from anthropologists' work in the same slave-exporting, sub-Saharan region examined by Nketia and Wilson, points to a minor deity who turns up in a wide swath of local religions and in similar religions across the diaspora.[23] Esu-Elegbara, who is both the god of divination and the gatekeeper to any communication with the spiritual world, loves to speak cryptically and elusively, demanding the worshiper decode his meaning; he is not above playing tricks to make this harder to do.[24] Esu-Elegbara's taunts, Gates says, act as a metaphor, or "trope," for a general, African-based strategy of criticism.[25] For Esu-Elegbara, indeterminacy becomes part of the challenge; it is why in the Yoruban pantheon Esu is the god of *divination*, rather than the god of *information*. Gates therefore uses the image of Esu-Elegbara to stand as a shorthand reference for a complex of (1) strategic elusiveness, by means of (2) playful, cryptic communication, only divinable through (3) expertise with its (4) ritualized form, collapsed into the term *Signifyin(g)*.[26]

In African American life, playing the Dozens, the elaborate game of trading insults, is one well-known form of Signifyin(g).[27] Signifyin(g) in this case means turning the insult (or more neutrally, a phrase) back on the hurler, but now with a twist and therefore a new meaning. Underlying this verbal jousting ritual is the basic requirement that *both* parties understand the form of the game as well as what the remarks mean. This mutual understanding depends on the players' shared sense of *facticity* ("the quality or state of being a fact").[28]

Gates's work, seen in combination with Wilson's "African conceptual approaches" and Gilroy's "changing same," helps to explain the importance of Africa in African American music generally and in *Head*

Hunters more pointedly. Samuel Floyd Jr. makes the Africa/African American musical connection plain:

> In African American music, musical figures Signify by commenting on other musical figures, on themselves, on performances of other music, on other performances of the same piece, and on completely new works of music. Moreover, genres Signify on other genres—ragtime on European and . . . early American dance music; blues on the ballad; the spiritual on the hymn; jazz on blues and ragtime; gospel on the hymn, the spiritual, and blues; soul on rhythm and blues, rock 'n' roll, and rock music; bebop on swing, ragtime rhythms, and blues; funk on soul; rap on funk; and so on.[29]

Both Gates's "Signifyin(g)" and Wilson's "heterogeneous sound ideal" depend on sustaining the strong individual "voice" amid the complexity of rhythms. Anlo-Ewe master drummer C. K. Ladzekpo, elaborating on what has commonly been termed the "cross-rhythms" of these individual voices (i.e., a Western perspective of separate metric lines, in opposition to each other), explains them additionally from an Anlo-Ewe perspective as a "composite" rhythm, fulfilling in part a cultural and moral imperative.[30]

To Ladzekpo, the composite rhythm both reinforces a main meter for dancers' feet (usually with a duple or quadruple feel) and presents a single, multitimbral pattern, with each musician's line contributing to the whole, patterns coordinated rather than opposed. The patterns interlace, "simulating the dynamics of contrasting moments or emotional stress phenomena likely to occur in actual human existence." These composite rhythms act as more than a metaphor for the stresses of life, serving also as "a preventive prescription for extreme uneasiness of mind," a training ground of "simulated stress phenomena" against which the players "hone alertness, singleness of purpose, and resolute fearlessness."[31] The ritual, moral underlay guides the performance expectation and requires a precise understanding of "part to whole." As Summers, who studied with Ladzekpo, also emphasized: "The African does not sit down on drums and jam. . . . If you study Ewe music, you realize that every note has got to be in the right place." [32] Beyond the sounds of the notes, the woven lines reflect a cultural and moral underlay. To play a part in the matrix, you must be mentally agile, quick of hand, confident, and attentive to your fellow players—all characteristics that *Head Hunters* demanded.[33]

As it turns out, Ladzekpo's faculty colleague Olly Wilson had a tangential connection to Summers's presence on *Head Hunters.* Wilson researched and wrote his study during the years just before the album's release, when Summers was his student at the University of California at Berkeley. Interviewing Summers in 1998, I mentioned the album cover photograph's African imagery and asked about his background in traditional music:

> Q: What was your background before you got to [your music studies at] Berkeley? Were you rooted in an African tradition already?
> Summers: Yeah. Definitely.
>
> Q: As opposed to any other kind of, like *salsa* tradition or Cuban, or whatever.
> Summers: Yeah. All of that. But that's African.
>
> Q: Sure. But I mean—
> Summers: I'm just answering you. I was involved in African music before I got to U.C. Berkeley.[34]

My disconnecting salsa and other Afro-Caribbean styles from African music was accidental, but Summers quickly corrected my slip of the tongue. Originally a saxophonist, he had found himself as a teenager drawn to percussion, particularly through Afro-Cuban music. This interest quickly spread to sub-Saharan styles. Summers, pursuing ethnomusicology under Wilson, studied music traditions from a broad geographical area precisely because he saw them as connected. He had noticed sub-Saharan West African musical figures in African American and Afro-Caribbean musical influences, occurring over generations.[35] Summers brought his expertise, of course, to *Head Hunters.*

In Anlo-Ewe music, the gankogui bell is key to individual agility and interactive coordination. The traditional bell pattern acts as a homing beacon for all the players. Afro-Cuban music—an ocean away—

depends in a similar way on *clave*.[36] Besides being the name for an instrument of two wooden sticks, one cupped in the hand and the other striking it, clave also means the underlying two-measure metronomic pattern that the instrument plays in a wide variety of Afro-Cuban music styles (see fig. 4).[37]

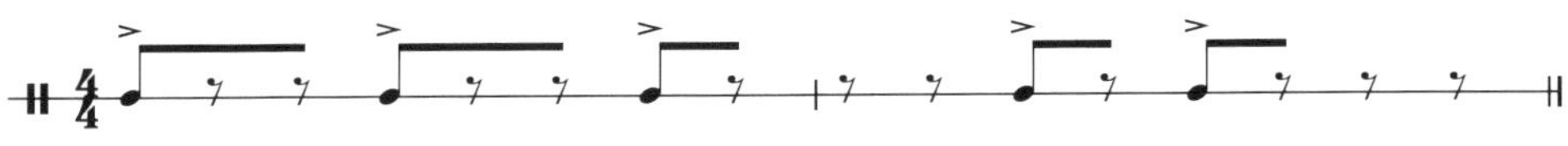

FIG. 4.

As with the gankogui pattern, clave provides the focal point used by all the players to establish and maintain facticity. Clave's syncopation Signifies on the beat, playing the trickster, alternately frustrating and then satisfying the expectation to land on a main pulse. In conversation, Bill Summers forcefully connected the clave function with Anlo-Ewe music, and with West Africa generally, calling it "definitely a part of Anlo-Ewe drumming. . . . Clave is African, totally. It has nothing to do with *Latin* [i.e., European] America, that's for sure. It's really an African thing." Summers went on to point out the drum set's historical connection with African aesthetics: "So with the African American, actually the most important African instrument in existence today in America, and in fact, the world at large, is the European marching drum set. If you notice, the patterns that are played by funk drummers, or played by jazz drummers, pretty much take their function from the *atsimevu* [lead drum] in an Ewe group."[38] Further, the instruments collected together into the drum set fill compatible roles with traditional Anlo-Ewe and Afro-Cuban drum ensembles:

> If you look at the hi-hat cymbal, that's your axatse [Ewe gourd rattle], that's your shekere [Afro-Cuban gourd rattle, also the identical instrument among the Nigerian Yoruba people]. That's your maraca. That's your fixed rhythmic group. You take your toms, there it is. The Native Americans contributed that to the first trap set. If you look at the trap sets from New Orleans, the first ones, they have Indian toms. Wooden

> drums, with skins on them. And what happened, my interpretation is this: [although] African [slaves] were not allowed to sit down together and play and perform together, the individuals *were* allowed to play in marching bands and military bands and given the opportunity to play European instruments.[39]

Summers was keenly aware that, whether acknowledged or not, African aesthetics infused African American music styles.

African Aesthetics in "Chameleon"

In "Chameleon," the first track on *Head Hunters*, Signifyin(g) pops up through the musicians' trickster approach to sound. As the song title suggests, the sounds are not always what they seem. The "bass" sound is not an electric bass; instead, it comes from two nearly identical synthesizer tracks, played together to create a stereo sound image. The "guitar" lick actually comes from an electric bass, played at its upper reaches (altissimo). And, contrary to the most basic of jazz aesthetics, which keep real-time interaction at the foreground, each instrument's track seems to have been recorded separately, so effectively has the engineer, Fred Catero, eliminated bleed-through; in reality, the song was recorded mostly "live."[40]

"Chameleon" also reinforces both Wilson's and Gates's conceptions through the music's organization. Despite the aural expectation to hear a song's melody right away, or at least soon after the song begins, Hancock puts it off for a minute and a half (1:29). "Chameleon"'s groove, not its melody, acts as the music's central organizing feature.[41] The "bass" two-measure pattern that begins the recording is repeated (00:05), setting the pattern as a two-cycle, four-measure ostinato figure (fig. 5), which continues to recycle, despite a couple of brief interruptions, for the next seven and a half minutes. After the fourth cycle, the drum set enters, with a recycling, two-measure groove of its own (fig. 6), which nonetheless complements the synthesized bass line.

With the "bass" and drum groove having been repeated until its presence is indelible, a new track layer appears (00:31). This time a "guitar"

FIG. 5. "Chameleon" ostinato groove—bass.

FIG. 6. "Chameleon" ostinato groove—bass and drums.

plays a muted-strings lick à la James Brown, its bent-note pickup (anacrusis) signaling each cycle's start.[42] Thus begins a layering process, building a *groove matrix:* after every fourth two-measure cycle, a new instrumental line joins, in a complementary, interlocking relationship with the others.[43] One by one, each new line entwines with its predecessors, until the sound space is filled (fig. 7).

How important is the groove in "Chameleon"'s overall plan? The answer lies in how much time the group spends assembling it, layer by layer, into a sonic edifice. As in the Anlo-Ewe example, each voice in the groove matrix refers to and complicates the synthesized bass ostinato, and each other, Signifyin(g) on each other. Throughout, the Anlo-Ewe gankogui bell pattern's organizing function is taken over by the bass ostinato. With the delayed melody entrance, the musicians thumb their noses at the melody's conventionally supreme place in the Western musical hierarchy, a position they emphasize with the melody's introduction. The four-phrase melody is halted (02:06) and begun again (02:15), as if to say, "Straight ahead? Guess again!"

FIG. 7. "Chameleon" ostinato groove—full matrix.

Although no one would mistake "Chameleon" for traditional African music or even Afro-pop, African aesthetics—as suggested by Wilson and Gates and dispersed across the diaspora, as identified by Gilroy—crop up almost at every turn. The transformation from the gankogui bell pattern to the bass line, a shift of instrument but not of function, suggests the "changing same" and replicates a similar transformation of the bell: the clave in Afro-Cuban music.

Herbie Hancock, describing how startling drummer Harvey Mason's syncopated backbeat sounded at the time, raved, "That beat on 'Chameleon,' nobody ever played that before."[44] The drum groove, reinforcing the bass ostinato, suggests a clave-like pattern, as well as fulfilling the normal clave organizing function. Figure 8 shows the basic drum motif, rewritten to emphasize both its halves, and compared with *son clave* (one of the most common clave patterns). The coordinated pattern between bass and snare drums omits only one note in the clave pattern, in the first measure; that note is supplied instead by the drum's partner, the "bass."

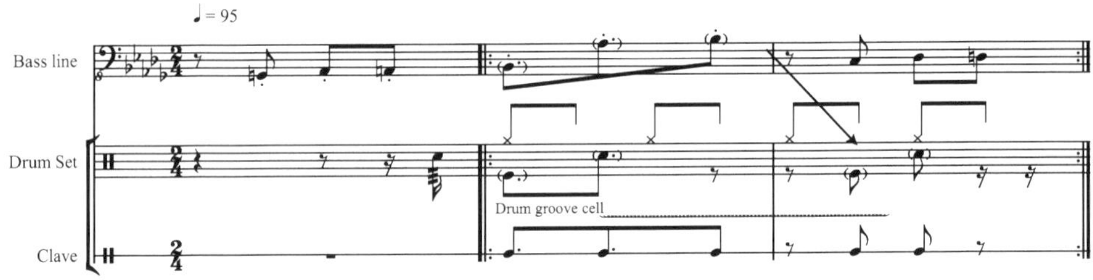

FIG. 8. Comparison of "Chameleon" groove cell with son clave.

The composite construction of this clave variation demonstrates the heterogeneous, matrixed construction described by both Ladzekpo and Wilson, in miniature. In the context of funk, Mason's backbeat snap just before it "should" happen (i.e., just before beat *three*) is startling. He is Signifyin(g) on the backbeat.

In jazz drumming, Signifyin(g) on the ride beat is not only allowable but desirable. But roles in African music tend to be more defined: the privilege of Signifyin(g) is granted to certain characters in the ensemble, while the rest of the group reinforces the groove. In "Chameleon," Harvey Mason's drumming style is highly interactive, Signifyin(g) on both traditions.[45] Mason establishes the groove in the first full measure of his entrance (at eleven seconds into the piece). Yet he Signifies on his groove almost immediately (fig. 9), his "ostinato" relegated to the listener's imagination. He varies the pattern by degrees, however, rather than radically shifting it before the pattern can be set firmly in the players' (and listeners') minds. Mason claims considerable latitude to vary his pattern, while still reinforcing the *sense* of stability by making sure to land on key notes in the groove.[46] As in the case of post-bebop drummers (e.g., Elvin Jones and Tony Williams), Mason refers to the groove frequently, dipping into the flow of it, while asserting his right to improvise on it, although in the context of funk. By simultaneously reinforcing and destabilizing this "stability," Mason Signifies on the groove, creating, to use Gates's terminology, "repetition with a signal difference." His improvisational style dances between traditions. It is simultaneously a case of the liberation of the drummer from the constraints of being "merely" the timekeeper, on the one hand (a freedom increasingly claimed since the advent of bebop), and, on the other, a transgression of the African-derived drum choir's traditional role (as embodied by the drummer) of reinforcing the groove.[47]

FIG. 9. "Chameleon": Harvey Mason establishing and then varying the groove.

His transgression is made possible because, similar to developments in jazz drumming in which players and listeners hold the ride beat in facticity, the backbeat in rhythm-and-blues (the parent of rock 'n' roll, soul, and funk), has become so endemic as to be internalized.[48] With the backbeat as anchor, the rest of the pattern could be elaborated in myriad ways without disrupting the dance groove. In fact, these various articulations take on identities: trap drummers strive to create identifiable patterns as "the beat" for particular songs, just as bass players—particularly in funk—will devise a particular ostinato pattern that becomes identified with a particular song.

Compare jazz drumming with funk drumming, embodied in the styles of Clyde Stubblefield (the JBs), David Garibaldi (Tower of Power), and Tiki Fulwood (Funkadelic). In place of the ride beat's swing triplet orientation, the main beats are subdivided as even eighth-notes, and in place of the shimmering ride cymbal, the metronome is primarily played as crisp clicks with the stick on the closed hi-hat. In jazz, not only the cymbal but also the drums reverberate, both beaten and resonating heads in place, tuned high and vibrating. Funk drum sets tend to be tuned low, often with the resonating head taken off and with a deadening pillow in the bass drum. While in jazz the ride beat is played on the ride cymbal and reinforced by the hi-hat pedaled "chick" on the backbeat, freeing the snare drum and bass drum for irregularly spaced "comping," the funk beat employs the sticked hi-hat, snare drum, and bass drum in a matrix. And while Williams's and Jones's fills occur throughout, using all the drum set's voices, funk drummers are more likely to keep the groove stable, filling at the ends of phrases; even fills tend to stay with hi-hat, snare, and bass drum interaction. Although both drumming styles exemplify African-based aesthetics, post-bebop drumming emphasizes Signifyin(g), while funk drumming emphasizes heterogeneity. Mason does both (fig. 10).

FIG. 10. "Chameleon" ostinato groove—bass and drums.

Keeping time on the hi-hat and playing a beat that owes much to the interplay of snare and bass drums, Mason plays on deeply tuned, dry-sounding instruments, the epitome of the funk style in 1973. Although coordinated, the three instruments are timbrally distinct, heterogeneous. Signifyin(g) relentlessly on the bass synthesizer groove, Mason nonetheless keeps his variations centered on interactive play between the closed hi-hat, snare drum, and bass drum. His playing style does much to complicate *Head Hunters*' identity (is it jazz or funk?) at the same time that it makes the aesthetic reference to Africa utterly unambiguous.

I am a Negro;
Black as the night is black;
Black like the depths of my Africa.
—*Langston Hughes, "I Am a Negro"*

Recurring charges of Herbie Hancock's having sold out in creating *Head Hunters* leave lingering questions.[49] Perhaps chief among them is, if Hancock wished to turn to popular music, why did he not turn to rock? Funk, and its parent soul (and its rhythm-and-blues grandparent), certainly had captured the commercial attention of the country by the early seventies, but rock was where the *serious* money lay. Hancock had ample opportunity to incorporate rock into his style.[50] His Miles Davis Quintet bandmate Tony Williams was an avid rock fan and recently, with Lifetime, had moved in a rock direction. Hancock's producer and manager, David Rubinson, had made his own name producing rock and pop acts; would soon become a partner of rock impresario Bill Graham; and was originally directed to Herbie Hancock through Jim Hilton, the Iron Butterfly's manager (of "In-A-Gadda-Da-Vida" fame).[51] If Hancock intended to prostitute himself, why not go all the way?

By the time of *Head Hunters*, Hancock (with Rubinson at the production helm) had already delved into African imagery and become attracted to Sly Stone's and James Brown's music, in part because of its sociopolitical significance.[52] Reconsiderations by Kofi Agawu and Paul Gilroy notwithstanding, in 1973 invoking Africa as an icon seemed unproblematic philosophically, in the face of its rapidly growing importance as a historical, cultural, and political touchstone.[53]

In the spring of that year, the last American units left Vietnam. The war had proved a disaster and had been focal point for countercultural activist alliances. With the war no longer an issue, the alliances, already tenuous, dissipated. The rhetoric of Black Consciousness was still in the air and growing, but many of the organizers for political action had left the scene or had been pushed from it. The formerly formidable Students for a Democratic Society (SDS), Student Nonviolent Coordinating Committee (SNCC), Black Panther Party, and other activist youth organizations lay in tatters, soon to fade altogether.[54] However, these movements still held sway as popular idealizations even though their political force was now tempered.

By 1973, Herbie Hancock had taken the name Mwandishi (Swahili for *composer*).[55] Asked about this in a 2001 interview by Cairo journalist Tarek Atia, Hancock explained:

> The early seventies were a period following the different kinds of social revolutions that were happening, and particularly in the United States, on various issues, Civil Rights being one of them, which included more of a recognition by the African American community of our heritage from Africa, . . . and adoption of Swahili names became one example of recognizing the African part of our heritage. . . . The sixties gave us a chance, because of the Civil Rights Movement, to kind of re-examine and make some sort of formal connection to our African-ness.[56]

Hancock, along with several other jazz musicians at the time, adopted a name in an East Coast, not West Coast, African language. Swahili, originally a lingua franca for trade in the Tanzania-Kenya coastal region, is the second most common language on the continent (Arabic is the first). Deprived of a specific homeland, black-conscious African Americans claimed Africa as a whole. Patrick Gleeson recounted reminiscing with Hancock about Julian Priester's influential presence:

> "He was the best trombone player in the world," [Hancock] said, "for that band [i.e., the Mwandishi group]." And then, you know, I understood what he meant. I think I took it quite correctly, that he wasn't saying that—there's lots of trombone players that are better technically; hell, there's better piano players than Herbie is technically, that's not the point. But that *Julian's Afrocentricity and his spirit and his spiritual honesty and clearness were part of the spirit of that band.* It was an important part of what he brought to that band. And just as every night, he showed up for work in a dashiki and with his African talisman around his neck, so did he spiritually. And that was part of what made that band that band.[57]

Departing from the romanticized African iconography of *Crossings* and *Sextant*, the mask on the *Head Hunters* album cover toys with jazz's early representations as primitive and uncontrolled.[58] Refashioning "primitivism" and "progress" as conjectural, the visual message clearly presents Hancock (and his music) as an in-your-face challenge to the polite, middle-of-the-road trajectory in jazz (addressing a "middle-of-the-road" that by now had been abandoned by anything resembling a numerically mainstream audience).[59]

Hancock's and funk's populism beckoned first to working-class black listeners.[60] Beyond this, the album broadened its populist stance along generational lines. Besides its parody of the Primitive, the album cover (and the album title) beckoned to hip, mind-expanding youth of any stripe. The album title and band name (*Head Hunters*/the Headhunters), slyly invoking youth's mind-expansionist argot, leave Hancock's meaning indeterminate. Left to the imagination is whether the heads he searches for are countercultural youth; Black Nationalists; expansionist-minded jazz, rock, or funk fans; or all of these, an example of Signifyin(g)'s indeterminacy.

Alongside the album cover's visual richness, Hancock and the other Headhunters Signify on the American "jazz tradition." Using rhythms and sounds from across the African diaspora (Brazilian samba-jazz, Ba-Benzélé pygmy *hindewhu*, Afro-Cuban percussion, and African American funk, to name a few), but employing forms and procedures long identified with jazz (emphasis on improvisation, extended solo form, jazz harmonic sonorities, and a small-group jazz instrumentation, albeit modified by the emphasis on electronics and amplification), they reinscribe jazz as populist, black, and adventurous. The result for Hancock's career was that, as he recalled to Bob Palmer the following year, he built a new connection with a young, black audience.[61]

For Bill Summers, the inscription of the music as Africa diasporic had political poignancy. For him, this identification was a form of outreach and education. "I've always applied [African musical concepts] to the commercial music that I come in contact with," he told me, "because I want to bring [up] the level of appreciation of the African experience and the African American, Afro-Caribbean, Afro–South American experience: I want to bring the level of consciousness up in people, so they realize how important a contribution that really was to the world of music. And it's been hidden, and it's been buried. And in many cases, not by White America, but by the musicians themselves, for having lack of respect for the origins of their own music."[62]

Commenting on the gap, routinely explored by jazz musicians, between sounded notes and their intertextual references (a "chain of associations"), Ingrid Monson argues that such a chain "may be set off that engages the listener and unites her or him with a community of other individuals who share a similar musical [or social, political, etc.] point of view." "The cultural knowledge of African American musicians," she points out, "includes familiarity with both 'black' and 'white' music and it is upon *all* of this knowledge that a musician draws in the act of performance."[63] This chain of associations, not only of "whiteness" and "blackness" but also of the histories of black slavery, European colonialism, and African postcolonialism, and the rhetorics of black cultural nationalism, holds true in both the music and the visual presentation of *Head Hunters.* Hancock issued no manifestos accompanying the album's release, nor did he with his earlier albums. Yet considering the climate of the times, his choice to close a gap of relevance with a young, hip, and politically engaged black audience was political on its face. The album's music, its image, its musicians, and its populism all expressed "an African thing."

CHAPTER 3

At the Crossroads of Genre

Funk in Action

> I think that the people that made that shift really occur were people like Lee Morgan, when he did "Sidewinder." People like Horace Silver, "Song for My Father." Hank Mobley. They started funkifying it. They started putting the funk in it, and then other people started feeling it. Even Herbie, when he did "Watermelon Man." OK, that was the beginning of the Headhunters stuff. That was really where it started.
>
> —*Bill Summers*

With *Head Hunters*, Herbie Hancock immersed himself in African-based aesthetics, but the entryway to that aesthetic fountainhead was through an African American music: funk. Though he might have seemed an unlikely member of the early seventies funk scene, Hancock had already started down the road to funkiness more than a decade earlier. He first burst upon the jazz world with the 1962 hit "Watermelon Man," a funky, R&B-influenced hard bop tune featuring Freddie Hubbard and Dexter Gordon.[1] Mongo Santamaria's *son*-inflected cover version the following year showed "Watermelon Man"'s affinity with Afro-Cuban musics and suggested R&B's kinship with Afro-Caribbean musics generally.[2] The *Head Hunters* recording of the song eleven years later connected it more explicitly to Africa, and this later version, played at slow-grind speed, demonstrates Hancock's grasp of funkiness gained over the intervening years.

The three versions of "Watermelon Man" offer insights on musical and cultural attractions to funkiness and how different expressions of funkiness relate to each other. The 1973 version, taken together with two other tracks, "Chameleon" and "Sly," shows intersections between funky jazz and the development of funk in the early seventies. Together, they offer details on Hancock's deepening attraction to black popular music. Funkiness carried with it the stamp of African American populist identity, which Hancock considered an aesthetic and social goal.[3] Funk music's influence on and relationship to *Head Hunters* is a key dimension in the album's extended web of affiliations.

The Funky Jazz Stream

In 1962, at age twenty-two, Herbie Hancock wrote and recorded "Watermelon Man" and gained national attention as part of a second wave of young jazz performers playing a substyle of hard bop called "funky jazz." It seemed to critics and fans that hard bop and its funky subsidiary amounted to a rejection of cool's "whitening" of jazz. David Rosenthal seconds this position: "Although some blacks—for example Miles Davis and pianist John Lewis—were involved, at least briefly, [cool jazz] was overwhelmingly a white phenomenon, both in its protagonists and its audience."[4] The association of cool jazz and the West Coast is not altogether accurate, as many have pointed out.[5] Ted Gioia, however, provides a guide to sonic markers of cool/West Coast by whatever title, such as a "strong compositional emphasis," an emphasis on counterpoint, less "dominating" drumming styles, clean note articulations, and "fluid and polished" execution.[6] While much has been said indicating hard bop as a reaction against cool jazz, Rosenthal argues against oversimplification. To him, while racial politics certainly play a part, hard bop also represents a reinterpretation of bebop's idioms and aesthetics.[7] Lewis Porter and Michael Ullman also argue that the racial politics assumed to be embedded in the two styles are overstated: "Cool players never lost the beat," and hard bop players weren't necessarily rejecting a cool style they had tired of, since as Porter and Ullman point out, "[Art Blakey] had been playing vigorously since the forties, and had nothing to prove."[8] But racial politics were not *absent* in the juxtaposition of styles, even if they were in the minds of jazz fans, and they were inscribed in hard bop song titles like "Opus de Funk," "The Preacher," and "Dis Heah."[9]

Musicians such as Horace Silver, Art Blakey, and Max Roach pared down their harmonies to basic triads, stripping their compositions of bebop's harmonic complexity, a complexity that cool endorsed wholeheartedly. They favored minor keys, turned melodic contours away from the mercurial leaps and turns of bebop, played generally slower tempos, and emphasized blues and gospel song structures. Where chamber music–like aesthetics seemed to dominate the "cool–West Coast style"—smooth ensemble blend, moderate to quiet volume, and discreetly supportive drumming—hard bop emphasized expressive, personalized timbres: horn players unpacked their storehouses of vibratos, shakes, rasps, and squeals, and drummers played aggressively. Unapologetically danceable, hard bop also reached for provocative expressions of personal styles and cultural truths.

Danceability seems to be a dividing line in portrayals of jazz as art or entertainment. Jump blues (sometimes called jump swing), in the style of Louis Jordan, Amos Milburn, and others, was another tributary of rhythm-and-blues in the late forties and throughout the fifties. Rosenthal and Baraka both mention Jordan, whose pared-down groups, shuffle rhythms, and novelty lyrics added much to rhythm-and-blues. David Ake discusses Jordan's slippery identity as both a rhythm-and-blues and a jazz figure and the historiographical problem his dual role suggests.[10] Ake's work adds to the growing body of scholarship that questions the more-or-less straight evolutionary line of development that dominates jazz historical scholarship (at least through bebop).[11]

To some, hard bop seemed a repudiation of bebop's advances, both artistic and social. Amiri Baraka argues that hard bop represents a squandered opportunity to press African American music's identity as artistically progressive and culturally revolutionary. Baraka feels a significant part of bebop's worth lay in its inattention to the whims of popularity: "To a certain extent, [bebop] resulted from conscious attempts to remove it from the danger of mainstream dilution or even understanding. For one thing, the young musicians began to think of themselves as *serious* musicians, even artists, not performers. And that attitude erased immediately the protective and parochial atmosphere of 'the folk expression' from jazz." Hard bop's references to black culture, incorporating rhythm-and-blues and gospel, had the virtue of marking the music ethnically, thereby reinforcing jazz ownership in African American territory. Yet by pointedly incorporating black working-class elements, Baraka writes, hard bop substituted "largeness of timbre and quasi-gospel influences for actual rhythmic or melodic diversity and freshness."[12]

Baraka focuses much of his disapproval on the "funky jazz" component of the broad hard bop movement. He complains that, with funky jazz, "*funky* (a word with as dubious a place in polite society as jazz) became the treasured adjective, where once cool had been." Baraka's complaint with *funky* and its companion term, *soul*, does not center on its baseness. Rather, he argues with its ersatz use as a cultural signifier, calling *soul* "a quality of expression, probably found only in Negroes wearing Italian suits . . . and merely calling tunes 'Dis Heah' or dropping *g*'s from titles is not going to make the music more compelling."[13]

In Baraka's view, hard bop's funkiness is disingenuous and mannered, "a self-conscious celebration of cliché and an actual debilitation of the most impressive ideas to come out of bebop." He sees hard bop, as a whole, as ultimately misguided. Despite its musicians distancing themselves from cool as a "middlebrow music," hard bop provided, "because of its musical and extra-musical affectations and its conspicuous 'exclusiveness' . . . a group of anthems for another kind of American middlebrow—a black one."[14] Baraka, although never mentioning social theorist Theodor Adorno, seems to echo Adorno's concerns that popular music's lack of intellectual challenge short-circuits its ability to foster and encourage redemptive, revolutionary social change.[15] Baraka sees jazz's progressivism—especially the change signaled by bebop, from jazz as "entertainment" to jazz as "art"—as a crucial step toward black social transformation to full membership in American society. Hard bop's place in this campaign, to Baraka, stems from neither its musical qualities nor its populism, which he sees as regressive, but from its role as a training ground for the jazz avant-garde, whom he sees as the real cultural heroes.

In contrast to Baraka's take on hard bop as middlebrow posturing, playacting one's roots, historian David Rosenthal sees vitality and optimism in the music and an extension of bebop's musical and social accomplishments. Adapting Stanley Dance's "mainstream," Rosenthal explains hard bop as occupying a broad swath of related and intersecting styles. Hard bop became the new jazz mainstream. "By 1955," he writes, "bebop was treated by jazzmen as but one genre among many. Hard bop functioned as an opening out in numerous directions."[16]

Rosenthal surveys hard bop's tributaries and sidestreams. He traces their stylistic intersections; musicians' shifting membership in groups and on recordings; and the nature of the jazz life, which is fragmented and contingent on the demands of the gig.[17] As an almost inevitable output of these factors, Rosenthal describes hard bop not as a style but as a collection of styles within an interpersonal musical practice. Rather than marking hard bop as a misguided digression from bebop's social and musical progressivism, or at best an exit point for frustrated artists anxious to jump into the avant-garde wilds, Rosenthal sees hard bop as a complex musical-social assemblage, which he calls "hard bop heterodoxy."[18]

To Rosenthal, hard bop is made up of not one but four currents, with plenty of intersection among them: (1) jazz infused with black vernacular idioms (also known as "funky jazz" or "soul jazz"); (2) "dark," moody expressiveness; (3) "lighter," lyrical playing, not normally associated with hard bop but nonetheless played by hard bop–associated musicians; and (4) experimentalists "consciously trying to expand jazz's structural and technical boundaries: for instance, Andrew Hill, Sonny Rollins, and John Coltrane prior to his 1965 record *Ascension*." Rosenthal, like Baraka, places emphasis on funky jazz, but in more approving terms. He describes it as the "borderline between jazz and black popular music, that [draws] heavily on urban blues, gospel, and Latin American music."[19] Recordings by Jimmy Smith, Horace Silver, Cannonball Adderley, and others conspicuously inhabit African American cultural territory. And to be sure, many non–African Americans who played this music in hard bop's heyday were nonetheless sympathetic to its expressiveness as black music.[20] Hard bop put black American life—all of it—in the foreground. And whether "funky," "lyrical," "astringent," or "experimentalist," this African American cultural linkage made it comfortable for players primarily associated with any of these subcategories to perform across their generic borders, depending on the requirements of the occasion.

Inherent in the permeability of these stylistic borders is the truth that jazz musicians—indeed, working musicians generally—release records not merely to document their art but also to sell it. To Baraka (and Adorno before him), trade and art are mutually antagonistic. While hard bop did not foment the revolution Baraka may have had in mind, the music's heterodoxy did disrupt fixed concepts of genre and, with them, rigidities of class within black cultural life. The conflict outlined by Baraka amounts to a showdown between commercial and art music, as if they could or should be held separate. In fact, funky jazz musicians played commercial music artistically *and* released art music commercially; the two musics were, in many cases, one and the same.

Herbie Hancock, recording such funky jazz tunes as "Cantaloupe Island" and "Watermelon Man," made the most of this blended role, just as he did later with *Head Hunters*, infusing his jazz style with the black popular music of the day. Even Hancock, though, was unaware at the time of other important diasporic intersections with this style.

Hard Bop and Afro-Caribbean Music

Besides its obvious lineage from bebop, hard bop is so often linked additionally to gospel music and rhythm-and-blues as to be considered sine qua non.[21] Straight-eighth (rather than swing) beat subdivisions, basic triadic harmony, and slower tempos draw directly from gospel, and their presence in fifties hard bop coincided with Ray Charles's blending of the same elements in the construction of soul music.[22] Observers less frequently spot a connection between hard bop and Afro-Caribbean music. Rosenthal does make the linkage, however, noting that "Afro-Cuban influences had been frequent in bebop" and were prominent features of hard bop recordings of the time (e.g., "Nica's Dream" and "Ecaroh," both on *The Jazz Messengers*, released in 1956).[23] Afro-Caribbean musics, especially the *montuno* in Afro-Cuban *son*-derived styles, attracted hard bop players partly because their forms lent themselves to improvisation and partly because they recaptured jazz's former dance orientation.[24]

The montuno, a solo-over-vamp section derived from rumba and son traditions, provided an opportunity to develop solos over an ostinato pattern.[25] In addition to rumba and son montuno, the later developments of mambo and salsa share this formal feature. In these and other Cuban and Puerto Rican son-based music traditions, the montuno provides an extended period of stability (most often as the final section of a piece): a harmonically static, cyclic rhythmic framework over which a soloist improvises. The benefit to the soloist in this situation is that, with the harmonic rhythm slowed to a standstill, and with the "tyranny of the chord progression" as the basis for soloing eliminated, the soloist—singer or instrumentalist—is free to explore rhythmic and melodic ideas to the fullest. In a montuno section, the soloist inspires the dancers and other musicians, fulfilling a *variable rhythmic* role; this role is highlighted in interaction with a rhythmic matrix (a *fixed rhythmic* group) made up of interlocking percussion instruments.[26] Short brass and/or vocal responses (*estribillos*) join the percussion matrix, making the fixed rhythmic group even more complex. In this context, fancy harmonic progressions are irrelevant and distracting. The primary interest centers on *ritmo*, the complex, sophisticated interplay of rhythmic clash and interaction realizable only through the interplay of distinct, heterogeneous timbres.

Dizzy Gillespie incorporated montunos as early as 1947 in such "Cubop" pieces as "Cubana Be" and "Manteca."[27] In doing so, he established the first post-bebop trend, predating Miles Davis's 1949 *Birth of the Cool* investigations of timbre by two years. Just a few years into bebop's revolutionary approaches to harmony, melody, rhythm, and phrasing, Gillespie actively sought to reconnect jazz's artistic aspirations to dance through Afro-Caribbean music, which demanded action on the dance floor. In his memoir, Gillespie links jazz with African approaches to rhythm, then writes: "Jazz was invented for people to dance. So when you play jazz and people don't feel like dancing or moving their feet, you're getting away from the idea of the music."[28] Gillespie's attraction to dance in the forties is echoed by Art Blakey, speaking about hard bop a decade later: "When we're on the stand, and we see that there are people in the audience who aren't patting their feet and who aren't nodding their heads to our music, we know we're doing something wrong. Because when we do get our message across, those heads and feet do move."[29] Likewise, "Watermelon Man" derives its place in history from its popularity as dance music.

"Watermelon Man," as Hancock first recorded it, foregrounds a bluesy, gospel quality while subtly suggesting the clave-based rhythm of Afro-Cuban music. But in this original recording, the clave-based rhythm is recessed into the mix, compared with any of the previous Cubop recordings (in the Gillespie mold) or with Cuban popular music (of any kind). Compared with those hard bop tunes that broadcast their Latin ties, "Watermelon Man"'s connection was inadvertent.[30] Hancock had not planned to Latinize the song. As a funky jazz recording, though, it shared common musical ground with gospel, rhythm-and-blues—and Afro-Caribbean musics.

Formally, "Watermelon Man" is a blues arrangement, elongated by the twice-delayed return to the tonic (fig. 11). The chart following (fig. 12) shows the paradigmatic twelve-bar blues structure (how "Watermelon Man" would be if it adhered to the normal form) with its alteration:

FIG. 11. "Watermelon Man" melody with harmonic plan.

											|----enlongation----|		
Measure Numbers	1	2	3	4	5	6	7	8	9	10	repeat 9 & 10 (2x)	11	12
12-bar blues form.	I	-	I	-	IV	-	I	-	V	IV		I	-

FIG. 12. Twelve-bar blues (showing alteration of blues form).

Hancock corroborated the conception of "Watermelon Man" as a funky blues, rather than an Afro-Cuban tune. Discussing the 1963 version, by Mongo Santamaria, I remarked, "In an interview, you talked about Mongo opening your eyes to the Latin aspect of that song, where before you had thought of it as just an R&B song." Hancock replied, "Right. Well, I thought of it as a jazz tune. Just a funky jazz tune. Not really an R&B tune, but kind of inspired from the R&B sensibility."[31] But Hancock would soon learn that his funky jazz tune was inextricably linked with an Afro-Caribbean sensibility:

> I got this gig with Mongo, in the fall or early winter of 1962. Now, my record was either not quite out or it had just come out the week before or something like that. I had never played Latin music before, I didn't have a clue about it. And Mongo's former piano player had quit, and his new piano player wasn't coming in till the following Monday. So there was this weekend, where Mongo had some gigs with no piano player. So I got the gig with him. They knew I hadn't played Latin piano, and they figured, well, they'd get some of the guys in the band just to show me some montunos. Just some basic stuff, so they could get through the weekend and get paid.
>
> One of the gigs we played was in the Bronx. And Donald Byrd and I shared an apartment in the Bronx, so Donald came by to hear how his "little brother" was doing, playing Latin music with Mongo Santamaria. And we were playing at this supper club. During a break, Donald and Mongo had this conversation . . . the gist of which I found out later: I actually was not involved in that conversation. I just once in a while would get a little whiff of something they were talking about. . . . The gist of it was that Mongo said that, considering the fact that African Americans and Afro-Cubans had this common heritage from West Africa, he had never really heard—*he was looking for the musical link that would link the Afro-Caribbean kind of music* (whether it's Afro-Cuban or whatever: he happened to be Afro-Cuban) *and the African American thing.*
>
> He had more or less what we'd call today a salsa band. . . . So I'm halfway hearing this conversation. Donald Byrd says, "Herbie, why don't you play 'Watermelon Man' for Mongo?" and I say, "Huh?" I'm thinking, "What's that got to do with what he's talking about? This is a serious conversation. It's like trying to find the missing link."
>
> So I started playing "Watermelon Man." And Mongo said, "Keep playing." So Mongo got up on the congas. As soon as he started playing, it was like a perfect fit. It was like a hand in a glove. And it just gave it a character that—it just blew everybody away.[32]

Jazz has been infused with Afro-Caribbean elements—which Jelly Roll Morton described as the "Spanish tinge"—from the beginning.[33] These elements have been reinforced over a century, in myriad ways, from the *habanera*-like "secondary rag" right-hand figures in ragtime piano (see figs. 13 and 14), through the succession of Latin dance crazes that filtered through much American popular music, from Tin Pan Alley songs of the earliest decades of the twentieth century to Bo Diddley and far beyond.[34] Afro-Caribbean idioms are tightly woven into the fabric of American music.

FIG. 13. Habanera rhythmic structure.

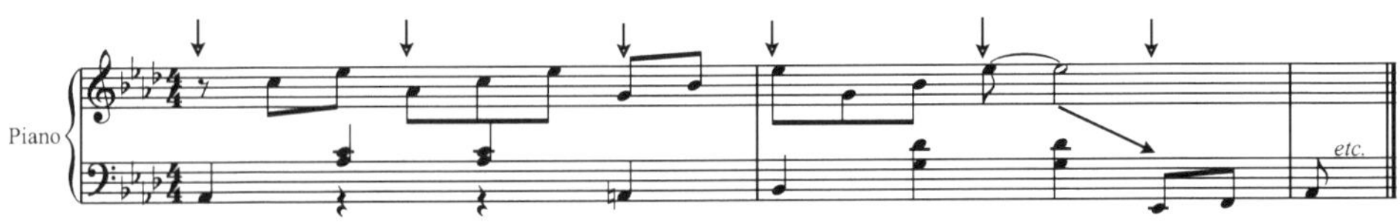

FIG. 14. Habanera as secondary rag rhythm in "Maple Leaf Rag."

Santamaria discovered, in "Watermelon Man," elements shared between his own Afro-Cuban music and funky jazz (and its tributaries), including rhythms, dance movement, and song forms. That these intersections could be news to both Santamaria and Hancock suggests that they derived from unconsciously shared cultural approaches to music-making, rather than particularly intentional or conscious cross-cultural study.

Hancock's firsthand experience with the powerful affinity of the two traditions was to become dramatized even further that evening:

> Little by little, the other guys in the band started joining in. And little by little, the people started getting up on the dance floor. Pretty soon, everybody was dancing and screaming. And the whole band was playing and laughing and having a great time. It was like a movie. I couldn't believe it. And then we finished the song, and everybody's jumping around and hugging and kissing. And everybody's saying, "This is a hit! This is a hit!" And I was overwhelmed. So Mongo Santamaria said, "Can I record this?" and I said, "By all means."[35]

Bebop in the forties had recast jazz as serious music, more appropriate to the crowded jazz club or the concert stage than to the dance hall. Jazz songs that claimed crossover success, like Dave Brubeck's "Take Five" and the Stan Getz–João Gilberto–Astrud Gilberto bossa nova "Girl from Ipanema," emphasizing this seriousness, kept to a chamber music–like sound, sophisticated harmony, and a lyrical approach to soloing. In contrast, as if to underscore the opinions of Dizzy Gillespie and Art Blakey, Santamaria's version of "Watermelon Man" became a gigantic pop hit—as a dance record. As in the case of other funky jazz tunes, Hancock's 1962 "Watermelon Man" appealed to both high art and populist aesthetics. Despite Hancock's lack of intention to create a syncretic tune, the Afro-Caribbean connection was clearly present. Santamaria's version made the most of the tune's cross-cultural relevance.

The personnel on Hancock's version do not suggest a successful marriage with Afro-Cuban music. Recorded with a typical small-group instrumentation, the players include Dexter Gordon (ts), Freddie Hubbard (t), Butch Warren (b), Billy Higgins (d), and Hancock (pno)—all of whom had jazz credentials aplenty, but little enough experience in Afro-Cuban music. In contrast, Santamaria's version incorporates jazz musicians, to be sure—Marty Sheller (t), Pat Patrick and Bobby Capers (ts, fl), and Rodgers Grant (pno)—but the "engine room" is made up of solidly Afro-Cuban instrumentation: Frank Hernandez (d), Victor Venegas (b), and a percussion section of Santamaria, Kako, Chihuahua Martinez, and Joseph Gorgas. In addition, Hancock had originally recorded the song in the normal jazz recording format of melody—extended solos—melody restatement, an outgrowth of the arrangement style associated with bebop. The seven-minute recording was much too long for a seven-inch 45-rpm release or mainstream radio format, and it was released on an album, *Takin' Off*. Santamaria's recording was more tautly timed (2:26), and it was released both as a single and as the lead song on an album. Santamaria's Afro-Cuban recording, not Hancock's, became the song's definitive version, rising to Top Ten positions on both the *Billboard* pop and rhythm-and-blues charts.

Santamaria's search for a missing link and Byrd's response, requesting Hancock to play "Watermelon Man," demonstrate the sensitivity of both musicians to the web of affiliations that binds jazz and Afro-

Caribbean musics together. Since Hancock's piano accompaniment style on the 1962 recording was far more commonly associated with gospel than with Afro-Cuban sensibilities, Byrd's attentiveness to the song's Afro-Cuban potential could have been missed by someone less perceptive. The reaction on the dance floor verified this connection. Not only did Santamaria's Cubanizing invigorate Hancock's piece, but the Cuban's audience, who came to dance as well as dine, were in turn aroused by the marriage of styles. The accidental quality of all this, illustrated by Hancock's initial "huh?" reaction, underscores how deep and pervasive this web is. Not only did Hancock *not* anticipate the Afro-Cuban connection, but, when I asked if this experience sparked a new interest in studying Latin rhythms, he said, "Nope. That was [Santamaria's] quest. It wasn't mine."[36] Hancock's interest in the tune remained with funkiness, as part of an African American aesthetic.[37]

Over the next few years, and primarily due to the Santamaria version's popularity, "Watermelon Man" would be covered over 250 times. Santamaria emerged as a leader in what John Storm Roberts has called a Latin-jazz-funk nexus, largely on the strength of "Watermelon Man," Santamaria's most successful recording.

Fifties Funky Jazz to Seventies Funk

As with funky jazz in the fifties, funkiness and funk music in the seventies became definable in aesthetic and political terms. Funk, as an outgrowth, or intensification, of soul, tapped a black populist consciousness, emphasizing the African-based aesthetics discussed earlier (see chap. 2). Rickey Vincent, in his book-length study of this music, writes, "More than a style, it is a means to a style." To Vincent, "jazz, the Caribbean Carnival, bebop, and The Funk" are mutually influential, each music an example of a generalized black popular self-expression. It is "an aesthetic of deliberate confusion, of uninhibited, soulful behavior that remains viable because of a faith in instinct, a joy of self, and a joy of life, particularly unassimilated black American life." First and foremost, funk in the seventies was people's music: "The implicit nature of The Funk, its inherent *nastayness*, which cannot help but drive people closer to their funky soul, peels off the veneer of pretense and exposes the unpackaged self for all to see."[38] For Vincent, "The Funk" stands as shorthand for a black working-class cultural identity ("their funky soul"), but funk's appeal in the seventies extended beyond this confined demographic.[39]

Funk played two sides of the street; by emphasizing black Otherness musically and textually, musicians and audiences portrayed funk as black music for black people, an Afrocentric stance that also appealed to non-black Others. Echoing an argument by Baraka, Vincent asserts that "aspects of black folks' funkiness are ultimately what have fueled mainstream American culture."[40] The cultural mainstream's attraction to funkiness is evident in its positive yet somewhat wistful response to funk—"wistful" because, though it is an expression of an Othered subculture, funkiness is emblematic of a hipness generally considered unattainable by that mainstream: an intersection between a romanticized marginalization (which might be attainable) and an actual one (which is less likely and in the end less desirable). The enormous crossover popularity of Tower of Power's "What Is Hip?" and "You've Got to Funkifize," as well as the Average White Band's "Pick Up the Pieces" and Wild Cherry's "Play That Funky Music," attest to this.[41] Beyond the anomalous ethnic makeup of the two bands (Tower of Power's mixed-race lineup and the Average White Band's white, Scottish members), "What Is Hip?" tries to locate the elusive cultural hipness embodied in funk, and "Play That Funky Music" tells of a white musician overcoming a potentially hostile challenge to play funk on a par with authentic, black musicians: "Play that funky music, white boy."

To love funk in the seventies was to build an alliance of difference, continuing a generational opposition to the encroaching, staid, Nixon-era world of the over-thirty set. Ingrid Monson, discussing hipness vis-à-vis jazz, links centuries-old associations between a complex of "blackness, social transgression, and pathology" with the "stereotype of the nonconformist, hip, deviant, jazz musician," associations whose scary but attractive image transferred, as she points out, "to musicians who developed the later styles of hard bop, cool, and free jazz."[42] Monson identifies an admiring yet patronizing primitivist view by the (white) mainstream of the hip black musician and of black identity, generally. As Monson notes, this stereotype is troubling, for it promulgates (even if unwittingly) a stereotype of black culture as transgressive: "Whether conceived as an absence of morality or of bourgeois pretensions, this view [by the mainstream] of blackness, paradoxically, buys into the historical legacy of primitivism and its concomitant exoticism of the 'Other.' "[43] Funk, writes Vincent, claimed a similar alterity: "The childlike, 'dirty' nature of some funk lyrics is also a deliberate return to an uninhibited state of mind, a state of childlike innocence and wonder, as a part of an adult state of sexual release and a state of African-rooted balance between Western and African opposites."[44] Vincent's comment shows that the same primitivist stereotyping extended to funk as well, and not always from outsiders. However, he seems relatively unconcerned about this view. He portrays funkiness as the wellspring of (black) hipness, from which American mainstream culture drinks deeply, but which is not necessarily, or at least not exclusively, transgressive. Rather, Vincent portrays funkiness as embodying black populism. "Unless you were living at the bottom of America's class structure and feeling the funk (or playing it)," he writes, "you may have missed the funk movement altogether."[45]

Ironically, funk's populism (i.e., its appeal to young, black, unassimilated working-class Americans) guaranteed its broad, crossover audience popularity. The music was "dirty and smelly, but it was *ours*, and it made its way into the music mainstream."[46] Funk became popular not by watering down its musical and social message but by refusing to do so.[47] It recaptured black popular music's badge of authenticity by peeling away the layers of suave sophistication so prominent in the Motown sound and many of the emerging rock styles, elements charged by some as blurring those musics' black identity.[48] Further, despite its basic, anti-sophisticated stance, funk was difficult music to play, a fact that drew Hancock and others to try to fathom it. To be funky was to be redolent of work, the body, the everyday, the Working People. Funk was hardly mainstream, in the sense of pushing black identity into the background in the quest for a larger audience. Rather, it emerged concurrently with the Black Power movement in the late sixties, shouting its black, populist identity ("Say It Loud"). Its lack of airs, and its association with the urban ghetto, appealed to a cross-section audience who sought to kiss the hem of the Other's garment.

Vincent attributes the birth of funk to James Brown and in so doing puts his finger on Brown's iconic image as a political symbol for Black Nationalism and pride in an unapologetic funky self: "The central locus of all funk, the representation of the total and complete *black man*, was James Brown. . . . Brown represented the political black man, the successful black man, the sexual black man, the relentless black warrior that was 'Black and Proud,' and, as the song says, 'ready to die on our feet, rather than be livin' on our knees.' Brown grabbed hold of the jugular vein of black aspirations and would not let go."[49] Musically, Vincent lays heavy emphasis on rhythmic, groove-oriented organization, his description reminiscent of the Anlo-Ewe rhythmic matrix: "His band backed up this no-nonsense message with a furious and unrelenting barrage of stripped-down rhythmic R&B, the primordial funk groove that had a gravitational pull so strong that, like a black hole, it moved the music of the world toward its core."[50] Vincent's expressive writing style, even in his descriptive analysis, conveys the taste of funk, missing in a strictly academic discussion. While he makes grandiose connections about the "total and complete" black man, he lands directly on Brown's funky expressiveness: direct, unapologetic, fully present, and without equivocation. Continuing, Vincent links this core with (sub-Saharan West) Africa, writing, that "the Godfather kick-started a new pop trend and made a rhythmic connection with Africa at the same time."[51]

Vincent connects sub-Saharan West African aesthetics to his own observations about funk music, pointedly adapting Wilson's "African conceptual approaches to music-making."[52] Citing one of these approaches, a "tendency to play in a percussive manner," Vincent describes, for example, the use of the rhythm guitar as a percussion instrument and the slap bass technique exemplified by pioneering funk bassists Bootsy Collins and Larry Graham. Illustrating how funk grooves are constructed of interlocking patterns employing many instrumental and vocal parts, all contributing to a whole, he points to Wilson's "heterogeneous sound ideal." This interlocking technique, prominent in James Brown's work beginning with "Papa's Got a Brand New Bag" (1965), mirrors the sound matrix organization of the typical Anlo-Ewe ensemble. The band members create a fixed rhythmic group, set against Brown's vocals, that acts in a *variable rhythmic* function. In much of Brown's music, this takes the form of instrumental (and verbal) responses to Brown's verbal calls.

If Brown is the founder of funk, he too has his precursors. Vincent looks backward through Brown's work in the sixties to funky jazz in the fifties, and both styles draw from Afro-Cuban musics.[53] All three styles, then, share a central aesthetic linkage with sub-Saharan West Africa.

They also share an orientation toward dancing as an integral part of the listening experience. Likewise, Herbie Hancock set out to create a recording that would produce sweat on the dance floor. *Head Hunters* is organized around the development of the funk groove and the groove's reinforcement of the *one* beat. Looking at groove construction in funk and in *Head Hunters* makes this centrality clear.

Laying Down a Funk Groove

Funk recordings live or die on their dance grooves. The groove, structurally a matrix of ostinato figures, is built to coordinate with funk dance steps. In a way, the dance steps become part of the matrix. The ostinatos, short, repeated melodic cycles of one- or two-measure duration, creatively combined as dance grooves, put bodies onto the dance floor. An effective funk groove needs a strong, bass-laden *one* beat. James Brown recalls his own role in developing the style of pioneer funk bassist Bootsy Collins: "I think Bootsy learned a lot from me. When I met him he was playing a lot of bass—the ifs, the ands, and the buts. I got him to see the importance of the *one* in funk—the downbeat at the beginning of every bar. I got him to key in on the dynamic parts of the *one* instead of playing all around it."[54]

Although the bass is given a primary role in establishing the groove, it is by no means alone. Rather, the bass acts as a focus within an interlocked group of instruments, which we can conceive of as a matrix, acting as a *fixed rhythmic* group. The matrix is constructed to set up the all-important arrival on the downbeat. The *one* beat is both prepared and commented upon: the rest of the one- or two-measure groove is either anticipatory (acting as a pickup gesture before the *one*) or reactive (acting as a response to the *one*).[55]

The groove, then, is made of a recurring preparation/arrival/follow-through cycle. It is the reliability of the *one*'s arrival, set up by the recurring preparatory gestures within the matrix, reinforced in the follow-through after the *one* (and Signified upon through syncopation), that gives the groove power on the dance floor. The grooves in James Brown's "Make It Funky, Pt.1" and Sly and the Family Stone's "Thank You (Falettinme Be Mice Elf Agin)" both illustrate this principle.[56] In Brown's groove on "Make It Funky" (fig. 15), the simultaneous bass drum arrival, beginning of the horn riff, and vocal emphasis on "funky" by the back-up singers all reinforce the *one* beat as the dance focus.

The drum pattern emphasizes the *one*, so much so that even the back-beats on the snare drum recede into the mix. The snares under the drum are tight against the resonating head, and the drum is tuned to a high pitch, almost matching the click of the sticked hi-hat eighth-notes. The effect is crisp but not loud. The bass drum note on the second half of beat *three* occurs as part of an interactive figure with the snare drum and is considerably quieter than the downbeat. At the same time, the electric guitarist plays a repeated chord on dampened strings, emphasizing a sixteenth-note counter-rhythm that strongly suggests son clave, played at double speed. The final gesture of this four-measure pattern is played on slightly open strings, ending on an eighth-note (4-ee-and) as a tag.[57]

While the bass guitar is foundational in groove construction, it can come with a twist. In "Make It Funky," the bass plays a pattern that stays on a single tone (the tonic note).[58] Beginning as it does, on the *one* beat, the bass pattern reinforces the rhythmic role of the horn riff, which also begins on the *one*. Once the pattern is established, however, the bass energizes all the subsequent arrivals on *one* further by anticipating each by a sixteenth-note, Signifyin(g) on the arrival (m. 1, last note, tied to m. 2, beat 1). Syncopating a note (either before or after a beat) is not a matter simply of presence or absence of sound but of frustrated and satisfied expectation. Momentarily disorienting, it forces the listener to work harder to keep the pulse in facticity, energizing the music. With so much of the matrix aligned with the *one* beat, then, the bass's anticipation pulls the listener/dancer to alertness, acting as a *super-one*.

Not only does the bass player rivet the listener to the *one* beat. He also rhythmically doubles the syncopated anticipation to beat *three*, an antic-

FIG. 15. "Make It Funky" groove matrix.

ipation that is also played by the horns. This sparse line orients the listener, not only to the focus on the *one* arrival but to the point of greatest rhythmic clash as well. The resolution of that clash on the following measure's *one* sets up the ostinato as a groove.

Brown's vocal responses just after the *one*, or alternatively the organ improvisations in the space left open, have the dual purpose of commenting on what has just happened—that is, the chorus singing "make it funky"—and propelling the cycle forward ("I got-ta") to the next choral lead-in of "make it," prior to their arrival on "funky" (fig. 16).

FIG. 16. "Make It Funky" interaction of James Brown, organ, with chorus.

This choral repetition ("make it funky") marks the *one* most prominently in the mix. The semisung "make it" functions both metrically and textually as preparation for the arrival on the *one* beat (FUNK-y).[59] The key simultaneity is of the vocal arrival on the downbeat with the beginning of the brass phrase and the bass drum note: all of these are added to the electric bass arrival of the *super-one.* Such a load adds force to the *one* beat, orienting the listener to it and impelling a dance response.

In a different way, Larry Graham's bass riff is the centerpiece of "Thank You (Falettinme Be Mice Elf Agin)."[60] It was this recording that spawned an entire new generation of bass players, using boldly creative note attacks as part of the timbral arsenal for the electric bass. As Vincent tells it, "Perhaps more than any other record, 'Thank You' introduced the Decade of Funk."[61]

"Thank You" has particular relevance to Herbie Hancock's approach with *Head Hunters.* This was brought home to me in a phone interview with him. At the time of the interview, I was teaching a course, Music in American Cultures, for which I had played Sly and the Family Stone's "Stand." I had been dismayed to learn that none of the students in my class had heard the song or, indeed, had heard of Sly. Talking with Hancock, I lamented this. He was dumbfounded: "They've heard of me, and never heard of Sly Stone?" He questioned my choice of "Stand" and advised me:

> Hancock: Play them "Thank You (Falletin Me Be Mice Elf Again)."
> Q: I'll do it today.
>
> Hancock: I bet they won't keep still [laughs].
> Q: I'll *definitely* do that today [laughs].
> Hancock: Because *that's the funkiest thing I ever heard in my life. To this day.*[62]

This is because of Graham's innovative string-slapping and -pulling techniques: "With bassist Larry Graham popping the bass on every note, Sly and Larry drove home a new force in funk, a punishing new standard of the nasty rhythm force that funk alone claims. . . . After 'Thank You,' both rhythm and melody became the territory of the bass."[63] In the case of "Thank You" (fig. 17), the notes as they appear in transcription do not fully convey the emphasis of the *one* beat.[64] The bass lands on a gesture at the *one* of each measure, not on the tonic *do* but on *te-do*, a move that would seem to soften the arrival on *one*.[65] If a solid, simultaneous landing on the downbeat was the clue to the primacy of the *one* in "Make It Funky," it is not as clearly the case here. The arrival comes not as a concrete tonic at the downbeat, as we might expect, but an eighth-note later. Remember that Signifyin(g) plays to a cultural aesthetic that says, "*Anyone* can make a direct point, but it is a sign of an alert, acute mind to speak allusively, through figuration." Graham's put-off arrival of *te-do* acts not as a hiccup but as Signifyin(g) on our expectation of the strong *one*.

FIG. 17. "Thank You (Falettinme Be Mice Elf Agin)" groove matrix.

If syncopation's power stems from delaying an expected arrival, "Thank You"'s *te-do* arrival, rather than simply *do*, makes a similar move in the realm of harmony. To the question of what could be stronger than landing on the tonic at the downbeat, the answer is that, by putting off the expected arrival point and by coming down on it just *after*, Larry Graham Signifies on it, setting up a frustration/satisfaction cycle that jolts the listener/dancer to alertness.

The bass establishes this frustration/satisfaction cycle through the *te-do* gesture, but also through timbre and register. The full-bodied low notes on the first two eighth-notes of each measure—*te-do*—have percussiveness and a weight that is different from the rest of the notes in the ostinato. Graham strikes the low string with his thumb, muting the second eighth-note (*do*) with the heel of his hand, creating separation from the rest of the pattern. The rest of the notes in each measure, all in a higher register, are played by a plucking-and-muting technique ("popping") developed by Graham. Overarching this measure-long call-and-response (labeled level 1 in fig. 18) is a two-measure pattern by the bass (level 2), with its "call" quality signified by the third popped note (e.g., m. 1, the second half of beat *three*) and its "response" signified by the more solid, cadential arrival and the two-beat rest setting it off as a completed idea (mm. 2 and 4). This in turn becomes half of a four-measure call-and-response pattern. The shift down an octave for the final *te-do* gesture makes it cadential, thereby making measures three and four consequent to measures one and two (level 3).

FIG. 18. "Thank You" bass pattern extracted.

The interaction between the guitar and drums reinforces call-and-response. Using an attack-and-muting technique similar to the *te-do* figure of the bass, the guitar likewise plays the *te-do* call on the *one*-beat of each measure. The response on the last beat and a half of measure one acts as a pickup to the second call, on beat *one* of the second measure (fig. 19). It is the response of the guitar, closely similar to guitar patterns on myriad James Brown recordings, that combines with the bass and defines the groove's overall length. The silence that follows affirms the closure, so that when the whole pattern starts again, on beat *one* of the now-repeated pattern, the sense of arrival on the downbeat is all the more emphatic. The drum pattern, in the tradition of all rhythm-and-blues-derived styles, places "calls" on beats *one* and *three* on the bass drum and backbeat "responses" on beats *two* and *four* on the snare drum. The bass drum note anacrusis (pickup) at the end of each measure propels the groove forward. What is at work through the interaction of guitar/bass/drums, then, is similar to the notion of clave, with its two-measure structure of rhythmic clash (m. 1, beats 2–4) and resolution (m. 2, beats 1 and 4).

Within the cast of characters of the small jazz group, the main responsibility for reinforcing the groove rests with the bass player.[66] As

FIG. 19. “Thank You” groove—bass and guitar interaction.

Larry Graham’s playing in “Thank You (Falletin Me Be Mice Elf Agin)” demonstrates, the bass plays a central role in establishing the groove in funk as well. Acknowledging a difference between funk “proper” and his own version, Hancock allowed the bass player a cornerstone role, giving him the freedom to improvise over it: “The biggest reason I enjoy playing this new kind of funk is the contrast between the wide open improvisation and the funky foundation at the bottom.”[67] In funk music, the “funky foundation,” that is, the locus of the dance groove, centers on the bass, depending in large measure on the bassist’s leadership role in the core relationship of the bass ostinato, the basic drum pattern, and a resulting shared understanding (facticity) of the *one* beat.

The Headhunters group’s attraction to the funkiness of “Thank You” reflects the importance of funk as dance music.[68] Saxophonist Bennie Maupin, who contributed the main ideas for “Chameleon”’s melody, found inspiration in funk dancing:

> I wrote that melody as the result of going to see the Wattstax concert in Los Angeles. . . . And I remember at the time, one of the dance steps that had been become really popular was called the *funky robot.* So I was sitting there, and I was just looking at these kids. When the music would start playing, everybody would start doing the funky robot. . . . The funky robot was popular. And so I was just sitting there, and I was watching these kids, and I was looking at their body movement. And I started to just hear in my mind melodies centered around that kind of movement. And that’s when the melody fragments for “Chameleon” came into my head. I was just sitting there.[69]

On *Head Hunters*, and generally in funk, the groove is often the center of attention, rather than simply providing support for the melody. In

"Chameleon," the funky foundation at the head is supplied by the signature synthesizer bass ostinato, its syncopation of beat *two* emphasized through doubling by the snare drum ("locking up" the bass and drums) against the steady beat reference point that is played on the hihat (fig. 20).[70]

FIG. 20. "Chameleon" groove—"bass" and drum interaction.

My personal experience with the prominence of the funky bass pattern in "Chameleon" was revealed in my interview with Bennie Maupin. As Maupin brought up the subject of writing the tune, I chimed in with the "melody" of the song: the bass ostinato. The mistake is not mine alone; whenever I ask students or colleagues to hum the melody of "Chameleon," they sing the bass ostinato. The melody itself, played by Maupin on tenor sax, is doubled by Hancock's synthesizer keyboard, recessed deeply into the record's mix.

I have been describing funk as based on an ostinato, a funk groove. Yet Hancock, attempting to create a funk album, created something else. If the rule in "Make It Funky" and "Thank You" is to keep up a stable, recycling groove, *Head Hunters* regularly violates it. The Headhunters group, while bowing deeply to the funk groove, struck a different path, based on their own sensibilities. The modus operandi of the group was to Signify on the funk groove. Both bassist Paul Jackson and drummer Harvey Mason had solid funk credentials. With a rhythm section made of players with such backgrounds, one would expect to hear a solid, stable funk groove. Certainly, Jackson knew how to lay down an ostinato and keep it going, unchanged; Mason, in high demand as a funk and R&B session drummer, likewise knew enough to play a beat, and to keep it stable, as a funky foundation. Summers was deeply immersed in trance music as a study and, both through his own research and as a student of Olly Wilson, understood the dynamic of *fixed* and *variable rhythmic* functions. Yet these musicians could not turn their backs on the jazz aesthetic's demand for improvisation. This point of rupture in the fusion of traditional African and jazz musics opened an uncharted creative space, through which the Headhunters group navigated. Throughout the album, the musicians hold the funk groove in dynamic tension: suggested and then varied but never allowed to go away, a push-pull that is at the heart of Signifyin(g).

The challenge for the Headhunters rhythm section players became how to establish a groove—held in facticity—while allowing for interaction and improvisation, both among themselves and between themselves as a group and the soloist. A comparative transcription of excerpts from the solo sections of "Sly" (figs. 21–22) demonstrates the process of establishing the groove and then taking the opportunity to let go, much like a parent teaching a child to ride a bicycle: running along with a tight control of the balance, gradually easing one's grip, and finally watching the child move on independently. Just so, in the first section Summers (playing congas) and Hancock (playing clavinet) both begin with a tight control of the beat pattern, playing only those fills that reinforce the pattern. Gradually they become more and more willing to stray outside the pattern, referring to it and commenting on it, in what we have come to understand as unmotivated Signifyin(g) (see chap. 2). The rest of the ensemble keeps to the ostinato as a *fixed rhythmic* group.

With the groove undergirding the action, even though that groove is quite variable at the surface level, solos by Bennie Maupin on soprano saxophone and (three minutes later) by Herbie Hancock proceed in a confident rhythmic atmosphere. This is made possible by (1) the bass guitar ostinato as absolutely reliable (similar to the gankogui bell-pattern function in Anlo-Ewe music) and (2) Mason's consistent reinforcement of the *one* beat (with its pickup note at the end of the preceding measure) and syncopated backbeat, on the second half of beat *two*. His pattern owes a debt to Afro-Brazilian samba, in which the march meter is energized by pickups.[71]

As the transcription sequence shows (fig. 22), Mason plays further

FIG. 21. "Sly" transition from groove to Signifyin(g). Establishing the groove: clavinet and congas vary their lines slightly.

FIG. 21. Continuation.

and further "out," Signifyin(g) on the groove, which nonetheless remains held in facticity. As the transcription also shows, however, Mason often refers to the downbeat and the syncopated backbeat, which are the essential notes for facticity to be maintained. This allows Bill Summers to add layers of percussion throughout the section (02:17–05:25) and, by doing so, to add complexity and texture to the mix, as well as provide sonic markers of the African diaspora. His beaded gourd and its rhythmic pattern suggest Anlo-Ewe, Afro-Brazilian, and Afro-Cuban traditions. Is the instrument an axatse? Then it's West African. A *xekere*? Afro-Brazilian. A shekere? From Cuba. Over this pattern, he plays a succession of (Afro-Cuban) rumba conga patterns, somewhat recessed into the instrumental mix—in the context of an

FIG. 22. Continuation of excerpt. As tenor sax solo begins, drum part becomes more varied.

adapted samba rhythmic underlay. This adds color to the sound mix but also suggests the kinds of layering we have come to expect with Africa-diasporic musics. The sonic identity of African-ness comes in large part from Summers's weaving of traditional sounds (i.e., traditional in diverse corners of the diaspora) into the matrix of sound.

But Summers's function is twofold; he establishes the groove with the shekere track and comments on it with the succession of conga patterns. By introducing the conga commentary, he adds rhythmic clash/resolution to the admixture and, therefore, excitement to the dance groove. Just as in the case of "Chameleon," the groove in "Sly," in its rich mixture of reinforcing and clashing with the beat, is an organizing anchor, highlighting the funk dance rhythm.[72]

What's Funky about HEAD HUNTERS' "Watermelon Man"?

The two earlier versions of "Watermelon Man" are part of the fabric of the African diaspora. Two elements in the 1973 version make this plain. First, Paul Jackson's bass pattern speaks "clave," this time a 2–3 clave pattern (fig. 23). The points of alignment with the beat are at the *one* (downbeat) of measure one and the *three* of measure two (the second of two possible backbeats), with syncopation at beats *two* and *three.* This pattern, again, speaks "clave," albeit misaligned by a quarter-note.

FIG. 23. "Watermelon Man" bass groove.

Rewriting the pattern (fig. 24), the aligned/unaligned character of clave is exposed, where the unaligned half is organized as a 3+3+2 eighth-note subdivision.

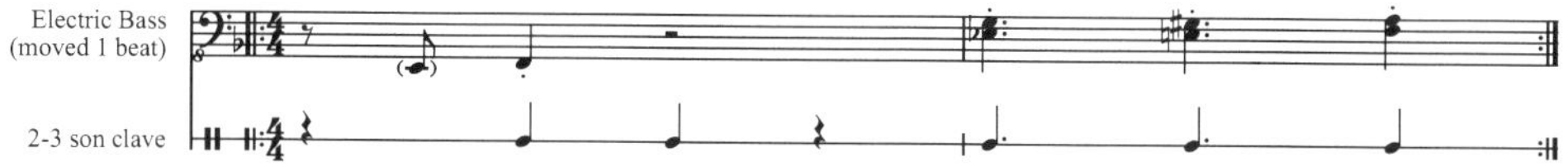

FIG. 24. "Watermelon Man" bass groove, realigned with clave pattern.

There are other points of alignment with African aesthetics and identity, as well. These include the percussive attack of Hancock's underlying synthesizer track (a "plucked" sound) and Bill Summers's performance of a Central African pygmy flute tradition (*hindewhu*) in the song's introduction and closing fade-out (fig. 25).[73] The hindewhu sound is a construction of five overdubbed tracks, all performed by Summers. All of the tracks, some made of alternating calls and notes, become interwoven, making a complex, dense matrix of calls, claps, and notes on a whistle.

FIG. 25. "Watermelon Man" hindewhu section.

The "traditional" one-note whistle is actually a beer bottle, filled with varying amounts of liquid to create different pitches for different tracks.[74] For the section, Summers adapted traditional calls of Ba-Benzélé pygmies in Central Africa. His original exposure to these flute-and-voice calls, in the course of his research on African music, came through a 1966 field recording, made by Simha Arom and Genevieve Taurelle, that subsequently had been commercially issued.[75] Summers wanted to place the African diaspora in the foreground of his music, "to bring [up] the level of appreciation of the African experience," his contribution to its African imprint.[76] The hindewhu section has subsequently become "Watermelon Man"'s signature sound.

The question is, in what sense is it funk? The tempo alone would seem to argue against identifying the 1973 version as a funk tune. At 73 beats per minute (bpm), it is hardly the dance groove described so far.

The typical dance tempo in funk is between 90 and 120 bpm.[77] At such a slow tempo, a dancer would find dancing the funky robot rather clumsy. The robotlike shifts from position to position at such a tempo would happen too gradually to be believable as robotic. Similarly, other up-tempo funk dances, often requiring pumping the pelvis, would jump the border from the rhythmical-but-suggestive to the bawdy. Other dances, like the hully-gully or the jerk (or rather, by the early seventies, their derivative replacements), which require a landing gesture on the *one* beat, would be difficult to time in synchronization with the beat: there would be a disconcerting period of "hang time" preparing to land on the *one.*

The tune, then, must be danced as a partnered slow-dance. But ballads tend to stay in the 50–65 bpm range; at 73 bpm, "Watermelon Man" would seem to be a bit brisk for a comfortable, swaying slow-drag.[78] I was twenty-two years old when *Head Hunters* was released and was present at many a party at which "Watermelon Man" was played. At first, couples were confused as to whether to dance to it as an up-tempo tune (quickly finding out how difficult this was) or as a slow-dance, with arms entwined (by far the better choice). Embracing couples soon learned, however, that this was no song for vagueness of foot. The music encouraged, perhaps required, a strong gesture on *one,* with a nearly equally strong gesture on *three.* In other words, it is a slow-dance, but one in which a funk sensitivity to the *one* is essential.

The 1973 version of "Watermelon Man" is funk-based, through its foregrounding of the *one* beat, and African-derived, through its rhythmic organization and the "hindewhu" sound. Africa certainly provided a cultural touchstone for *Head Hunters,* but not merely in evoking a sense of homeland or even in an underlying set of aesthetics. Funk carried musical punch and a political charge as well, a "plain and funky truth."

CHAPTER 4

The Pasts They Brought with Them

In 1973, Herbie Hancock wanted to make a funk record, not a jazz one; nevertheless, he could not ignore his own musical past. That past included his six years with the Miles Davis Quintet, one of the top small jazz groups of all time. The group solidified Davis's attraction to modal harmonies, open-ended forms, and group interaction, all features that Hancock internalized and developed in the context of *Head Hunters*.[1] But by the time he commenced the *Head Hunters* album, Hancock had also recorded his own work, composed soundtracks for television and film, worked as a sideman on many recordings, experimented with electronic music, and made a personal study of early twentieth-century orchestration. These were not his only musical influences; less visible ones included Hancock's attraction to the music of Maurice Ravel and other early twentieth-century Western art composers who had influenced his music with the Davis group. His interest in these figures, as well as in midcentury avant-garde composers such as Karlheinz Stockhausen and Pierre Boulez, influenced his post-Davis avant-garde recordings with the Mwandishi sextet/septet, which in turn served as background for *Head Hunters*.[2]

Head Hunters also carried the influences of several popular styles: early sixties funky jazz, late sixties James Brown proto-funk, and seventies funk, each of them reflecting an engagement between European- and African-based aesthetics. These somewhat disparate styles drew from the wellspring of African conceptual approaches to music-making, outlined by Olly Wilson. *Head Hunters* became the most audible of Hancock's explorations into the African roots of African American music to date. As a fusion of funk and jazz, the recording projected a multifaceted identity of race (black), class (populist), cultural background (Africa), and generation (youth).

The album that evolved was far from a clear-cut realization of Hancock's inclination going in. Neither was it solely a manifestation of social forces and tendencies. As in many small-group jazz recordings, it was a highly collaborative endeavor. Each musician brought to it his own personal experiences and musical tastes. The album's aesthetic projection of black-populist-youth social identity met in unavoidable confluence, daily, with each player's style, history, personality, aesthetics, and individual ideology.

Bennie Maupin's work with Davis on the *Bitches Brew* project, and his subsequent position with the Mwandishi group, brought a measure of continuity to the *Head Hunters* recording. Both Maupin and Hancock adapted aspects of the avant-garde jazz movement, as well as several more mainstream jazz idioms and funk. In doing so, they reinscribed avant-garde jazz's association with a general Afrocentrist arts movement, extending that movement's philosophical attraction to Africa as a cultural trope.[3]

Each of the other musicians made contributions from his own background. Bill Summers's involvement with African and Afro-Caribbean ritual musics further exemplified and extended this musical expression of Black Nationalism. Additionally, Harvey Mason's career as a pop and rhythm-and-blues sideman, and Paul Jackson's dual immersions in acoustic bass style and in the Bay Area funk scene, influenced the sound, and the identity, of the album. The project, even considering Hancock's leadership, bore the stamp of all the musicians and their past experiences—personal, cultural, and musical. These experiences intersected repeatedly in a "web of affiliations."

Hard Bop, Modal Jazz, and the Avant-garde: Difference, Convergence, and Transcendence

Historian John Szwed problematizes the way most jazz histories track style developments: "The most common mistake made with jazz styles is to focus on the differences between them instead of seeing what they share in common, and this is where a definition of jazz—if one is possible—is likely to be found."[4] Although some recent historians have acknowledged the slipperiness of genre, jazz histories generally make a point of distinguishing between various post-bebop categories.[5] Hard bop is commonly portrayed as a reaction to cool jazz (which may or may not be conflated with West Coast jazz), and these are both compared to the avant-garde (or "new thing").[6] Modal jazz is described alternatively as a category and as a harmonic (i.e., stylistic) practice but in most cases is separated from hard bop and the other styles.

Herbie Hancock played all of these, as did Miles Davis, John Coltrane, Eric Dolphy, and many others. This fact raises the question of difference: Are the aims of these currents really so different as to justify their historical parsing? How does the picture change when we consider their similarities as well as their differences?

In 1963, Amiri Baraka lauded an emerging group of young jazz musicians whose commitment to experimentalism argued against what Baraka found to be two artistically and socially limiting jazz forms—cool and hard bop. For Baraka, cool is "almost in its intentions, a middle brow music," a problem hardly corrected by hard bop, which he associates with an equally banal, black middlebrow mentality.[7]

In place of these "middlebrow" styles, Baraka finds renewed vitality in the experimentalist work of John Coltrane, Sonny Rollins, Elvin Jones, and other "young musicians I will call, for lack of a more specific term, 'avant-garde.' " The paradox is that "their way had been prepared to a great extent by the 'funky' style."[8] David Rosenthal, seizing on this seeming paradox, embraces hard bop's categorical slipperiness. Rosenthal parses the style into a "heterodoxy" of funky, lyrical, astringent, and experimentalist subtrends, of which funky jazz has already been discussed.[9] While all the categories are indeed slippery in the extreme, I want to focus briefly on the experimentalist current. To Baraka, Rollins and Coltrane represent the avant-garde and a move away from hard bop, a style "sagging under its own weight," while Rosenthal counts those same musicians (within an overlapping time frame—e.g., Coltrane before 1965) as "experimentalist" hard bop.[10]

Experimentalist to what end? Rosenthal develops two themes as basic to hard bop: a delving into jazz's African roots and a preoccupation with personal expressivity.[11] With harmonies still rooted in nineteenth-century functionality but increasingly stripped of obfuscating chord extensions, the melody, especially a melodic orientation in improvisation, seemed poised to take center stage in hard bop generally. But the melodies of these experimentalists were often becoming less "melodic": squeals (Lee Morgan), "sheets of sound" (Coltrane and Dolphy), and silence (Horace Silver, Thelonious Monk, and Miles Davis) were encroaching on the realm of the melodic. The trend moved toward altering the traditional materials of melody—figure, motive, subject, theme, and contour—and removing from them the narrative quality associated with the tradition.[12] Increasingly, these techniques were being used to create meta-melody, expressive gestures that largely bypassed melody. Or otherwise put, since tonal melodies unfold in time as narrative successions of tones from start to finish, they now could be heard not as deep personal expressions but as conveyances, mediations, or filters of such expressions; in the place of these tonal melodies, jazz musicians increasingly tapped into a long-standing African American tradition of personalizing a melody with unique manipulations of timbre, alterations of the "set" melody, interpolating notes and sounds, and other expressions—embodied in Olly Wilson's notion of the heterogeneous sound ideal.[13] Meta-melodic materials, as they developed in experimentalist hard bop, were abstractions *from* melody in that, increasingly, they conveyed line, timbre, and shape as melodic lines did but bypassed the narrative qualities of melody and therefore tapped more directly into the realm of expression.[14] Analogous to abstract expressionist art, in which the artist rejects the ideal of representation, the squeals, silences, and sheets of sound could be heard as attempts to do away with narrative melody so as to go *more directly* to an expression of deep personal meaning.[15] Significantly, these meta-melodic flights soared over a ground of self-consciously African-based rhythmic and timbral underlay.[16] Free jazz, from this standpoint, released meta-melody from the tether of functional harmony.

At about the same time, Miles Davis found his own escape route from functional harmony, adopting modal scales. Explaining to Nat Hentoff, Davis expressed a desire to move "away from the conventional string of chords, and [return] to emphasis on melodic rather than harmonic variation. *There will be fewer chords but infinite possibilities as to what to do with them.*"[17] Rooted in a desire to become more exploratory in his improvised soloing, Davis nevertheless kept his explorations largely within various modes during the last years of the fifties and the first years of the sixties, prescribing the modes as part of the precomposition process. This provided a sense of harmonic movement without the weight of narrative inevitability associated with major and minor tonality (and embodied in the term "running the changes"). Over the course of the sixties, Davis constructed pieces that owed ever less to harmonic inevitability, opening doors for other kinds of exploration: melodic, timbral, and interactive among musicians.

Davis alum John Coltrane took a different path to arrive at a similar destination. His use of modes in the early sixties became an increasingly flexible extension of the modalism he had played with the Davis group (cf. *Kind of Blue*), especially beginning with "My Favorite Things."[18] Coltrane's use of modes continued to expand past doctrinaire confines throughout the rest of his life.[19] Coltrane's use of modalism opened expressive doors for his rhythm section players ("They don't have to keep their strict chordal structure"), while still providing the soloist with plenty of freedom ("And the soloist can play any structure he wants to. But the rhythm section is totally unhindered or uncluttered").[20] An example of this flexible use of mode is heard in "Alabama" (1963). After a slow, nonmetrical introduction in which he sets both the dolorous affect and the mode (dorian), a swing-eighth middle section begins, with Coltrane soloing. His first gesture of the section is a descending tritone that is highly dissonant to the mode, creating a jarring tension and intensifying the affect suggested by the title.[21]

As we have seen, the use of modes, prominent in recordings by Davis, Coltrane, Dolphy, and others, had replaced "running the changes," with a slowed rate of change from one harmony to the next (known as "harmonic rhythm") and a shift away from harmonies that led inexorably forward to the piece's end (i.e., a shift away from the expectation implicit in the term "chord progression").[22] Thus freed, the soloist could allow improvisational ideas to emerge gradually, to be fully explored to completion.

To be sure, in playing hard bop and modal jazz, Davis and Coltrane, although the most prominent small-group leaders of the time, were not the only musicians seeking relief from the confinement of melodic and harmonic expectation. The developments in Coltrane's and Davis's styles reflected changes elsewhere in the jazz field. Their styles intersected with a burgeoning avant-garde movement in jazz. Figures associated with this latter movement, collectively characterized as *free jazz, new thing*, or *avant-garde* musicians, with George Russell, Ornette Coleman, Sun Ra, and Cecil Taylor prominent among them, had been ridding themselves of functional harmony (i.e., chord progressions) in jazz throughout the fifties. The line of development extended throughout the sixties with Sonny Rollins, Albert Ayler, Eric Dolphy, the Art Ensemble of Chicago, and Anthony Braxton.[23]

Although their procedures were different, free improvisers and modal performers shared similar goals. The primary focus was to shift from a reinterpretation of a standard song's structure (by means of reharmonizing the tune, as well as group players' musically interacting on the bandstand) toward an exploration of group interaction (by means of limiting the degree of compositional structure, which necessitated close, sympathetic listening). Discussing "Flamenco Sketches" from *Kind of Blue* as the modal piece par excellence, in which players "[improvise] on a number of modes whose sequence is established but whose duration is variable," Ekkehard Jost makes the "fundamental importance" of modal playing's relationship to free jazz explicit: "The moment the convention of a standardized bar pattern is dropped, the members of a group are forced to listen to each other with intensified concentration."[24]

All this made possible a resurgence of group improvisation, now transformed from the New Orleans collective improvisation model of the early decades of the twentieth century. Whether improvising individually or simultaneously within the group, the goal became to allow a forum for ideas to flow freely and allow reaction to one another's improvisational gestures to be instantaneous, rather than tied to waiting for the measure to come around.

Ornette Coleman played a central role in the development of avant-garde jazz, with his landmark recording *Free Jazz* (1960). Expressive materials used in Coleman's improvisations, for example, included such devices as bi- and polytonality; archaic, non-Western, and synthetic modes; altissimo squeals—all of which could be employed or altered at the player's discretion (and all of which Coltrane was then currently exploring, although in a more modally based harmonic context).[25] As a whole, these materials took the form of what Jost has called "motivic chain-associations," in which "ideas introduced by the 'soloist' of a given section are spontaneously paraphrased by the other players, developed further, and handed back to the originator in altered form," the goal being the formation of an "interlocking collective." Coleman sought to transform the notion of collective improvisation, now as simultaneously a personal and a collective expressionism, its coherence depending "almost exclusively on the players' readiness to interact."[26] Jost's analysis provides a key unifying element in avant-garde jazz. Collective improvisation, as it developed from early jazz in New Orleans, had been more melodically interdependent, the polyphony tied to the underpinning harmonic progression and the instrumentalists staying out of each other's way through largely tacit, traditional agreements as to register and density of material. Jost's "interlocking" collectivization and "motivic chain-associations" suggest a new guiding principle. Motivic chain-associations as Jost describes them—or, even better, *gestural* chain-associations—are ways of receiving, reinterpreting, then retransmitting ideas; and interlocking improvisation implies a coordination of parts, none of which comprises a whole, as in the interlocking drum choir of Anlo-Ewe drumming.[27] Integrating the two models involves attempting to react instantaneously to an improvisational idea and to reinterpret the idea as it unfolds, a technique we will shortly visit in the Miles Davis group of which Herbie Hancock was a member. This synthesis is of (improvised) personal expression combined with the overall (also improvised) expressive goals of the ensemble. Such instantaneous reaction is possible only through a deep emphasis on sympathetic listening (concentrated on the present), grounded in a shared understanding of the jazz tradition (concentrated on the past). In this sense, *Free Jazz* exemplifies an overarching characteristic in avant-garde jazz: the reinvestment in music as *process* over *product*. Amiri Baraka's article naming the avant-garde contrasts this emergent style with a continuity of swing, West Coast jazz, and "even . . . the artificially exciting, comparatively staid regular rhythms of hard bop traditionalism," which he says "demonstrates how the African elements of the music can be rendered almost to neutrality."[28] Baraka's problematic identification of rhythm notwithstanding, the predictability of form, dictated by conventions of functional harmony, had indeed become a straitjacket, which Coltrane, Coleman, Davis, and others sought to transcend in highly individual ways. In a "genre" of music as ruggedly individualistic as avant-garde jazz, the flexibility of form developed from and depended on an overarching exploration of new expressive ideas ("melodic" now in quotation marks).[29]

Seen in overview, hard bop experimentalists, modal players, *and* avant-gardists shared the same project, although the musical details differed greatly. For all of them, melodies and harmonies had become confining; rather than a medium for deep personal expression, melody and harmony had become the expressions themselves. Although the specific escape route differed among these groups of players according to personal inclinations and style developments, the process of confronting these musical elements as filters—and ultimately as barriers—to some deeper expression was common to all.

Herbie Hancock and Stylistic Convergence

When Herbie Hancock joined the Miles Davis quintet in 1963, Davis had been playing mode-based jazz for half a decade. Earlier, the 1959 landmark recording of the idiom, *Kind of Blue*, had brought to the jazz mainstream a major shift in jazz composition. One source of this change, acknowledged by Davis, had been the playing of Bill Evans. Identified though it is with Davis, the album also has the stamp of Evans upon it, supplying harmonies and arrangement ideas, one of the compositions for the album, and the liner notes. The influence on Hancock of Evans's style from the 1959–60 Davis sextet has been observed elsewhere. Davis biographer Jack Chambers, for example, notes Hancock's "delicate touch" as evocative of Evans.[30] Others cite his "chord voicings and mode-based thinking."[31] Other mutual loves reinforced the connection:

both men were drawn to the mode-based compositions of Claude Debussy and Maurice Ravel.[32]

Yet Evans, influential though his style was, was not alone in musically stimulating Hancock; the free jazz movement beckoned as well: "Both Hancock and [Tony] Williams kept close tabs on the freer forms of Ornette Coleman, Cecil Taylor, and Eric Dolphy. Those forms were, after all, among the main currents of their formative years . . . and they made their strongest impact on jazz just when Hancock and Williams arrived in New York to begin their professional careers. . . . [Hancock's] favorite job before joining Davis was a short-lived but influential engagement under the leadership of Eric Dolphy."[33] By 1963, then, Hancock had already played modal jazz, had become attracted to freer forms, and had recently produced a significant hard bop hit in "Watermelon Man." Did Hancock's varied style background represent a peripatetic inability to keep to a given style or perhaps a "growth" cycle, in which each style superceded the previous one? Or was there something that drew all of these styles together for him?

Hancock quickly became a central figure in the Miles Davis quintet, which would develop its name as one of the best small groups in jazz history. This group of young lions included (besides Davis and Hancock) Tony Williams (d), Ron Carter (b), and Wayne Shorter (preceded first by Sam Rivers and then by George Coleman) on reeds. The ensemble was responsible for E.S.P. (1965), the album that signaled a major change for Davis. Hancock recalled in an interview with Ben Sidran that, at this early stage in his tenure with the Davis group, he and the other young sidemen thought highly of the more "outside" music being recorded by John Coltrane and Ornette Coleman.[34]

As of the time of Herbie Hancock's entry into the Davis group, Davis and Coltrane represented two diverging solutions to the problem of dislodging functional harmony through modalism. The difference between the two styles lay in Davis's relative fathomability, stemming both from his astringent melodic sense and from his relative fealty in improvisations to the modal pitch set he had established. Ultimately, however, adhering to a pitch set, even if a new one, could prove stultifying. The members of Davis's young rhythm section, and in particular his saxophonist George Coleman, were attracted to Coltrane's expansiveness.

Although inclined to play Coltrane's freer style of jazz behind George Coleman, Davis's rhythm section tended to play more conservatively during Davis's solos: "Behind Miles, we would play in a way that was more reminiscent of what we were accustomed to hearing behind Miles. You know, I would be thinking more in terms of Wynton Kelly and Bill Evans. [But behind George Coleman,] we'd play all kinds of figures . . . things that were considered more toward the avant-garde. Things that were more expected of a sound that you'd hear behind John Coltrane."[35] Taking note of the difference in treatment, Davis demanded that the rhythm section play similarly behind him: "And I looked at Tony. Tony said, 'Really?' We said, 'Okay.' So we started doing that stuff. I mean, playing with the rhythms and doing all kinds of wild things behind Miles. Things that we never heard on Miles's records before."[36] Davis struggled at first—Hancock recalled it as bobbing and weaving, like a prizefighter looking for an opening—but by the third night, as Hancock recalled, "not only was he not bobbing and weaving, I was the one bobbing and weaving and trying to find my place, 'cause Miles had it then." Davis had assimilated the new sound into his own conception: "And right after we played that set, that third night, Miles said 'I don't wanna play any chords anymore.' So, okay, you know. And the next album was the E.S.P."[37]

With Coleman now replaced by Wayne Shorter, the group's recording of E.S.P. caused a sensation. The music, although under Davis's leadership, came about through collaboration. Davis later recalled, "I didn't have to write for the band; all I did was arrange the music in a way we could play it after they wrote it, put the finishing touches on it." Regarding Hancock's assimilation of styles, Davis said, "Herbie was like a sponge. Anything you played was cool with him; he just soaked up everything."[38] Musicians, critics, and fans recognized a major shift in Davis's music. As Jack Chambers recounts:

> For Davis's perennial fans, E.S.P. served notice not only of a change in direction but also of an about-face in his stated position on Ornette Coleman and the exponents of freer forms. That change was also implied in the title, E.S.P., which seemed to reflect the cliché current among both the adherents and the detractors of free forms that the

> only way bands would play unstructured music together was through extrasensory perception or mental telepathy [cf. Jost's comments, quoted earlier]. Davis offered his listeners music held together by less rigid structural principles than he had formerly used, and he was showing off a new, young band capable of suffusing each piece with a remarkable unity. If they were not exactly appealing to [extrasensory perception], they were nevertheless giving up the familiar hallmarks of melody and tempo in favor of the much more elusive notions of mood and atmosphere.[39]

Where melodies had been composed and tempos established beforehand, even as jumping-off places, the emphasis now centered on improvisation, based on group members' intensive listening and interaction.

For their part, the Coltrane group now found their attention to improvisation expanding radically. Anecdotes of the group playing a single song for up to three hours abound. While the pitch material in Davis's and Coltrane's recordings of the time tended toward church modes, strict adherence to these modes became less important, not necessarily an end in itself. Speaking of his own playing style of the time, as a young pianist in the Coltrane group, McCoy Tyner later explained cryptically that his choices of pitch collection were not intended to substitute a new harmonic orthodoxy for an old one: "Sometimes you're not even thinking about what chord you're playing. I mean, because the chord is just a symbol. The chord signatures are just symbols of a particular *sound*. [Q: Do you then ultimately approach the keyboard as just one big chord?] Yeah, yeah. Well, more or less that way. Because it's how you resolve things that matters."[40]

Tyner's discussion of resolving chords as a central concept suggests a shift in the function of the scales on which these chords are based. For him, the *sound* of the music seems to incorporate a flexible intersection of the scale, voice leading, and interaction with whatever the other musicians are doing ("it's how you resolve things that matters").

Lewis Porter confirms a similar approach in John Coltrane's music, actually a complex of related tools. These tools include scales outside the major-minor norm but related enough to the norm to give Coltrane (and others) the option of adding notes outside the mode, absence of an expected chord progression within the mode, and a slowed or even static harmonic rhythm.[41] All of these techniques combine to break what some have called the "tyranny of harmony."[42] Coltrane's approach to modalism affected Tyner's, Coltrane serving as Tyner's bandleader and mentor during the better part of the 1960s. Speaking with Ben Sidran, Tyner explained that "although any scale carries implications of what 'fits,' I find [that] when you're playing a blues it doesn't matter if you play a B-flat seventh or a B-flat minor. It's the scale that counts. You know you're really playing off a *sound*, rather than just defining what the notes are."[43] On one hand, Tyner's comment can be read as an explanation of the indeterminacy of the major and minor thirds in the blues, codified in the blues scale as containing both notes. But Tyner's comment also mirrors a similar orientation revealed by Herbie Hancock. Hearing me identify one of the songs on *Head Hunters*, "Watermelon Man," as being in a mixolydian mode, he hesitated before agreeing, adding: "But I don't think of it that way. . . . I think of pitches in terms of degrees of tension and release. I'm aware of the notes of the scale that would fit [the modes], but I don't want to be tied down."[44]

To Hancock, modalism in the avant-garde jazz movement of the early sixties represented a process, a tool for discarding harmonic constraints, similar to moves in twentieth-century academic music some four decades earlier, and for reconsidering the principles of voice leading ("tension and release" being analogous to "dissonance and resolution") that gave rise to rules of functional harmony in the first place. As the decade unfolded, the Davis group continued to treat modalism more fluidly. Davis, Hancock, and Shorter spent more time incorporating "tension and release," straying outside the confines of mode.

BITCHES BREW Reconsidered

I said earlier that the trajectory of hard bop experimentalism, and likewise avant-gardism, pointed to an exploration of increasingly metamelodic expression over a self-consciously black rhythmic and timbral overlay. From this perspective, the Miles Davis albums leading to and culminating in *Bitches Brew* can be seen as a fusion of jazz and rock, but as a type of fusion previously undescribed. The intersection includes modalism, avant-garde jazz, academic avant-gardism, *and* rock (especially as these relate to African conceptual models of music-making).

Using modal melodic materials, as well as avant-garde meta-melodic techniques, the improvisations on the album blend the two streams. This is an extension of the Coltrane model of flexible modalism, toward collective improvisation, foregrounding process over product. Yet the album disgruntled critics, who saw it as foregrounding product over process.

Critics did not like the inclusion of rock elements, especially since rock, firmly entrenched within the popular music industry, epitomized a music-as-product orientation. The negative comments focused on two rock components in *Bitches Brew*: the rock industry's production technique of cut-and-paste editing and rock's orientation to amplified and distorted sound.[45]

Much of the critical response to *Bitches Brew* centered on rock's sonic markers: the use of amplified instruments, rock vamps, and multiple percussionists. Regarding the latter two, Davis, in his autobiography, recalled the influence of Tony Williams in Davis's mid-sixties quintet. In retrospect, this influence seems to have set the course for the remainder of Davis's career:

> The way I had been playing before these guys came into the band was kind of getting on my nerves. Like a favorite pair of shoes that you wear all the time, after a while you've got to change them. What was good about Ornette Coleman was that his musical ideas and his melodies were independent of styles, and being independent like that would make you appear to be creating spontaneously. I have an almost perfect sense of melodic order. But then I discovered after really paying attention to some of the things Ornette was playing and talking about—especially after Tony came into the band, and listening to what he had to say about what Ornette was doing—that when I played one note from my trumpet I was really playing about four and that I was transposing guitar solos to my trumpet voice. *In my music with Tony, I started putting the backbeat in the drums out front and on top of everything, like in African music. In Western music, white people at this time were trying to suppress*

> *rhythm because of where it comes from—Africa—and its racial overtones. But rhythm is like breathing.* So that's what I began to learn in this group and it just pointed the way forward.[46]

As Olly Wilson points out, and as I reiterate (see chap. 2), sub-Saharan West African conceptual approaches to making music suffuse African American musics generally. To the extent that all the jazz styles I've mentioned until now share a cultural memory of Africa, they also share this sensibility with rock music, particularly as an outgrowth of rhythm-and-blues of the forties and early fifties.[47] Parallel to this, there has been a close, ongoing relationship between rhythm-and-blues (and its derivative styles, including urban blues, soul, and funk) and rock.

While the differences of musical *means* in hard bop, modal jazz, and avant-garde jazz have tended to cloud their similarities of *aims*, described earlier, the similarities of musical means in rhythm-and-blues, urban blues, soul, and rock 'n' roll have tended to obscure their cultural differences. All share the same or at least closely similar instrumentation and amplification, similarities of singing style, similarities of form (blues, thirty-two-bar song form, and stanza-with-bridge), and prominent backbeat rhythms.[48] Yet the differences in audience, distribution, iconography, and social commentary are robust and plentiful.[49] Under each umbrella there is a dialectic, a struggle between moving toward innovation on the one hand and remaining grounded in core aesthetic principles on the other. In general, we expect jazz to favor innovation and rhythm-and-blues to favor reinforcement of the tradition. Miles Davis's last albums of the sixties seem an attempt to create a synthesis of these oppositions. Yet in terms of the critical response, the incorporation of elements associated with both rock and rhythm-and-blues into a jazz framework worked to his advantage and disadvantage.

Jack Chambers typifies the dismissive tone given to rock elements in Davis's music of the time:

> "Stuff" locks Hancock into a *little rock vamp* on the electric piano and stifles—or at least tries—Williams into boogaloo rhythms that are infectious, toe-tapping, and trite. For Williams, the cadences seem ridiculously easy, and he executes them with a dutiful clarity as long as

> he can hold himself to them. For Hancock, the vamp may or may not be absurdly easy—it sounds as if it should be—but in either case he is willing to stick with it all the way. In doing so, he gives one of the first indications of the adaptability that in the next decade would permit him to court and find considerable pop fame.[50]

Chambers is correct in noticing the rock elements in the "little rock vamp," the use of electric piano, and the straight-eighth "boogaloo" rhythm (as opposed to *búgalú*) played by Williams. But focused as he is on Westernized aesthetics of virtuosity (the general understanding of which assumes complexity) and innovation, Chambers overlooks the African aesthetics of cyclical song structures, ostinatos, orientation to dance and body involvement, and other elements articulated by Wilson, which may or may not have anything to do with such a view of virtuosity. One person's "cyclic structure" is another's "little rock vamp": Chambers and others fail to notice an aesthetic shift to these values. The fact that they simultaneously reinforce similar values in white rock music confuses the issue, and it is this cloudiness that is one cause of debate surrounding Davis's later career.[51]

Chambers elsewhere notes that rock audiences were not as confused as Davis's critics were: "A few [of Davis's peers] noticed that *Bitches Brew* did not in any way pander to teenaged tastes. It was probably more unlike anything that rock fans had ever heard than it was unlike what jazz fans were used to."[52]

Rather than a simple fusion of jazz and rock, I understand *Bitches Brew* as an extension of modal jazz and the meta-melodic material associated with avant-garde jazz, *as well as* rock. What sealed the album's identity was the fact that these were grafted onto elements shared by rhythm-and-blues and rock, *coupled with* the strong sales of the album in the white rock market. Since, as described earlier, rock rhythms themselves tap into groove aesthetics associated with black music (of myriad forms but prominently in rhythm-and-blues), and since these grooves are in turn expressive of African conceptual approaches to music-making, Davis (in *Bitches Brew*) and white rockers (generally) were tapping the same source. Since the cross-cultural popularity of the album appealed to a developing market strategy on the part of Davis's record company

(Columbia), and since the popularity also appealed to Davis's restless desire both to grow his music *and* to flourish financially, Davis continued in that direction.[53]

The conspicuous use of editing techniques, however, drew the most searing criticism of *Bitches Brew*. Critics interpreted the extensive editing by producer Teo Macero (in collaboration with Davis) as an unwelcome rock-industry intrusion into the jazz milieu, since rock producers (and popular music producers generally) edit avidly. Macero and Davis's editing can also be read as related to *musique concrète*, crafting sound recordings by splicing together preexisting snippets of recorded material, which Macero likely would have encountered as a Juilliard composition student in the fifties. In fact, Macero saw his role in the editing room as a composer-collaborator and alter ego of Davis.[54] Davis biographer Jack Chambers observes that Davis and Macero were comfortable in this role: "Neither Macero nor Davis seems to have had any qualms at all about what they were doing to Davis's music. . . . Many jazz fans accepted recordings at least partly created in the editing room with the same equanimity Macero and Davis showed in producing them."[55] The equanimity Chambers mentions was anything but universal.[56] If avant-gardism (especially under the *free jazz* name) represented a reinvestment in the improvisational process over a crafted product, then post-production editing seemed to subvert that goal.

Of course, not only the rock industry employed editing (and later, sampling). Academic avant-garde composers, such as Karlheinz Stockhausen, also kept the editing blade handy, along with various electronic studio techniques, to manipulate sound.[57] Miles Davis had studied Stockhausen's music for close to a decade by the time of *Bitches Brew*, and Hancock became exposed to this music during his tenure with Davis.

The point is not to deny rock's influence on *Bitches Brew* but to contextualize its influence as blended with all of Davis's interests of the time. *Bitches Brew* fused several kinds of music-making, and this multiplicity of influences in turn affected Hancock's post-Davis musical ideas. It was a period of transition for both musicians. Hancock had not completely severed his relationship with Davis and was still gaining insights during this time; he recorded "Great Expectations" with Davis during the *Bitches Brew* sessions, in November 1969, despite the fact that the song does not appear on the album's original release.[58] Besides, the lessons of *Bitches Brew* had started earlier. Davis's approach to the album had begun with the *Miles in the Sky* sessions in 1968, while Hancock was still integral to the group.

Hancock's Mwandishi Group: Process and Product in Détente

By the time of *Bitches Brew*, Herbie Hancock had officially left Davis's group.[59] However, he had appeared on the preceding albums, *Miles in the Sky* (1968), *Filles de Kilimanjaro* (1968), and *In a Silent Way* (1969). Having recorded periodically as a leader throughout the sixties, Hancock decided to move on to full-time leadership by mid-1968.[60]

Hancock had enjoyed two successful soundtrack projects, for Michelangelo Antonioni's film *Blow Up* (1966) and the Bill Cosby television cartoon *Hey, Hey, Hey, It's Fat Albert* (1969). These led to a recording contract with Warner Brothers and formation of the Herbie Hancock Sextet, known informally as the Mwandishi group, after the Swahili name ("composer") that Hancock had recently taken.[61] It is here that the extension of the fusion principle of *Bitches Brew* becomes clear in Hancock's post-Davis work. The blend is of various jazz styles—hard bop, modal jazz, and avant-garde jazz, which we now comprehend as part of an overall expressive trajectory—combined with academic avant-gardism and the African-based characteristics of both rock- and rhythm-and-blues-based styles, as well as more direct influences from Africa.

The Mwandishi group shared a taste for experimentalism and a broad range of backgrounds. Trombonist Pepo Mtoto Julian Priester played a wide variety of styles and had recorded with Sun Ra's Arkestra (1954–58) and appeared on Max Roach's *Freedom Now Suite* (1960), as well as with hard boppers Blue Mitchell, Stanley Turrentine, and Lee Morgan and Latin-jazz artists Cal Tjader and Eddie Palmieri. Jabali Billy Hart (d) had played with a similar variety of headliners, including Jimmy Smith, Stan Getz, McCoy Tyner, and Pharoah Sanders. Mganga Eddie

Henderson (tpt, flugelhorn) was less well-known, a San Franciscan trained as a doctor but fully committed to music.[62] He had studied as a teenager at the San Francisco Conservatory of Music and had been influenced by Miles Davis's *Bitches Brew*, an album Mwile Bennie Maupin (ss, ts, b clar) had played on. Mchezaji Buster Williams had made a name for himself as a sideman, playing behind Gene Ammons, Sonny Stitt, Betty Carter, and Nancy Wilson, among others. Williams had played on *Fat Albert Rotunda* (coincidentally, he and Maupin had been friends since their early days in Detroit) and was the only holdover from that project.

The group produced two recordings for Warner, *Mwandishi* (1970, issued 1971) and *Crossings* (1971), now augmented by Patrick Gleeson on synthesizer. In 1972, the Mwandishi group (now officially a septet, with the addition of Gleeson) left Warner Brothers for Columbia, producing a third album, *Sextant* (1972).

With a group so capable, and guided by a desire to expand into the realm of avant-gardist collective improvisation, the addition of Gleeson was problematic on several fronts. Although not a musician by training, Gleeson had been experimenting with multimedia art, a self-described *artiste manqué*, as early as the late fifties. Inspired in the late sixties by a recording of Bartòk's posthumous violin concerto, Gleeson, by now a professor in the English department at San Francisco State College (now San Francisco State University), resolved to enter into the world of music. As he related to me:

> I started getting all sorts of tape recording equipment out of the vis ed, whatever it was called, department. And began making *musique concrète*. And then I felt very limited by that, of course, and had heard that there was a—I had known about the Bell Lab at Columbia project, the computer music lab. And then I heard that there was a new kind of synthesizer that was being made by a guy by the name of Don Buchla, and that it was over at the Divisidero Street Dancers' Workshop [Anna Halperin's dance company]. I had actually been doing some scores for dancers at the Dance Workshop, so I got over there and got there just in time to see the thing being moved from there to Mills College. I mean literally. I followed the synthesizer across to Mills. And started

> hanging out with—I can't remember Tony's last name, but then Robert Ashley came later. Just getting more and more involved with that synthesizer. I finally gave them a thousand dollars to help them buy a four-track recorder, and for that I got one night per week in perpetuity all night long on the Buchla.[63]

The synthesizer developed by Donald Buchla at Mills College ranked with those at Columbia University and the University of Michigan as the state of the art at that time.[64] Gleeson continued: "So at that point I quit teaching. And I had saved a little money to live on and also to invest with another guy in what turned out to be, I think, the tenth Moog synthesizer ever built. So with that, you know, we had then this music commune, which became Different Fur [recording studio]. John Vieira and I—my partner in this synthesizer—began building this studio." By the early seventies Gleeson and Vieira had established Different Fur Trading Co. as a premier recording facility in San Francisco, recording studio albums for many Bay Area rock, jazz, and funk acts, including the Herbie Hancock sextet's *Crossings*. While *Crossings* was being recorded:

> I'd worked for a couple of different producers, David Rubinson being one of them, doing little synthesizer tasks on a few pop and funk albums. And I had been telling David that I had been playing, which was true. I had been putting *In a Silent Way* and *Bitches Brew* as a two-track on my eight-track recorder. I had just gotten a sixteen-track before we started *Crossings*. And then, you know, I had been overdubbing synthesizer stuff on it. I said, "Gee, it's really great, David. It really works. Let me—" I'd heard that he was signing Herbie, and I said, "Let me play with Herbie." So he told Herbie. He said, "Look, this guy is not really a musician. He's a knob-twister. But if you go down there, he can set the synthesizer up for you, and you can play it." So Herbie came down, and—thank God, you know. I'd be selling insurance today if he didn't. And he said, "Well, you know. Let's put the tape up and listen." And he said, "Right here I've kind of thought of something." I said, "Well, let me show you what I could possibly do here." I had no idea that I was ever going to be employed, just as a knob-twister. And so Herbie said, "To me it sounds kind of, maybe we could do that but maybe come out of the solo a little slower or faster or something." I

> said, "Fine." So I did that. And he was so noncommittal. He just said, "Well, why don't I come back in a couple of days and listen to what you're doing." So when he came back, he listened and he got that kind of funny smile. And said, "That's good. Well, let me get the rest of the album." He got the rest of the album, and I played on the rest of the album. But he said later that he—he was very generous about it. And he said in print several times that I just blew him away, that he'd never heard anything like that. Of course I hadn't either. I was just making it up, you know.[65]

The synthesized sounds on *Crossings* amount to post-production overlay. Gleeson would begin with tapes of the other musicians, which had been recorded "live," and overdub multiple tracks of effects with the synthesizer. The process was laborious and anything but improvisational, as Gleeson recalled: "On *Crossings* as I did the tracks, I was thinking of the total result of the tracks."[66] The technique had the synthesized sound of the academic avant-garde, grafted onto an improvised avant-garde jazz performance.

But by the next album, *Sextant*, the synthesizer gained full integration into the recording project. As Gleeson relates: "On *Sextant* the first piece, 'Raindance,' was done by running this loop of a synthesizer sample-and-hold pattern. Then we all played to that, and I played live to that, as well. Then I also overdubbed a lot of tracks on that. Some when Herbie was in the studio and some when he wasn't. And then Herbie came in and overdubbed at least one synthesizer track on that. There were a lot of synthesizer tracks."[67] The technique retained the earlier multitrack technique but now had moved beyond simply a sonic overlay. Moreover, Gleeson had by this time developed techniques for setting synthesized timbres in advance and switching them in real time, allowing him to improvise on synthesizer onstage. This was no easy feat during the period before miniaturized and multitimbral keyboard synthesizers, when changing to a new timbre meant reordering a complicated configuration of patch cords and knobs (see illustration). Bill Summers described Gleeson's ability, as well as the impact on *Head Hunters*: "Now, that's what made the difference [in *Head Hunters*]: Herbie coming up, after his being influenced by Pat Gleeson. Pat Gleeson had an ARP [2600]. And it was a piece of equipment that required a bunch of patch cords. And to change the patch, to change the sound, you had to go through hell. And he used to do it on the gig. He knew the instrument that well that he could do that. And Herbie, I think, got swept up in the technology."[68] The synthesizer by now had become more than an addition to the group's mostly acoustic sound. Hancock became interested in producing synthesized sounds himself.[69] Hancock's work with the Mwandishi group, especially the latter-day incarnation on *Sextant*, may seem to be an avant-garde exploration of *product* (layered synthesis over improvised music). The sextet, however, was reconciling product and process even then, since Gleeson was by then playing synthesizer in real time. This accord became extended with *Head Hunters*, with Hancock layering "produced" synthesized lines over improvised material, as well as the reverse: improvising over a prerecorded synthesizer groove (e.g., "Chameleon").[70]

Second, Hancock's musical tastes led to Gleeson's own compositional development. Gleeson describes his synthesized tracks on *Crossings* as influenced by Ravel and Debussy. The observation has already been made that Hancock's piano voicings were influenced by these composers from the beginning of the Davis quintet period. But the attraction was ongoing, as was Hancock's penchant for studying orchestration:

> One time I was listening to [Ravel's] *Daphnis et Chloë*, and he said, "Hmm." He said, "Is that the complete?" and I said, "Yeah." He picked up the tape and said, "Oh no, it's not. It's not the complete." And I said, "Well, yes it is," and he said, "Oh no, it's not." He said, "There's two different suites and this is just one of them." He said, "You should get the complete and listen to that." So I said, "OK." And I did; I bought it. And that became the high point—in my room, I mean we all hung out with each other a lot. And he came by the room. And he said, "Oh, now you're listening to the complete," you know [laughs]. "I told you I was right." I said, "Yeah." He said, "Are you listening to it a lot?" I said, "Oh man, I listen to this a lot." He said, "How many times have you listened to it?" I said, "You mean this tour or ever?" He said, "Well, like ever." I said, "I don't know, I must have listened to this about thirty or forty times." He looked at me in disbelief. He said, "Thirty or forty times?" He said, "You should be listening to this every day. You should listen to it once a day." And then he backed up a little bit; he said, "Well, you know, not necessarily the whole thing every day. But you

> should listen to it once a day, reading the whole score." And then he kind of backed up, and he said, "Well, you don't need to read the whole score all the time, but you can refer to it." And he said, "And not necessarily every day, but, you know, well, *maybe every day for a year*."[71]

The story, Gleeson later told me, was a slight raconteur's exaggeration, but it does convey the group's palpable commitment to experimentalism and profound study. "Herbie went in streaks," he said. "Herbie, like many working musicians, enjoyed listening to music intensely, not primarily for pleasure but rather to absorb and learn."[72]

Alongside Ravel's approach to orchestration, Karlheinz Stockhausen's compositional techniques interested Hancock, an interest he had evidently picked up from his days with Miles Davis.[73] Often, on the road, the group would congregate in Hancock's room, listening to tapes of their latest performances and, on one tour, to Stockhausen's *Gesang der Jüngling*.[74]

Later, on the *Head Hunters* project, Hancock would continue using the techniques he had developed within the Mwandishi group, in a complex interaction between process and product. While using such product-oriented techniques as synthesis and overdubbing, as well as funk, which tended to be tightly arranged, as its guiding idiom, *Head Hunters* nonetheless was rooted in improvisation as a process. Given Hancock's experimentalist mentality, the Mwandishi group's incorporation of synthesis, far from abandoning the improvisational aesthetic of avant-garde jazz, can be seen as Signifyin(g) on both the academic avant-garde *and* the avant-garde jazz movements, appropriating those movements' methods and sounds to the Mwandishi group's own expressive ends. *Head Hunters*, in turn, would become a way of extending Mwandishi's avant-gardism, now recast as a populist, dance-based avant-gardism.

The Mwandishi Group and Black Protest

Gleeson's presence in the group presented an additional problem. As the lone white player during a climate of heightened racial suspicions and antipathies, his presence was a thorn in the side of many black observers: "So there was the feeling at first that, 'What the fuck is Herbie doing now? Jesus Christ, the brother is so confused he doesn't know who he is,' you know. . . . And then this wonderful thing gradually happened, you know, that was we bonded."[75] Within the group, the "problem" of Gleeson became humorous:

> There was a little resistance to me, on a couple of grounds. I mean, this was during the days of Black Power, and I was the only white guy in the group. In fact later, once I was accepted, there were some very funny jokes about that. I remember we were down in David Rubinson's swimming pool, after the first album. . . . By that time I had been asked to join the group. So Herbie's sister, Jean, a wonderful woman, said, "Everybody else has a Swahili name. We're going to have to think of a Swahili name for Pat." And she must have conjured up this whole thing, because everybody's looking at her. And she said, "Oh, I know. *Bwana*."[76]

Gleeson's inclusion in the band notwithstanding, album cover art for *Crossings* and *Sextant*, featuring paintings of griots and a Masai dancer, allows no ambiguity about the group's affinity for Africa, which continued to be strikingly evident on the cover art of *Head Hunters*.[77] The titles of several songs ("Sleeping Giant," "Rain Dance," "Wandering Spirit Song") reinforce this notion, as does the groove of even such synthesizer-laden pieces as "Rain Dance."

Thus, Hancock's Mwandishi work, as an amalgamation of hard bop with modal jazz and avant-garde jazz, expresses an Afrocentric experimentalism. The amalgamation is the point: a focus on any of these contributing streams distorts the picture of the whole. The admixture is made even more complex (and richer) by the orientation toward groove in *Head Hunters*. The change in this admixture is evident in "Vein Melter" (*Head Hunters*) as a distillation of "Water Torture" (*Crossings*).

"Vein Melter" and "Water Torture"

In "Water Torture," Jabali Billy Hart's drum pattern begins 1:13 into the piece, setting a rhythmic framework against which a bass clarinet theme is played by Bennie Maupin. The drum pattern is thematic, a pattern that is set, abandoned, and reprised. In contrast, the theme in "Vein Melter," also played on the bass clarinet by Maupin, precedes the funereal drum cadence by Harvey Mason (which retains the slight accent on beat *three* with a rest on beat *four*). The startling accent chord at the end of the theme, similar to the recurring sforzando chord in "Water Torture," jump-starts the drum cadence on "Vein Melter," which continues without variation throughout the piece. Once the cadence begins, it never stops, until it fades out nine minutes later (fig. 26). Here the funeral cadence is so constant that it becomes more than thematic: it is the anchor of the piece.[78]

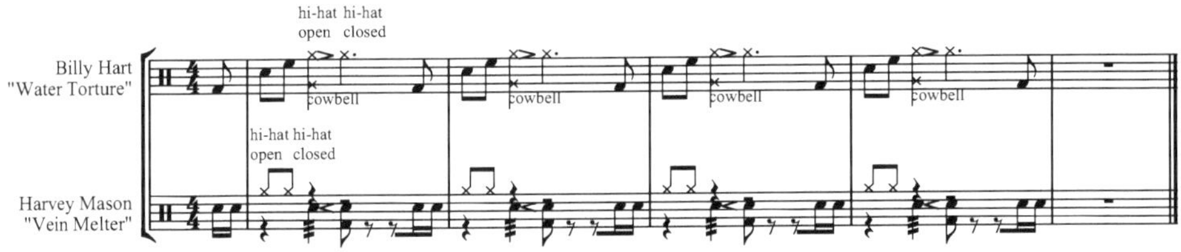

FIG. 26. Comparison of drum cadences in "Water Torture" and "Vein Melter."

The recurring melodic theme of "Water Torture" is similar to the opening theme of "Vein Melter." Both frame a pentatonic mode, based on A*b* in "Water Torture" and B*b* in "Vein Melter." The two themes, though not identical, are clearly related. In fact, if one were to rewrite them together (after transposing the latter to A*b*), with the first gesture of "Water Torture" as a call and the first gesture of "Vein Melter" as a response, the two would combine seamlessly (fig. 27). The theme of "Water Torture" is fragmented, with coloristic interludes, as if such a call-and-response structure were invited.

An abrupt sforzando interrupts the melody in "Water Torture" immediately after—or at least it seems to—but by the fourth such fragment and sforzando, the two are heard together, as theme and tag. In "Vein Melter," the theme runs to a clearer close before the sforzando: the moment therefore sounds like punctuation, rather than like some-

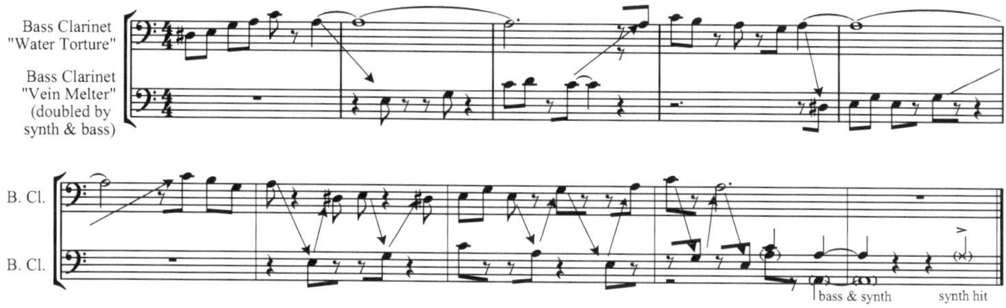

FIG. 27. Composite of "Water Torture" and "Vein Melter" themes.

thing integrated into the theme. It is then discarded until reprised as a closing gesture to the piece. Harmonically, both pieces are nearly static, staying on a dorian/minor tonic pedal (although "Vein Melter" shifts briefly to a mixolydian/major tonic pedal).[79] Section development in "Vein Melter" is marked by shifts in ostinato pattern by Paul Jackson's electric bass, rather than by harmonic means.

Overall, the affect of "Water Torture" and "Vein Melter" is closely similar: a dirge quality permeates both. Indeed, Bennie Maupin, listed as the composer, referred to "Water Torture" as a funeral dirge, while Herbie Hancock, who composed "Vein Melter," described it as a meditation on a friend who had died of heroin addiction.[80]

Because of the static accompaniment in "Vein Melter," one might think of it as an example of product, rather than process, orientation. Yet it is an extension—one might almost think of it as a recomposition—of an avant-garde piece that already makes such distinctions irrelevant.

Bennie Maupin

The earlier career of Bennie Maupin, the composer of "Water Torture" and the only holdover from the Mwandishi group on *Head Hunters*, further illustrates the intersections among avant-gardism, the hard bop movement, and fusion jazz. From 1963 to 1966, Maupin played with key players of the developing avant-garde movement, including Marion Brown and Pharoah Sanders.[81] (Sanders's later collaborations with John Coltrane [1966–67] were to establish him firmly in the primary ranks of the movement.) Maupin also played with various hard bop groups, including groups led by Horace Silver (1968–69), Lee Morgan (1970), and Woody Shaw (1970)—all in the same time period as his involvement with Miles Davis's *Bitches Brew* project (recorded 1969, issued 1970).[82] Sonny Rollins, a friend and associate, first introduced Maupin to Hancock.[83] Prior to the time period just mentioned, from 1966 to 1968, Maupin played in a group led by hard bop drummer Roy Haynes. This reinforces the point that, despite claims to the contrary, the borders between hard bop and the avant-garde jazz movement were somewhat permeable, apparent in the eclecticism of Sun Ra, the Art Ensemble of Chicago, and Charles Mingus, to name a prominent few.[84] Baraka, in his landmark essay "The Jazz Avant-Garde," lists emblematic players' names rather than style descriptions, explaining that "each of these men have their *own* way of playing, but they represent, as a group, at least to me, a definite line of departure."[85]

Not only were players apt to play in either style during the same time frame (or in close succession), but avant-garde and hard bop styles shared many characteristics. Not the least of these was a growing black consciousness, as well as a wide diversity of expressions of this consciousness. Indeed, both styles can be seen as highly individualized attempts to resolve the dynamic tension of extending jazz's expressive boundaries, on the one hand, and reinvesting in jazz as a black cultural tradition, on the other. From this standpoint, *Bitches Brew*, the Miles Davis album emblematic of the rise of "jazz-rock" (and the album that brought important exposure to Maupin), became not only an early and prominent example of fusion jazz but also an example of the crossable borders—not only between jazz and rock but also between hard bop and the avant-garde.[86] Just so, Maupin's involvement with the Mwandishi group and with the *Head Hunters* project extended that cross-pollination of styles.

Jack Chambers makes the observation, noted earlier, that *Bitches Brew* was not as strikingly rock oriented as it was purported to be.[87] The album conferred visibility and, to a degree, legitimacy to "jazz-rock." It used rock elements, to be sure, such as added percussion; straight-eighth note orientation; and electric piano, bass, and guitar instrumentation. But, as we have seen, thematic material tended to modalism (an extension of Davis's work of the previous decade), juxtaposed with the extreme dissonance associated with avant-gardism. And moments of free collective improvisation abound.[88] The underlying approach was clearly experimentalist and eclectic: there is little besides the straight-eighth vamp, for example, in "Pharaoh's Dance" to signify rock-ness to the listener. Ralph J. Gleason's liner notes to the album encapsulate this approach: "Somehow [people] have the automatic reflex that if something is labeled one way then that is all there is in it. . . . So be it with the music we have called jazz and which I never knew what it was because it was so many different things to so many different people each apparently contradicting the other and one day I flashed that it was music. That's all."[89] Herbie Hancock hired musicians with predictable sensibilities for his projects. His choice of rhythm section clearly facilitated his drive toward a funk sound in *Head Hunters.* Likewise, the presence of Maupin, whose background included various jazz styles but comparatively limited experience in funk, ensured that the album would not abandon Hancock's basic jazz orientation. Maupin's solo in "Sly" affirms this (fig. 28).[90]

Maupin's choice of soprano saxophone argues prima facie a jazz orientation. (Elsewhere on the album, Maupin plays tenor sax and bass clarinet.) Soprano saxophone had not yet penetrated the sound of rhythm-and-blues derivatives. It could be argued, in fact, that the use of soprano sax by a core of fusion jazz players—notably Maupin, Wayne Shorter, and Grover Washington, all influenced by John Coltrane—ushered the instrument into fashion within R&B.

Additionally, Maupin's meta-melodic gestures—particularly the "sheets of sound" runs, silences, and altissimo squeals—use the language of avant-gardism, and the emphasis on modal scales furthers the accord of modal jazz with avant-gardism that stands as a hallmark of Coltrane's middle and later career and as a theme of Davis's *Bitches Brew.* The application of these jazz sensibilities over an Africanized rhythmic overlay—that is, funk bass and clavinet ostinato patterns, African percussion, and a drumming style that is funk-based but also "out"—extends the aesthetic we first encountered with funky jazz.

FIG. 28. Bennie Maupin solo in "Sly" (beginning).

Bill Summers

Percussionist Bill Summers was a natural choice for Hancock's new group. He, like Hancock, had been grounded in European classical music as a boy, playing piano but specializing in reeds. Exposed (by his parents' extensive record collection) to Afro-Cuban music, he began playing hand percussion at the age of twelve, by which time he was already playing jazz saxophone and flute. Attracted to Afro-Cuban and West African ritual drumming traditions, pointedly as an alternative to European classical music, Summers entered the music program at the University of California at Berkeley in the late sixties, pursuing an interest in ethnomusicology. Shortly thereafter, Olly Wilson and Ghanaian master drummer C. K. Ladzekpo joined the faculty.[91] Summers worked closely with both mentors. He had a band on the side at the time, and he first met Hancock in the context of this group. Hancock had been contracted to play during the inauguration period of a new university art museum. As Summers relates:

> They had just built that museum. And I had a group called Bàtá Koto. Bàtá Koto did music from West Africa and the Caribbean, and South America. Brazil, stuff like that. And it was the only group in the area of its kind. . . . So we opened for Herbie. Herbie, after the show, invited me to come to San Francisco and sit in with his group. And I was very excited about it. I took my instruments—I think I may have brought about twenty instruments to the show. It's not a lot of instruments for a percussionist, in the sense that I had maybe two or three congas and some bongos. And then a bunch of hand percussion stuff, like gankoguis and bells, and axatses and shekeres. Small things, you know what I'm saying? Triangles. So you could have twenty things and not have it be a big thing. But what I did was, when I got to the club, I took my instruments and I put them on the side of the stage. I wasn't so egotistical or crazy as to say, "Oh wow, I'm playing with Herbie. I'll set my stuff up on the stage." I didn't do that; I set my stuff to the side of the stage. And he walked in the door, and I was sitting in the club, in a chair. And he walked by, and he turned around and looked over at the stage and saw my stuff sitting on the side of the stage. Off the stage, on the side. He said, "What's all this shit?" Just like that. And he went to the dressing room. Well, I took all my shit and left.[92]

Summers met Hancock again the next year:

> Herbie came to do a lecture at U.C. Berkeley, for Olly Wilson's class. And I was the T.A. I had to meet him at the gate, at Sather Gate, and drive him up to the class. Well, I got into the car, and we drove up to the class. I didn't really have too much to say to him. But after the class, we talked. All of this came out. And he said, "I did that?" He was surprised that he did that. I said, "Yeah, well. That's what happened." He said, "Well, man, why don't you sit in with me tonight?" And so, that time I came in and sat in with him. A couple of weeks later, he called me and asked me if I wanted to play with him and Alice Coltrane at Santa Monica Civic [Auditorium]. It was just me, him, and Alice. That really started it.[93]

With the band now comprised of Hancock, Maupin, and Summers, Hancock searched for new members to complete the ensemble. Summers described his own involvement in the process to me as "taking him to many, many places. And looking in some very unusual places for musicians. Like guys that were young, that were just hanging out. They were, you know, pretty good. They were just playing in the house, in the basement, doing gigs. But he was looking for new, fresh meat, new ideas."[94] Summers facilitated Hancock's search for new talent.[95] Summers's position in the local funk scene enabled him to expose Hancock to a broad range of players (and playing styles) in the idiom.

Summers attributes much of the album's success to the groove foundation—the Africanized rhythmic underlay mentioned earlier—laid out by himself, Jackson, and drummer Harvey Mason. Prominent in this foundation was (and for Summers has continued to be) a loyalty to African sensibilities, although this role often has been overlooked in the reception of the album.

Summers's contribution to one of the album's strongest sonic images is sadly underestimated, primarily due to a historical placement of percussionists as providers of exotic atmosphere. Partially, the secondary role given to percussionists emanates out of a lingering association of percussion with the exotic rather than as foundational, even within communities of musicians creating under the philosophical and cultural shadow of Africa.[96] Under such a perception of percussion as exotic, the small-group jazz format, although altered to allow for the presence of synthesizer, electric piano, and electric bass, was still basic, at least as of *Head Hunters*.[97] This is made audible in the mix: Summers's percussion is recessed into the sonic landscape (e.g., "Chameleon").

Summers's influence can also be felt in the Africanized composite rhythms and percussive playing style that suffuse the album. That is, not only can Hancock's playing of the clavinet as a percussion instrument be attributed to his attraction to the guitar line in James Brown's recordings, but it is also a response to the African and Afro-Caribbean playing of Summers throughout the album.[98] Similarly, Harvey Mason enjoys the freedom to play fast and loose with the groove patterns of both "Chameleon" and "Sly," relying on a shared sense of what and where those patterns are, established through the playing of Summers and Jackson.

Harvey Mason

When Herbie Hancock broke up the Mwandishi group, he told drummer Billy Hart of his plans for the upcoming *Head Hunters* project. Hancock needed a funk-oriented drummer whom he could also relate to musically and personally. Hart recommended Harvey Mason without hesitation. Mason at the time was hot property as a session musician (to date he has appeared on well over one thousand recordings), could play film music, could play jazz, but had a primary association with rhythm-and-blues.

Mason had attended Berklee School of Music in Boston and had graduated from the New England Conservatory. Despite his current popularity in R&B recording, he originally worked extensively as a jazz drummer. He had played with masters of the jazz mainstream: Erroll Garner (in 1970) and George Shearing (1970–71). Additionally, however, he had played rhythm-and-blues-oriented fusion jazz as a founding recording member of the Blackbyrds.[99] Having settled in the early seventies in Los Angeles, Mason over time had become a leading session player with a broad catalog of leaders, styles, and genres, although with particular success in rhythm-and-blues.[100]

Like bassist Paul Jackson, Mason had the ability to create imaginative yet solid groove patterns; it was a benchmark of his playing style. As Hancock enthused: "Every beat on the album was original. He [Mason] created his own funk. That beat on 'Chameleon,' nobody ever played that before. And Harvey swings his tail off! He plays with a lot of dynamics, and that's missing in a lot of funk."[101] Mason brought together the strongest dance groove possible, part of a rhythmic matrix, playing with sensitivity to dynamics combined with virtuosity. His deviation from playing the groove "straight," as part of a fixed rhythmic function, did much to distinguish *Head Hunters* from strictly a funk album, making it "something else."

Mason, like the other musicians, incorporated his own past into his playing. The wealth of these musical and personal pasts came together and bounced outward and back again, in ways that Hancock cultivated but could not have predicted with precision. Hancock "fortunately paid attention to where it was going, and followed that," shifting from his original plan of creating a funk album to what we now know as the *Head Hunters* album.[102]

Head Hunters (1973). The gourd rattles Bill Summers holds in his hands and his Afro hairstyle let us know where this music comes from. If there is any question, though, the focal point of the photograph removes doubt. In blazing yellow and orange tones, and in sharp contrast with the background, we see Herbie Hancock, hands poised above a synthesizer keyboard, his head replaced with an African ritual mask that has radio knobs for eyes and a VU meter for a mouth. A trickster god. (Courtesy of Columbia Records.)

Takin' Off (1962). The cover of Hancock's first album features him as the genius at work, alert and sophisticated, framed by a suit, crisp shirt, tie, and conservatively styled hair. The suited look tapped into mainstream images of power and control; the accompanying respectability factor fit neatly into the integrationist atmosphere of the Kennedy New Frontier era. (Courtesy of Blue Note Records.)

Sextant (1972). One of three Africa/space-fantasy paintings by Rob Springett used on Herbie Hancock's album covers. David Rubinson commissioned the paintings for the covers. The painting's futuristic reinterpretation of African roots visually represents Hancock's musical interest at the time. (Courtesy of Columbia Records.)

Herbie Hancock and Patrick Gleeson in performance, 1972. Gleeson changed patches in real-time improvisation with Hancock and the others on stage. (Photographer unknown; courtesy of Bennie Maupin.)

Herbie Hancock and Patrick Gleeson at the studio, probably 1977. Gleeson: "Herbie is patching an EMU modular of mine (one of the first few machines that EMU had built). Behind us is the customized ARP 2600 I played on the road with Herbie and on *Sextant*." (Photographer unknown; courtesy of Patrick Gleeson.)

The Headhunters arrive for their first tour of Japan, 1974. They were hosted by a Buddhist-affiliated world peace organization, Soka-Gakai. Left to right: Mike Clark, Bennie Maupin, Herbie Hancock, Bill Summers, Paul Jackson. (Photographer unknown; courtesy of Bennie Maupin.)

The Headhunters in concert, Japan, 1994. Left to right: Blackbird McKnight, Herbie Hancock, Bennie Maupin, Paul Jackson (partially hidden, b), Mike Clark (partially hidden, d). (Photographer unknown; courtesy of Bennie Maupin.)

The Headhunters on tour at the Smiling Dog Saloon, 1974. Left to right: Mike Clark (d), Paul Jackson (b), Herbie Hancock (keyboard partially hidden), Bennie Maupin (sax). The same week, both Weather Report and the Oblivion Express were also playing in Cleveland. Wayne Shorter and Brian Auger sat in. (Photographer unknown; courtesy of Bennie Maupin.)

Fred Catero and Herbie Hancock in the Wally Heider recording studio, 1976. (Photographer: Kaz Tsuruta; courtesy of Fred Catero.)

At the Lyricon synthesizer factory, Boston, 1974. This was a spur-of-the-moment tour. Left to right: Wayne Shorter (back to camera), Bennie Maupin (glasses), Paul Jackson (knit cap), Bill Bernardi (seated, back to camera, inventor of the Lyricon), Rahsaan Roland Kirk (dark glasses), Herbie Hancock, Joe Texador (Kirk's valet). (Photographer unknown; courtesy of Bennie Maupin.)

At a Buddhist meeting while on tour, probably 1974. Buster Williams introduced Hancock to Buddhism in the late sixties; most members of the Mwandishi and Headhunters groups practiced the religion and frequently stopped at meetings while on tour. Left to right: Paul Jackson, Herbie Hancock, Mike Clark. (Photographer unknown; courtesy of Bennie Maupin.)

David Rubinson, mugging in the Automatt studio. In addition to his producing and management duties, Rubinson owned the Automatt, one of the leading studios of the day. He also formed a partnership with Bill Graham during the seventies. (© 2005 Ed Perlstein/MusicImages.com, used by permission.)

David Rubinson with Herbie Hancock and Bill Graham, probably late 1970s. (© Ed Perlstein/MusicImages.com, used by permission.)

Performing at the Berkeley Jazz Festival, 1977. The festival featured an all-star set with the leading fusion jazz artists of the time. Left to right: Herbie Hancock, Stanley Clarke, and Carlos Santana. (© 2005 Ed Perlstein/MusicImages.com, used by permission.)

Performing at the Berkeley Jazz Festival, 1977. Another shot from the same set; Herbie Hancock with John McLaughlin. (© 2005 Ed Perlstein/MusicImages.com, used by permission.)

Backstage at the Berkeley Jazz Festival, 1977. Left to right: Joni Mitchell, Mimi Fariña, Herbie Hancock. Fariña has just received a sizable donation for her Bread and Roses charity. (© 2005 Ed Perlstein/MusicImages.com, used by permission.)

Vernon Slaughter with CBS recording stars at an annual sales convention, probably early 1980s. Left to right: Webster Lewis, Marlena Shaw, Herbie Hancock, Rodney Franklin, Deniece Williams, Verdine White (of Earth, Wind, and Fire), James Mtume, DJ Rogers, George Duke, Stanley Clarke, Leon Ndugu Chancler, Vernon Slaughter. (Photographer unknown; courtesy of Vernon Slaughter.)

Vernon Slaughter with Fred Ware, regional promotional manager, at CBS annual sales convention, late 1970s. (Photographer unknown; courtesy of Vernon Slaughter.)

CHAPTER 5

Hands on the Knobs

How Production Techniques Changed the Music

Is it "cheating" in jazz to use multitrack recording, post-production editing techniques, and other tools of the studio? Is there something about the sound of synthesizers, or of electrically amplified and distorted instruments, that is anti-jazz? A vocal assortment of critics, musicians, and purist fans thought so in 1973, when *Head Hunters* was released. The abundance of fancy production, to them, sniffed of pandering to the large pop audience, an audience whose "virtue" was their sales potential, rather than their discerning jazz tastes. The implication was that *Head Hunters*, like Miles Davis's *Bitches Brew* and the many hot-selling fusion jazz albums since, resonated with the sound of the cash register at the expense of jazz.

For proponents and detractors alike, the linkage of sales with style was and has continued to be in the foreground of any critical assessment of fusion jazz; and because *Head Hunters* was the first jazz album to be certified platinum by *Billboard*, both factions point to it as a prime example of this presumed linkage. For the album's foes, robust sales demonstrate the extent to which Hancock had "dumbed down" his art; for its fans, those same sales proclaim Hancock's desire to look beyond established confines to achieve a populist relevance.

Whether the influence of the music industry on fusion jazz was beneficial or malign, influential it was.

Plugging In: Electronics, Sound Production, and the Recording Arts

During the last half of the sixties, musicians in general played a burgeoning array of amplified and synthesized instruments. But this development had largely left the field of jazz untouched. To be sure, the Hammond B3 organ had had a bearing (as the prominence of Jimmy Smith, Jimmy McGriff, and Ray Charles attests), as had the electric guitar, beginning with Charlie Christian in the late thirties and exemplified by Wes Montgomery in the sixties. A minority of jazz musicians continued to be among the first to experiment with new instruments; nonetheless, the majority stayed acoustic altogether. The aesthetic of clear timbres and clean melodic lines in these instruments, even when amplified, continued to dominate.

The rules of the game in rock and rhythm-and-blues were quite different from jazz. Those idioms, which tended to draw on similar, confined approaches to harmony, melody, and form, distinguished themselves in other directions: the quest for the perfect "hook," the most exciting dance beat, and avid explorations of new sounds. This exploration included making the sounds louder, of course, but just as central was rock's tendency toward sound distortion. Also, in contrast with the growing demand for powerful amplification associated with the larger-growing venues for rock and rhythm-and-blues, jazz performances in clubs reflected the more intimate (read: smaller and dwindling) audience for jazz in general. This intimacy revealed itself in the predominance of acoustic instruments rather than electric ones and in musicians balancing the relative loudness of each instrument through playing technique, as opposed to amplification and electronic mixing. In contrast, the pop industry, among others, made concerted use of the new technology in live performance. With the introduction of new distortions and "effects," and more powerful amplification, the expressive possibilities expanded dramatically, and pop, R&B, and rock performers were able to play in ever-larger venues.[1]

Live performance, however, was not the only beneficiary of the technology boom. Labels, producers, and artists, from classical to pop, embraced new tools in record production. Rapidly expanding options for sound modification, editing, and multitracking offered expanded creative potential in recording and post-production phases, as well as the economic flexibility of adjusting studio time and space to suit the specific job at hand. Splice-editing (discussed later in the chapter) had held a role in the aesthetic framework of many recordings since the advent of magnetic recording tape (around 1948). By the mid-sixties, that role had significantly enlarged, with precise, far cleaner editing capability allowing for multiple, sometimes minute fixes within a song, in the quest for the best composite take.[2]

With these tools in hand, there was a sense in pop, rock, and R&B that a record producer, if he could crack the code, could construct a hit almost at will. This was mainly not true, but an industry myth held that astute producers, using past hit recordings as a guide and adding their own input, could potentially push a modestly talented group over the edge of popularity by using the recording techniques and signature musical styling, if not the actual sounds, from proven hit records.[3]

At the same time, performers were promoting their recorded music with live performance tours, and the expectation was that the performance on stage had to sound more or less equivalent to the studio recording.

In pop, live performance operates in a symbiotic relationship with radio airplay. With repetition of a particular song comes audience recognition and (if listeners like the song) a building desire to hear the song again. Replaying the song builds associations of pleasure and pain for which the song becomes a sort of personal, emotional soundtrack. If all goes according to the marketing plan, the expectation that the radio will play it again, coupled with the hope that they will play it *soon*, keeps radios and listeners' ears tuned in. Repetition provides the key to the format. Repeated radio play builds demand for the recording, now internalized as an expression of the listener's own personality. The listener, if all goes well, will be driven to own—not so much the product as the musical experience—and will become a buyer. In promotional tours, live performances of songs should replicate the original as much as possible, while including enough "live" difference to make the audience feel the excitement of having the song played *just for them*.

Rock and pop music's use of the technology allowed easier replication of the recorded sounds that sold the records, in a large live venue. But in both live performances and studio recordings the *sound* became a highly affective component of the music. Despite similarities of form, harmony, and melody, rock 'n' roll of the fifties and early sixties was radically changed in sound by the end of the sixties decade. As pop music scholar and cultural critic Simon Frith describes it, the shift from "rock 'n' roll" to "rock"—that is, a shift to a new aesthetic—was driven "not just by the power of its sound, but also its cultural power." Using the Beatles as a key example, Frith links this identity with a self-conscious move toward art: "The Beatles' success suggested that it was possible to have a mass cultural impact while preserving one's status as a 'real' musician."[4] Frith turns his focus to rock's *cultural* influence, largely leaving *timbre's* culturally affective powers underexplored ("not just by the power of its sound"). Yet much of rock's cultural power derives from the affective power of its sound, as does jazz's. Rock musicians, beginning in the mid-sixties, made striking innovations in timbre. The Beatles' landmark *Sgt. Pepper's Lonely Hearts Club Band*, for example, keeps largely to previous uses of verse/chorus song structures, harmonies, rhythms, meters, and melodies.[5] What *does* mark *Sgt. Pepper* as a different approach is largely the pursuit of expressive timbres.[6] This exploration takes many forms, including unique combinations of instruments, inclusion of instruments not normally associated with rock, *musique concrète* techniques, distortion and other "effects," addition of synthesizers, and other techniques.[7] Many of these experiments utilized new developments in recording and amplification technology, and in turn the intense interest in using innovative timbres drove additional technological developments.[8]

While major shifts were happening in the sounds of rock, the *notes* in rock recordings made liberal use of a storehouse of traditional riffs, harmonies, rhythmic figures, danceable ostinato grooves, and song structures such as twelve-bar blues, all outgrowths of the music's rhythm-and-blues and country roots.[9] As in the case of the Anlo-Ewe master drummer whose creative use of preexisting, traditional patterns marks his music as excellent, traditional patterns continue to play a large role in rock aesthetics. In both cases, the aesthetic is to favor preexisting patterns but to execute them in ways that simultaneously move the music along as a composite and also "say something" uniquely expressive. This sameness and predictability, translated by some as marks of impoverished creativity, really play a fundamental role in all rhythm-and-blues derivatives, including rock, soul, and funk.

Given the misalignment of the aesthetic basis for each idiom, jazz partisans' baleful appraisal of rock should not surprise us. Rock musicians made use of the innovations in recording technology to push out timbral horizons, while staying grounded in traditional figures; "purist" jazz musicians and fans saw the same innovations as yet another attack on jazz's sense of adventure. To them, reliance on technology impinged on or even removed in-the-moment improvisation opportunities or disguised a lack of instrumental mastery.[10] The marriage of jazz with rock—or any of the styles derived from rhythm-and-blues—was destined to be a troubled one, at least in the reception by observers steeped in the jazz tradition.

Pointing to the rise of the rock 'n' roll industry during the fifties, historian Jonathan Kamin has shown how the territory was staked: "Jazz was touted by some critics as America's only true native art form and improvisation was considered one of its saving graces."[11] Kamin describes a key relationship to keep in mind: jazz's art identity and improvisation as its major standard of quality. Good jazz, then, equals or at least depends on good improvisation. Mainstream jazz musicians claimed that fusion players were incorporating a style with mass appeal but with limited display of improvisational skills.

The "saving grace" of improvisation was one of the few aspects of jazz that all the bebop and post-bebop styles had in common. However much these various camps disagreed on *how* improvised music should sound, the *standard* of live improvisation—that is, improvising, in interaction with fellow band members, in real time—was a given. The stereo recording process, first brought into play in the fifties, revealed this standard. All the players except the featured soloist were recorded simultaneously onto two tracks—left and right, for stereophonic richness—that could be edited only in limited ways.[12] With two-track technology, the excitement and implicit risk of irrecoverable error in one's improvisation were always present, much as in the live performance environment. In contrast, fusion musicians, especially after *Bitches Brew*, began making extensive use of recording studio technology commonly used in rock and R&B production by that time, including multitrack technology that allowed musicians to add their performances as a new layer synchronizing with previously recorded tracks playing through their headphones. This sel-sync technique replaced the original mode of overdubbing, used with mono or two-track recording, where previously recorded tracks could only be consolidated with a new live performer by copying both simultaneously onto a new tape machine.[13]

Observers steeped in the tradition of live improvisation held multitrack's expanded capability to add tracks after the initial recording in suspicion. Even though these recording "constructions" had occurred before, to some degree, multitracking seemed to threaten trading the documentation of a live, real-time event for a manufactured one.[14]

The notion of "manufactured moments" implied that this was a move toward rock and pop that would call into question the improvisational competence of the performer. In hindsight, the furor surrounding the new recording technology was overwrought, at least insofar as its qualitative effect on jazz improvisation was concerned. Three decades have passed since *Bitches Brew.* While advances in recording technology have made significant changes in the ways recordings are crafted, improvisation is still prominent in jazz, as it was in both *Bitches Brew* and *Head Hunters.*[15] Instead, the anxiety in the early 1970s over the anticipated loss of improvisation masked deeper worries. The first of these was that musicians would need to develop new skills, over and above having "chops" on their instruments. These skills included new areas of competence in knowing how to work within the multitrack recording process, which often required new abilities in working with effects-processing, mixing, and editing, collectively known as the *post-production process,* or at the very least becoming comfortable enough with the results of these techniques to insert their playing seamlessly into the process. The new practices also often required developing expertise in new instruments. The synthesizer, for example, was undergoing rapid development and deployment across many genres in the sixties and seventies. All this change was both a boon and a curse. To those ready to embrace the new gadgetry, it could give them entry into the control room. Those fearful or disdainful could legitimately worry about their viability in the evolving studio.

Musicians weren't the only participants worrying about the potential loss of control to technologies driven from behind the control-booth glass. *Head Hunters* producer David Rubinson explained to me that the members of the production team and the record labels for which they worked often sensed their own imminent loss of control in the production process—to the musicians.[16] Fusion jazz musicians were developing expertise in these expanded studio techniques very quickly. In many cases, notably Herbie Hancock and Weather Report's Josef Zawinul, their interest in the production and recording technology and their abilities with the new developments outstripped those of the recording engineer. With knowledge comes power: the glass barrier of the control-room window had suddenly become permeable. As Rubinson explained:

> Rubinson: The musicians, as I know it, were thrilled. Because they got to put their hands on the knobs. They got to control how the music was sounding. They got to put their own creative input in and control their own creative destiny. And got the other guys away from the console and out of control.
>
> Q: Now, how did that happen?
>
> Rubinson: Very simple. The music started to evolve from piano, bass, drums, and two horns. And basically, the older engineers didn't know what the fuck was happening. They had no idea what was going on with synthesizers or electronic instruments. And as the musicians were able to make their own sounds, and as they got exposed to the white rock 'n' roll and the white forward-looking music, they said, "Well, these guys can do anything they want. Why don't we do anything we want?" I mean, that's the way it was with Herbie, anyway. . . . Working with young, creative people, those terrible barriers weren't there. So Herbie [previously] had never been at a mix session. He basically said, "Mix? What do you mean?". . . . He made fabulous leader records, but they'd go out to [Rudy Van Gelder's studio in] New Jersey, and Rudy would record and say "this is it" when it was done. The next they ever knew of it was when the record came out.

> So if anybody said, "You know, maybe a little more hi-hat," Rudy would say, "You gonna come here, you get my sound." So it was not fundamentally a creative process. They were really kind of cut off. And that was the old style. It was, "You go in and you record and you leave. You pick up some cash and get the hell out of there." But what they do with the product is up to them. So the whole creative process started to include electronic devices, echo devices, post-production techniques—and musicians took control of it.[17]

Rubinson also identified the ideological struggle that accompanied these developments: "The technical revolution brought about the creative revolution . . . [because] the new technology gave the power to the musicians . . . [who could then take control of] the edits, choices, balances, takes, and—the ultimate control—the mixing process."[18]

Herbie Hancock became rapt with the production process along several planes. As a former engineering student during his Grinnell College days, he became infatuated with the technology that was developing. He had composed for film and television, which generally provided for tighter authorial control than the kind of small-group compositional process that was a vehicle for improvisation. And as a member of Miles Davis's quintet and as a leader of his own groups, he had learned the rewards, freedom, and final voice granted to whoever has control in the production process.

The Synthesizer's Ascendance

One of the new challenges for fusion jazz musicians was how to incorporate the synthesizer into the ensemble. Patrick Gleeson became the seventh member of Hancock's pre–*Head Hunters* group, Mwandishi.[19] Gleeson encountered some resistance to his contribution from the acoustic-oriented band members at first:

> When I went to New York, the first gig I played live with the band was at the Village Vanguard. And we were to have a rehearsal. In fact, we were to have several before the opening. And [laughs] one guy comes

> to the rehearsal, which was [bassist] Buster Williams, who came late. I don't know if he ever took his bass out of the case; he may have. But I remember he looked at me, and he sneered and he said, "It sounds like a big vacuum cleaner" [laughs]. So, you know, there was not a lot of enthusiasm about me.[20]

In Gleeson's case, he had entered the field of music through technology, rather than entering the technology through an already present expertise in music. This caused him some degree of anxiety: "Here I was, you know, never been on the road before. Compared to the other guys, [I had] slight musical skills. Really. I mean these guys were masters of [their instruments]—and nobody was a master of the synthesizer because [it had just been invented]. And I was, you know, a keyboard player that at that time couldn't have cut it in a Top Forty band."[21]

What might have proved a disastrous combination of mismatched skills became instead a ground for developing a new sound together. Gleeson related to me that, at some point, the other members accepted him into the band. He had hurdled the suspicion among the other musicians that the inclusion of the synthesizer in the sound was a gimmick; he had gotten through the disparity between their "chops" and his own, as well as the suspicion that he had merely arrived on the coattails of his associate, producer David Rubinson. As he explained to me, he did this by gradually "getting and then demonstrating the seriousness of the music."[22] As a result, he later said: "The feeling in the band, rather than that they had expanded to meet me, was that I had bought in. . . . *And now this synthesizer was a part of this music. The music hadn't changed; the synthesizer had become part of it.*"[23] Comments from others in the group bear this out. The task was not merely for Gleeson to blend into the existing sound of the others but to do so in a way that enhanced the musical values already in place. Bennie Maupin exemplified the group's enthusiasm: "We became accustomed to the fact that there was another entity and that it was a performing entity. Nobody really knows anything about Pat Gleeson [laughs] and what a tremendous innovator he really is. . . . I was always thrilled with his ideas. Because any time you can make music that's *totally* different, what could be better than that?"[24]

Of course, liking the new sound and developing the expertise to incorporate it into the new music were different issues. Especially in his early involvement with the Mwandishi group, Gleeson would add his synthesized tracks after the live playing had ended. Maupin, continuing, discussed how the live musicians allowed aesthetic room for Gleeson:

Q: But how would you leave room for it? Because a lot of that stuff he couldn't do on the fly, right? He would have to do it after—

Maupin: We just listened and listened and listened to each other. I mean, you had to really listen. Herbie was not telling anybody what to play, when to lay out, when to come in. It wasn't even about that. It was just about listening and having that trust in each other that led to what we created. Because sometimes it would be so dense with sound, there would be no room for anything. All the space was full. But then we would just thin out all the textures. Thin out everything. I mean, we'd have our moments when it would just be out there, and then we would thin it way down. And at those times, I think that there would be opportunities for Pat to create shapes and swoops and all kinds of little things that no one had ever heard, ever.

I think that just the nature of what we were doing, after a certain point, everybody was very concerned with how we used the space. So I think really on a more intuitive level, we maybe prepared the way for things to be placed here and there.

Q: You know somebody well enough so that you intuitively know what he's going to want to insert something into?

Maupin: Mm-hmm. And those things that happened, when Herbie and Pat would get the tapes, and they would go over to Different Fur and just start putting things in there. Pat has such a sensitivity, that he's always had. He's always been very conscious of the fact that he started really wanting to do music late, and all of that. But he's far better than a lot of people who have been doing music all their lives. And he's more conscientious than a lot of guys I know who may even be classified as great.[25]

The things that Hancock and Gleeson started "putting in there" were neither precisely melodic nor harmonic; the sounds are perhaps best described as timbral events. Gleeson's and Hancock's incorporations of the synthesizer sounds allowed for an added dimension of orchestration in the small-group format. Both men emphasized this orientation in interviews. According to Gleeson:

> Debussy and Ravel and Gil Evans [laughs] were my spiritual betters and antecedents. And so I always thought of an orchestral extension of what was going on in the music. And I was always interested, and am still interested, in the area where the live instrument ends and the synthesizer extends it in a way that it isn't necessarily possible to tell. . . . I thought of it as extensions of the instrumental performances and, probably as much or more than, as "wash." Just because of my own sensibility, it probably turned into something that was "washy," but I was thinking of it more as extensions of the instruments.[26]

An inherent problem with synthesis was (and remains) the choice of synthesized timbre to be used at any given moment. During the early seventies, synthesizers were exclusively analog, were difficult to configure, and had severe limitations on their choices of sounds. The term *computer music* surfaced as much because of the highly technological appearance and operation of the new medium as because of the sounds produced. Early synthesizers were not as user-friendly as current models; one had to set the sounds in advance, severely limiting the notion of real time improvisation. Gleeson's contributions occurred at first in the studio, with Gleeson listening to tapes of his fellow band members and filling the spaces left open for him. But as the technology improved, timbres could be chosen more in the moment and therefore could be improvised in real time. As this became possible, notes and instrumental colors became inseparable, a complex to which the musicians responded improvisationally.

These developments affected Hancock profoundly. Bill Summers told me that

> what happened with *Head Hunters*, what Lee Morgan and the others did not have before was electronics. That's what made the difference, Her-

> bie coming up, after his being influenced by Pat Gleeson. And Herbie, I think, got swept up in the technology. . . . Herbie, still to this day, has every new toy known to man. And he keeps it in his environment. And he's very up on interactive media, multimedia sorts of things. As a result of me being around Herbie and being around David, I'm exactly the same way, even though I have one foot in 2000 B.C. and one foot in 2000 A.D.[27]

The synthesizer was not the only generator of new sounds. At the time of *Head Hunters*, acoustic instruments in a jazz session typically would be recorded via microphone, and adjustments of tone would happen largely through the musician's playing technique. However, a panoply of timbral effects for nonacoustic instruments, such as fuzz tone, wah-wah, and chorusing, were available for the musician to control. Studio effects, such as doubling delay (an echo effect) and EQ, remained under the purview of the recording engineer, in collaboration with the producer or whoever had final touch on the control board.[28] Although much of the originating sound was under the control of the musician at the point of performance, the final vote stayed with the person in charge in the control room. However, with early synthesizers plugged directly into the control-room console and largely out of the producer's realm of expertise, that glass barrier was breached.[29] Once disturbed, the hierarchy of control was no longer stable. This is not to suggest that the control room was *completely* closed to musicians previously, but the new technological shifts lent them unprecedented access. With their hands on the soundboard knobs and faders, musicians developed the core skills to begin to exert their will on aspects of the recording process, beyond performance. Multitrack recording and tape-editing techniques provided additional tools to join other real-time improvisations added later, in Gleeson's case with *Crossings* and *Sextant*, and for Hancock with post-production auteurism.[30]

Developments in Recording Technology

Monaural (mono) jazz recording done on a single track continued the recording industry's way of operating from its earliest days, although the medium had changed to erasable magnetic tape around 1948. This new medium allowed the freedom of cut-and-splice editing (splicing), in which physical tape sections of a preferred rendition could be cut and inserted into the tape of another rendition, replacing material or adding to it. Stereophonic recordings, available to the public in the late fifties, were another major innovation.[31] With separate tracks for left and right speakers, stereophonic sound produced something closer to the directional dynamics of a "live" listening environment:

> This allowed a stereo image to be recorded—the material on one channel only was heard from the left. The material on the other channel was heard from the right. The material that was shared equally was heard [as if] from the center. And proportionately across the spectrum left to right in this way. There was no "center" channel. Three audio images, but only two channels on the tape machine. So, the invention of the three-track machine. This gives you a real channel for the material you want in the center. . . . Controlling the center material [was] invented primarily for classical and pop musicians [i.e., featured musicians or soloists]. Typically, this allowed the orchestra to be recorded in full stereo, on two tracks, and the featured artist to be recorded separately on the third track. This allowed complete control over the star's performance and is the beginning of "multitrack" recording.
>
> In mono or two-track recording the only way to fix was (1) splice-editing (which could still allow for using takes [i.e., incorporating tape segments] from different performances); (2) overdubbing, which meant recording the band or orchestra first and then playing back the mono or two-track tape of the band, while simultaneously recording the featured performer, and combining the two onto a second tape (on a second machine). This had been going on for years. It had been going on since mono tape recording started (Les Paul etc.) and the advent of the three-track machine changed everything. Why? Because before, in order for the band to be in sync with the singer, the playback of the band tracks had to be made off the ERASE heads of the tape machine. In overdubbing [i.e., prior to three-track tape recording], you just played back the band tape and sang along. Everything was in sync. You were copying the band from the original tape, and recording the singer singing along, on a separate dubbing (copying) machine. But now it was all being done on one (three-track) machine. This is the

advent of true multitrack layering, called “sel-sync,” as differentiated from overdubbing.[32]

To explain further, three-track technology was initially developed with classical music and pop recording in mind for two reasons. First, recording an orchestra separately and then joining it with the soloist’s performance on the same tape prevented the introduction of unwanted noise (“hiss”) caused, in the earlier process, when dubbing from two machines onto a copying machine. Hiss was undesirable, to say the least, in the hi-fi aesthetics associated with classical music recordings. Second, it allowed an orchestra to be recorded in stereo, in a large recording studio, with the soloist recorded separately or even at a later time in a small, acoustically controlled booth. This improved the producer’s ability to control the balance and tone of the solo performance relative to the larger envelope of the orchestra. Additionally, starting with a cleaner-sounding tape enhanced the ability to edit. Editing for the backing tracks of the large orchestra, for instance, before the featured artist entered the studio further streamlined the process. Also, although one could splice-edit any magnetic tape, the disruption of the sound at the edit’s seam risked a “pop” on the finished tape. Therefore, as the technology continued to develop, with more and more tracks (by the time of *Head Hunters*, twenty-four track was the standard for commercial recordings), errors could be fixed creatively. One possibility was to “punch in” (“drop in”) a fix, that is, to re-record only the few notes that needed fixing directly onto a track of the recording tape, fixing the original tape and avoiding adding irritating tape “hiss.”

Another advantage was that, by recording multiple parts as isolated sounds on dedicated tracks of the tape, the recording engineer could make tone adjustments to the sound of each track and blend the tracks together (“mixing”) with greatly enhanced flexibility. When the tracks were recorded at different times, this was no problem, but for individual tracks recorded simultaneously, great care was taken to obtain separation of the sounds coming from each musician (eliminating “bleed-through”). Further, the engineer could do an initial pass of the mix during the recording process, if he wished, but had the ability now, with the producer, to revise the mix at later sessions, finalizing the mix ("mixing down") to a two-track stereo master format. Multitrack recording thus offered increased production options and inherent editing advantages.

Multitracking also saved production costs. Facilities and add-on equipment could be scheduled to fit the needs physically and technically of the particular recording segment, whether a rhythm section, horns, strings, or soloists—miking one performer or twenty. It minimized the inevitable scheduling conflicts, technical snafus, retakes, and other delays that could drive up production costs. Expensive and/or highly scheduled soloists could be accommodated with prime-time studio slots (with the highest per-hour studio rentals) and a luxury recording environment to record to a playback tape (which sealed the background context as utterly predictable). Session string players would show up at the early-morning economy-rate time, whereas high-demand rhythm section players often groaned over recording dates starting before one o'clock in the afternoon. Low-rent studios could be used for isolated or preliminary segments, the master multitrack tape then transported to more expensive studios for the finishing work.[33]

In contrast, at least from the producer's and engineer's point of view, small-group jazz recording, from bebop recordings in the forties through the sixties and beyond, was particularly well suited to two-track technology. With improvisation and live interaction at the forefront of the music anyway, clients were less likely to demand overdubbing capability, although splice-editing was always possible. Setting up the instruments and microphones was simple, with less need for the separation of instruments, although the drums were sometimes separated. Because the instrumentation format was quite stable—a rhythm section of piano/bass/drums, with one or two solo horns—the setup and mix were also standard or, at worst, easily adapted. To the record label, this meant that, although the market for this kind of music was relatively small, the investment for producing a record was minimal, and the number of records needed to return the investment was a fraction of that for a pop recording. The aesthetics of small-group jazz thus remained symbiotic with the low cost of two- or three-track recording.

Using the Studio as an Instrument

Arbitrary limitations of the term *jazz-rock fusion*, as the earlier discussion shows (see chap. 1), obscure what was being fused musically. However, the term does describe one element of this music well. What draws fusion jazz recordings together is not the notes being played but how the notes got there: jazz musicians used rock and R&B production techniques.

Most of the developments in technology described earlier took place over twenty years, roughly from 1950 to 1970. Over the same period, rock 'n' roll emerged, ascended in importance, and dominated the pop music industry. With pop sales figures spiraling upward, record labels increasingly were inclined to invest in ever higher production quality, with the corollary of ever higher production budgets. Record labels used these same studio production techniques to make products more palatable to consumer tastes. As playback equipment quality improved, customers increasingly looked for and could expect higher production values. Bowing to the importance of radio airplay, pop producers up to the late sixties routinely calibrated their final mixes to cheap car speakers, which could accommodate only a limited frequency range. Similarly, home stereos usually "read" only midrange frequencies—fancy woofers and tweeters were the province of audiophile classical and jazz listeners. As home stereos became increasingly sophisticated and as car radios began to offer FM's fidelity in the late sixties, however, producers began to adjust their mixes accordingly. For example, Sly and the Family Stone's landmark 1969 "Thank You (Falletin Me Be Mice Elf Again)," which showcases Larry Graham's funk bass, sounds shockingly thin compared to the bass sound in "Chameleon" just four years later. Production and playback technology did not advance only to attract customers; no doubt many changes were generated by inventors' and production personnel's natural predilection to build a better mousetrap. As production-related manipulations of sound increased, so did the contestation among record label, producer, engineer, and artist for control of the final creative product.

The producer's role in pop music, especially in the recording's planning stages, is described by music industry historian Michael Fink. The pop producer exerts "considerable influence on the choice of songs" to be recorded. Another choice the producer routinely makes, or at least has a powerful voice in, is hiring arrangers (or creating arrangements), which entails both "a rhythm arrangement, including the vocal routine and rhythm section (piano, rhythm guitars, drums, and bass); and an arrangement for all the other parts, including background vocals." The producer usually assumes responsibility for booking the studio and engineers, musicians (including a rhythm section if the artist does not have one), special recording equipment, and copyists and will usually act as a bridge between the performers and the label. In-house producers are most likely to use studios owned or primarily used by the label, but independent producers will take care to choose "a studio that combines the right size, 'sound,' ambiance, recording equipment, and engineering personnel for the artist and for the recording's concept."[34] The imposing, activist producer's role that Fink portrays fits, say, Phil Spector's "wall of sound" recordings during the sixties. The musicians still perform, but much of the ultimate power over the finished product—beyond the musicians' efforts that we actually hear—rests in the producer's hands: in the pre-production arrangements and in the decisions made in the control booth throughout the recording and post-production process.

With the explosion in sales power of the small-group rock band in the mid-sixties, exemplified by the Beatles, the ability to wrest away or at least share control of the recording process grew exponentially.[35] With this sharing of control, the rock performer was able to use the editing and multitrack resources of the studio as part of his or her creative process.

But in jazz circles, as this studio creativity grew, the ability to "fix" performance problems that occurred within improvised segments raised fears that instrumental technique would suffer. Small wonder, then, that jazz critic Bill Cole complained about Hancock's *Mwandishi* album: "The album is highly arranged, so there's very little room for improvisation. It really sounds beautiful, but it's so contrived."[36]

In fusion jazz, the most profound influence from rock was in this use of the recording studio: the configuration of the room itself, as well as the equipment and techniques that went with it. As David Rubinson put it: "The studio became part of the creative process. The artist's canvas. Not a crutch—a creative tool."[37]

Editing as Part of the Creative Process

Clearly, the influence of Miles Davis on Herbie Hancock's music appeared in Hancock's use of modalism and rhythmic structures and in his orientation toward collective improvisation. Davis was also indirectly influential in Hancock's choice of musicians. Both Bennie Maupin, who played on the *Bitches Brew* sessions, and Buster Williams, who played with Davis briefly in 1967, would join Hancock in the Mwandishi band, and Maupin would remain for *Head Hunters.* Beyond these factors, Davis's assumption of increased control in the production process provided a model for Hancock.

From the latter years of the sixties, Davis grew increasingly involved in the editing process, in partnership with his producer, Teo Macero. According to Macero, their working relationship was so close that he saw himself as Davis's alter ego: "From the time the studio musicians start playing, we take down every note of music . . . I make masters of everything. I may have 15 reels, so Miles and I cut those reels down. . . . I keep listening to it over and over with the engineer and finally Miles comes in and listens to it and he sort of smiles and he walks out. That's all there is to it."[38] Macero's description refers to a later album, but the procedure was the same with *Bitches Brew.* The daily routine for *Bitches Brew* of recording every note would be followed by an early-morning routine of reviewing the tapes of the previous day, as Maupin recalled:

> I would come to the studio. If the session was at 10:00, I would make it a point to be at the studio by at least 9:15, just so I could see what the prerecording thing was about. Since I had the opportunity to go into Columbia studios for the first time, I said, "Well, who knows? This may be my last time. I want to see how the big guys do it." I would come in there—they would already be working. I don't know how long they had been in there, but Miles was always there before the musicians came in.[39]

But Davis would not allow his musicians to listen to more than a fraction of their output:

> The thing that I remember most about the recording was that he never let anyone hear anything. We didn't do a take and say, "OK, let's go back and listen to that." If we did, it would be every bit of about ten seconds. Then he would say, "OK Teo, shut it off. Let's go on." And then we would go on. So you didn't have an opportunity to hear what you played. And I realized after a while that he did that so that no one would imitate themselves. Because he knew that if you get a group of young musicians in the studio like that, and you give them an opportunity to hear what they're playing, then they're going to stop creating and start imitating themselves.[40]

Davis's involvement in the editing process was made possible by a combination of his understanding of his own powerful position in the jazz market, his strong-willed personality, and his long working relationship with Macero. Davis had entered the control room, but not to liberate it generally: he claimed control only to keep it himself, or rather in collaboration with Macero. Bennie Maupin recalled the shock of hearing *Bitches Brew* for the first time:

> I didn't hear any of that music until the recording was released. I was in San Francisco the first time I ever heard it on the radio, in my car. . . . And I was going crazy. I was saying, "What is that?" I said, "It sounds familiar, but I don't know what that is." You know, that sound. And then finally after—you know how long those tracks are—the guy says, "Well, that's the new Miles Davis recording, *Bitches Brew*. It's quite long, but we're going to play it anyway." And that's when I first heard it. We just parked the car. This guy played the entire thing. We listened for hours. Listening to it, I was so—it just took me over. I had no idea that that music sounded so beautiful. Because I couldn't tell anything during the recording sessions.[41]

Hancock involved himself in the production process in a similar way. As in the case of *Bitches Brew*, the recordings for *Mwandishi* and later albums included an extensive editing process in the post-production phase of preparing the albums for release. This seems to be the basis for Bill Cole's complaint that the *Mwandishi* album was "highly arranged," "contrived," with "very little room for improvisation," despite its beauty. In fact, according to the album's producer, Rubinson, the music was played in real-time interaction, mostly, if not completely, improvised: "Herbie and the others had music that they had written, melodies, or in the case of 'Ostinato' [on the *Mwandishi* album], just a bass line and groove. Everything else was improvised."[42] Patrick Gleeson, who became a member of the group about this time, provides a window into the process:

> The conversation was very concise. He'd say [mumbles], "Say. Let me see. So. Do that. [aloud] Oh, I know. All the horns, why don't you guys play the melody in unison. Or, you know, you could play it, you might want to play it an octave higher (or an octave lower)." And—boom—then we'd try that. And each guy would take his own line about it [i.e., try his own interpretation of the idea]. And then, you know, some guy would find some slightly different way of ending it. And Herbie would just say, "Hmm. Mmm-mmm." And that "Mmm" would become part of that tune. And then he'd say, "Well, uh, you know, let's try it." And then coming right out of the head, Herbie for the first time, we would know what the rest of the track was going to sound like, because Herbie would be playing. And of course as jazz musicians, Buster and Billy would be playing with him. And there would be the groove. And sometimes Buster would say, "Uh, is that like a sus4 [chord]?" And Herbie said, "Mmm. Mmm." And so Buster would play the sus4 on the bass. Which, when you think about it, changes the chord entirely. And kind of make it an altered form of some other chord. And so there would be this very tradition-steeped approach to it, even though it was, you know, funk-jazz or fusion or whatever else. It was a brief rehearsal on the head. . . . And then everybody in the group knew each other and everybody's playing so much that at a certain point Herbie would look up and play something that would obviously—but not so obviously—be leading back to the head. Then everybody would know—you know, it was a skill—and—bang—we're going back to the head right now. And you'd go to the head. And then Herbie likes something and says, "We could play that twice maybe there." Or he'd say, "When we come

> back to there let's take it at G, instead of B-flat" or "B-flat instead of G." So then the whole thing would be transposed from that point on. And it relied on extremely skillful players being able to adjust very, very quickly. So even though it was very organized in a way, *it was organized through a series of improvisational processes, based on a very, very slight sketch of a head.*[43]

As in the case of Davis with *Bitches Brew*, Hancock took the opportunity to be an equal partner in the post-production process. In his case, he became even more hands-on than Davis had been:

> Herbie had access to the complete—the complete—creative process—including editing, mixing, splicing, layering—and he used it all. . . . The solos and the group improvisations were all recorded full length in the studio. The new techniques *made real freedom possible.* The old way, [for example, with Charlie] Parker [or Lester] Young, [they would have] only three and a half minutes to get it all out. Then with the LP, they could stretch out, but only for a few more choruses. The new studio techniques allowed for unstinted playing, and then just keeping the best parts.[44]

Two aspects of Rubinson's comment bear explaining. First, one criticism leveled at the fusion jazz movement in general, and *Bitches Brew* in particular, is that it encouraged chopping up a musician's improvisation, disrupting the music as it had flowed in the moment, potentially doing grave damage to the musical integrity of the piece. While this was undoubtedly true in some cases, there is more to the story. I was curious about this, because if the players knew the final recording would be spliced, I reasoned that it might cause them to shift strategically from building an overall shape in improvising to playing moment to moment.

Interviewing Josef Zawinul about the shortened improvisation on "Pharaoh's Dance," I learned that the musicians did not know that the tape would be edited; in fact, at the time of the interview, Zawinul mentioned that a reissue that would preserve the entire original was in the works.[45] Zawinul described his keyboard soloing style as creating an "arch," bringing into play an overall narrative plan. This would seem to buttress the position of Davis biographer Jack Chambers, that this wholesale wrenching of his playing from its original context was an unconscionable violation of Zawinul's art.[46] This is one half of Chambers's point. Paradoxically, he also laments the long duration of the finished product. When I posed this interpretation, Rubinson's response was emphatic: "More unconscionable than telling Prez [Lester Young] that he had only two choruses?? Worse than letting Bird [Charlie Parker] have only one take? Horseshit. Letting them do one song of their own, if they did a standard in return? An LP in 1970 could contain [a maximum of] forty to forty-five minutes total. Because of the technical limits of the disk. The longer time, the less dynamic range, the lower the audio level, the worse the signal-to-noise ratio. Simple. Certainly not unconscionable."[47] Rubinson's irate response stems from the second aspect of his earlier comment: despite the purist lament over splice-editing, editing was a traditional practice in record production of all types. Even before tape splicing vastly expanded editing options, Rubinson points out, musicians routinely self-edited to deal with time limits enforced by the technology. A ten-inch 78-rpm record could reproduce up to slightly over three minutes of sound. Ideas that musicians wanted to express would have to come in under the time limit; to accomplish this, they would have to either plan ahead (plan the number of choruses), respond to cues, or redo the take. The advent of microgroove recording technology made possible a twelve-inch 33-rpm record that could carry twenty minutes of recorded material on each side. As Rubinson points out, however, the time strictures were elongated but not eliminated.

In contrast, the sextet recorded *Mwandishi* at leisure, exhausting any ideas they wanted to express. Then the editing process took over. With his hands on the editing blade, Hancock was able to extend his authorial will deeper into the finished product. This post-production editing process, with its implication of who would have the final creative word, occurred in the pre-tape era as well, when musicians were frequently excluded from the choice of which take would be released. Generalizing about the shift, Rubinson enthused: "This was fantastic. This was the revolution. In Marxian terms, the workers took over the means of production. [Earlier,] the musicians used to just split, and [the producer] would send them a copy later. Not any more."[48] Gaining final control required moving into the control room, the producer's territory, no matter what the technology. The early seventies was a moment of tremendous flux in the recording industry, and in the jazz arm of that industry in particular. The earlier two-track small-group jazz model had faltered, and fusion jazz now enjoyed ascendance. But whether this was a permanent shift or not, no one knew. Record labels simply had no reliable crystal ball that would allow them to be confidently dictatorial as in the past; their hesitation became a window through which the strong of will jumped.

Which portion of seizing control was motivated by creative aspirations and political concerns, and which by business economics, is not clear. What is clear, though, is that Hancock, having seized a large measure of control, chose to continue highly collaborative work with his fellow musicians while retaining the leader's position, a fact made plain in his quarterbacking compositional style. As Gleeson describes, much of the material was worked out interactively in the moment, although, as leader, Hancock retained primary control over the process as well as the overall musical plan: "And then . . . we would know what the rest of the track was going to sound like, because Herbie would be playing."

With the recording of *Mwandishi*, then, Hancock developed the studio recording session as a compositional tool, in much the same way as a more traditional composer might use a piano, as a way of checking and then editing an idea. This became a model for his subsequent recordings, including *Head Hunters*, although with a significant alteration in that album.

Other recording groups at this time also used adaptations of the model. The funk/Latin fusion group War utilized the editing process for their 1971 hit "Slippin' into Darkness" (*All Day Music*): " '"Slippin' into Darkness" was the first time I used editing to create a song out of a jam,' [producer Jerry] Goldstein says. 'It took me five days to figure out how to edit a single out of what we had. The only way to do it was to let the band play free and then figure out what to do with it later.' "[49] For Hancock, the studio, and the advantages of editing, multitrack recording, and the other techniques discussed so far, blended the processes of pre- and post-production with composition:

> I remember that the bass line for "Chameleon," I felt that the notes were a little long. And I wanted to try doing the bass line again, but with the notes shorter. Punchier. So we pulled up a sound on this synthesizer, and so I recorded—I guess we had a click track to work to. And so I played it, you know. Then, when I went back to David Rubinson's studio, and besides this, entered the other thing that I had done, which was the reason I had gone to Pat Gleeson's [recording studio, Different Fur Trading Co.], I said, "Oh, I also did another version of that bass line on 'Chameleon.'" And he said, "OK, let's put it up." So he puts the tape on, rolls the tape, and plays it back. And I said, "Whoa, wait a minute." He says, "You've got both bass parts up now." And then I said, "Now waaaait a minute." So normally, because bass has a low-frequency sound, and the lower the frequencies are, the more difficult it is to locate where the sound comes from, it's nondirectional. But in this case, since they were done on two different—I think on two different synthesizers, but at any rate, the sound that I used for each one was slightly different. And so it meant that I could put one on one [channel] and one on the other. And you get a sense of a wider bass. Sort of stereo bass. Which is what you never get on records. Usually the bass comes right through the center.[50]

In contrast to editing as strictly a post-production technique, and in contrast to his own earlier compositional model, Hancock used editing in composition, which he then tested in live playing situations. It was a multiple-step process. First, as Bill Summers reveals, basic ideas were developed:

> And so the band was solidified. And I remember going to this place called Funky Jack's in San Francisco, which was in this guy's apartment. It was a twenty-four-track studio. And we went up in there. David [Rubinson] may have been there, maybe not. I think he was there. I don't think he was there all the time, though. But what we did for at least two or three days was play and tape. There was no real structure that I can remember. And the tapes were then sifted through and the ideas extracted that built that album.[51]

So far, the process recalls that of "Slippin' into Darkness," but with a crucial difference in who's doing the sifting; that is, the producer's presence is felt, to be sure, but as one of many players in the game.

Once the basic ideas had been extracted, the process of composition continued largely as a process of editing. Further, although Hancock maintained authorial control over his compositions and arrangements, the procedure fostered a high degree of cooperation in fomenting and building improvisational ideas. Maupin elaborated: "Once we started doing those rehearsals here in LA, getting ready to do the recording, we just turned the tape recorder on, and we jammed. On our lunch break, or whatever, we'd just go back and listen to see what the jams were about. And we'd extract from it whatever we thought we could maybe build on and just kind of work around that. The tune that really broke *Head Hunters* was 'Chameleon.' And that was a jam."[52] Rather than layering a track over another track to build a piece, the procedure was to use ideas from jams as part of the composition process. The newly solidified ideas coalesced into larger compositions, which the group then tested in front of live audiences for further refinement. As Maupin told me:

> The way we did our rehearsals, we rehearsed Monday through Friday. The first couple weeks, we just rehearsed. And, I think, by the third week, we'd take a gig, someplace like the Lion's Share over in Marin. We rehearsed in LA. But David Rubinson's office was up in San Francisco. And so he'd hook up a gig for us so we could come and try the music out. So we rehearsed and got enough tunes together that we could play for at least one evening. And we'd come up and just try the music out on the public. Because by the time they found out that Herbie was going to be there, the joint would be sold out for two shows. I mean it would be [whew] instantaneous. And so those weekends were very good for us, because we got to get the feedback from the audience. But we went in there and just created these tunes. And we collaborated in a way that we hadn't prior to that recording. And it went rather smoothly. There were no hitches in the music we were doing. We enjoyed collaborating on the music.[53]

Hancock elaborated:

> Hancock: So [Rubinson] had us working in some clubs in Marin. Just to try it out. And people went nuts over it.

Q: Were they prepared for it? Because what had been going on before that was totally different.

Hancock: Well, first of all, San Francisco is a very forgiving place. I mean, you can try things there. And audiences are more willing to listen to something new. Which is really great about the attitude of San Franciscans. And they do listen. That's the thing about it. It's not just that they just listen to the words—I mean they listen to what's going on. They listen to the groove; they listen to the solos, and they were dancing to it. Oh, they loved it. They danced to it, and it was a totally new experience for them. And they thought it was hot. And so that really inspired us and encouraged us. And it really shaped—*it helped us shape the music, to refine what it was that we were doing.* Playing it in front of a live audience like that before recording it. Then we went back into the recording studio and recorded it.

Q: And you recorded more or less live? Well, you recorded it live with some synth overdubs, I guess.

Hancock: Yeah, with synth overdubs. We had the whole rhythm section live. I did all the clavinet parts live.[54]

Maupin underscored this last point:

Maupin: There are very few overdubs on that recording. I think some of the only things that might be overdubbed were some of the synthesizer work that Herbie did.

Q: Because there are two or three lines going on?

Maupin: Yeah, right. So you couldn't play those things live. But he covered quite a bit of it, just right there. As we were actually going through it. *And so those gigs that we would do on the weekend enabled us to develop a way of playing through the forms of the tunes and just doing it all live. Because that was an important part of what we wanted to capture: the live playing.*[55]

In the recording studio, the collaborative spirit continued. Laying down live tracks with all musicians playing interactively maximized their ability to improvise together. The recording was done via multitrack; yet instead of laying down individual lines and then layering them together, the tracks were recorded together, with each instrument on a separate track. All the musicians were in a single room, with sound baffling around each of them to prevent leakage, for instance, from the horn track to the bass guitar track. The goal was interaction: with baffling placed so as to preserve sight lines among the players, the open room facilitated this.[56]

With the basic tracks laid and initial edits done, Hancock then layered additional synthesizer tracks. In this way Hancock used multitrack layering to solve musical problems, which the groove matrix on "Chameleon" illustrates. Hancock's use of a layering approach had resonance in African and African American traditions. Members of a jazz rhythm section function collectively as a *fixed rhythmic* group in Wilson's sense of providing a cohesive matrix against which a solo—the *variable rhythmic* component—takes place.[57] In a jazz setting, the instrumentalists of the matrix, while imparting stability, do not surrender their improvising role. So in a typical small-group jazz format, there are two types of interaction happening: interaction within the *fixed rhythmic* group to create this matrix and interaction between the soloist and the matrix as a whole. Hancock's "bass" lines were prerecorded, and Hancock then recorded a clavinet line in real time, in interaction with the drums, percussion, and electric bass. The second synthesizer clavinet line, functioning as part of the *fixed rhythmic* group matrix, was recorded *after* the basic tracks were laid. The result (fig. 29) sounds to our ears as if Hancock had played his solo to the complete *fixed rhythmic* matrix, although the methodology disrupts the matrix conceptually as a unit. Hancock's ability to manipulate multitrack recording techniques enabled him simultaneously to reinforce and to revise a prevalent African and African American musical practice.

I have been discussing collaboration as informing the *Head Hunters* album. More accurately put, it was a modified collaboration. Although there was much give-and-take in the entire process, the leadership role rested with Hancock. Fred Catero, engineer on the album, confirmed this:

FIG. 29. "Chameleon" rhythmic matrix, all parts performed by Herbie Hancock.

> Herbie generally had a pretty good idea of what he wanted. Sometimes he would change it on the date. But I don't recall him ever coming in and saying, "No, we're going to redo this, in this manner. And I'm going to change the whole structure of it by editing." I mean, that was not his style. He generally knew what he wanted. It was just a matter of that it was expedient for him to keep recording and take the best groove, rather than just do it from beginning to end and then keep doing a bunch of takes. You know what I'm saying? Because that's another way to do it. You do a take, you listen, and you say, "Well, it really locked in halfway through. Let's do it again." And then hopefully you get a good front and a good middle and a good end [laughs]. But he didn't do that. A lot of times he would do one or two takes, and they were "longies," and then he'd edit.[58]

This modified collaboration extended to the post-production process, according to Bennie Maupin:

Q: How collaborative was it? I mean, was it pretty much Herbie's show, as far as that post-production part?

Maupin: In many cases, we would be there, listening. From the beginning of the project, from pre-production, right on through the recording, and then on to post-production. We'd have an opportunity to just be there, because you'd never know when they might want to have something redone. So I would be in San Francisco sometimes all week. I'd come home on the weekend and fly right back up there on Monday. And we'd *work*, you know. So I would say that there was an opportunity to be involved right on through to the very end of the project.[59]

The production hierarchy was clearly undergoing redefinition, but it was still not egalitarian. However, although Hancock had achieved a great deal in controlling his creative output, his control was not absolute. Maupin indicated this:

> A lot of guys, even today, relinquish [post-production] to the producer and the engineer. They don't want too much to do with whatever happens during the mixing sessions. Some guys don't even come to the mixing sessions, for whatever reason. Herbie was very interested in the technology, as you know. So he was present, for the most part, when those sessions were happening, unless we were away or something. And sometimes when we were away, the decisions would be David's. And I could always tell when they were his because, in some cases, the horn sound would not be right. For me. *Herbie just heard it a different way.* But, you know, it's all done now. So be it.[60]

What was that "different way" of hearing? Maupin's comment makes clear that Hancock had something in mind that he sought to achieve through the production and post-production processes. Equally clear, what he had in mind included the notes that were played but also went beyond them. The collaborative experimentalism in rehearsal, described by Patrick Gleeson, suggests this. Beyond the notes lay the timbre, the "sound" of the album. The technologies that made the new timbres possible—in synthesis, amplification, effects, and sound layering—disrupted historical notions of what jazz should sound like.

Timbre, then, contributed to *Head Hunters'* genre confusion and opened the door to marketing the album beyond the confines of a single category.

The Linkage of Timbre and Genre

Any discussion of fusion jazz as a genre brings up the use of amplified and electronic instruments as one dividing line between fusion and "straight-ahead" jazz. A secondary demarcation occurs over the inclusion of acoustic instruments not normally associated with jazz, such as sitar and other East Indian instruments, various African instruments, and other non-Western instruments. This points to a timbral orientation in fusion. If one imagines a continuum in instrumentation from the standard small-group jazz format (saxophone and/or trumpet, acoustic piano, acoustic bass, drums) through the standard small-group rock format (lead and rhythm electric guitars, electronic keyboard, electric bass, drums) and onward to a liberation from traditional instrumentation formats (e.g., inclusion of non-Western instruments, sampling, and synthesis), earlier recordings by Miles Davis and others emerge as transitional toward fusion. What's less fusion-like is the *sound* of these albums, which suggests the importance of timbre in fusion's identity. Tony Williams's drumming, for example, shows the importance of timbre, particularly on Davis's "transitional" albums prior to *Bitches Brew*.

Discussing "Frelon Brun (Brown Hornet)" on Davis's *Filles de Kilimanjaro*, Davis biographer Ian Carr describes the central roles of Dave Holland's steady bass riff and Chick Corea's "fairly static chording" on the piano as setting an atmosphere against which Williams's and Davis's "violent interplay" is "fresh and exhilarating."[61] Carr's discussion of this song, and of *Filles de Kilimanjaro* as a whole, pays insightful analytical attention both to musical details and to Davis's increasing attention to timbre. In particular, the electric piano plays a central role. "Although the acoustic piano is featured from time to time," Carr writes, the electric piano's prominence "colors the ensemble sound, and it is also used to point up the bass figures."[62]

The new sound (and its associations with rock and soul) is undoubtedly an important marker for Davis's move toward rock, as Carr describes, and Davis's continued use of electric guitar and bass guitar is a hallmark of his new sound. But interestingly, the drums—not only Tony Williams's playing of figures but also the sound of the drums themselves—help to keep the album tethered to the "jazz" side of jazz-rock. Williams's straight eighth-notes set the piece's groove, and Williams plays accents in interplay between the bass drum and snare drum, with an eighth-note metronomic pattern favoring the closed hi-hat. Williams blends rock and jazz aesthetics: although the groove says "rock," Williams plays around it, in the language of jazz, Signifyin(g) on it as if the groove were a given, understood by the listener.[63] Even though Williams's style diverges from the rock ideal of a steady metronomic beat with a minimum of fills in prescribed places (primarily phrase endings), the overall pulse and straight-eighth subdivisions suggest rock. However, the *sound* is still on the "jazz" side of the jazz-rock divide.

To identify a record from the late sixties as jazz (as opposed to rock), listen to the sound of the bass drum. The typical jazz drum set of the time featured a relatively small bass drum (often eighteen inches in diameter), tuned high, with both batter and resonating heads in place. The bass drum beater tended to be made of a softer felt than that used with rock drums. The result was a quasi-tonal sound, with a "mushy" attack and a long, ringing die-off. The playing style tended to favor a soft attack, known as "feathering," which had its roots in the swing era of the thirties.

Although rock drumming saw an explosion of drum sizes and configurations during the late sixties, jazz drum sets had became increasingly standardized since the fifties. The typical jazz drum set of the time was fairly compact, with a bass drum, a snare drum, a mounted and a floor tom-tom, and two cymbals (ride and crash) plus a hi-hat cymbal. Earlier, bass drum attacks during the swing era varied, depending somewhat on the music's medium. On the bandstand, the drummer most likely played with a heavy foot on the main beats, reinforcing the walking acoustic bass line. Recording technology in the thirties, however, favored a "feathered" touch, so as not to overload the recording stylus with too much bass. The acoustic bassist, miked, could instead deliver the needed main-beat touchstone. During the forties and the rise of bebop, drummers tended either to feather the main beats or to omit them entirely, in order to allow sonic room for accented bass drum "bombs." Given the tiny clubs and lack of amplification (much less the modern-day presence of sound men, mixing boards, and stage monitors), all of these elements—the high-pitched, ringing drums, coupled with a playing style that foregrounded the ride and hi-hat cymbals and backgrounded heavy bass drum hits—made it possible (and desirable) to play softly enough to accompany a small, unamplified jazz group. Tony Williams's loud, aggressive playing style set him apart from most jazz drummers of the sixties, yet his approach to tuning largely reinforced the jazz aesthetics in place.

In contrast, rock and funk aesthetics, especially by 1973, tended to favor a "dry" sound, with minimal ring.[64] The bass drum tended to be tuned looser, partly to provide a deeper tone ("thud") and partly to lessen the length of reverberation and decay ("die-off"). Often the drum would be muffled from the inside with a pillow. Engineer Fred Catero recalled his treatment of Harvey Mason's bass drum for *Head Hunters*: "Usually it was one of these things where they put pillows in things. Which is sort of 'rock,' because in a true jazz date, you don't do that. Because you want the drum to ring a little bit. But remember, Herbie's sound as it progressed, in fact, that may be one of the reasons he was so successful—because he was one of the pioneers who was able to take jazz and make it appealing to people who didn't like jazz. By giving it that contemporary rock sound."[65] The deep, dry "thud" of the rock bass drum was consistent with funk aesthetics as well, reflecting the overall attraction to the "funky foundation" embodied in the bass guitar sound and prominent in Harvey Mason's drum sound on *Head Hunters*.[66]

Speaking with David Rubinson, I asked about the differences in sound, particularly with regard to "Vein Melter" on *Head Hunters* and the thematically similar "Water Torture" on *Crossings*. Rubinson's response was that the drum sound did indeed indicate the genre or at least the association of genre. Rubinson and Catero had first experimented with these differences in sound on *Mwandishi*, with the inclusion of Ndugu Leon Chancler as an "additional drummer" on "Ostinato," and continued these experiments on various tracks, as well as on later albums:

Q: Billy Hart plays the notes he plays, but the *sound* of his drums sounds like jazz drums.
Rubinson: Because on *Mwandishi* we had two drummers. We had Billy Hart to be the jazz drummer and we had Ndugu to be the funk drummer. And the sound of their two drum sets is totally different.

Q: The sound of the way they were tuned and everything?
Rubinson: The set itself. Right.

Q: Was that planned or what?
Rubinson: Of course it was planned. That was the whole concept.

Q: OK. So what sounded "white" about the rock sound, and what sounded "black" about the—
Rubinson: No. It didn't sound "white" or "black." In this case, there was no rock sound; *it was a funk thing and a jazz thing.*[67]

The importance of the drum sound to "jazz-ness" can be seen in the attention given to reclaiming the earlier sound by "neo-bop" drummers in the eighties, audible, for example, in Jeff "Tain" Watts's recordings with Wynton Marsalis.

To be sure, there are differences in the playing styles on "Water Torture" and "Vein Melter." The unwavering, funereal cadence played by Mason in "Vein Melter" does much to separate the piece from previously held notions of jazz as improvisation oriented. But even more interesting, the *sound* of the drums, foregrounding the deep bass drum note, disclaims the "jazz-ness" of the piece. We hear an echo effect, but it is not an internal ring of the drum itself. Rather, it is a studio echo effect common in rock and funk music of the time: a slow echo, substantially quieter than the initial attack note. The effect conveys affect: a "thud" bass drum note, which nonetheless carries an echo, conveys a gravitas of distance, in space or time.

Curious about the difference between "a funk thing and a jazz thing," I asked Fred Catero to describe his approach to recording Mason's drums for *Head Hunters*. He confirmed that Billy Hart would have both heads on his bass drum, whereas Mason would take off the outside head. Expanding his response, he noted that not only were the techniques and aesthetics in play derived from rock and funk but the very structure of the studio promoted this derivation:

> Well, it was basically the studio. Because remember, this was done in the seventies. And in the mid-seventies, it reached its peak of dead-ism. I mean studios were made like clothes closets. You know, full of fur coats. It was the worst god-awful sound in the world. And the idea—it was all born of necessity. *It was born of the rock necessity to have no leakage. And so the attempt was to design studios that sucked up as much sound as possible, so there would be no resonance possible in the room, so that it could be as "dead" as possible.* In addition to which, they had just discovered all these wonderful reverbs and flangers and stuff like that; and if there were some kind of resonance in the room, and then you tried to add reverb, it sounded kind of weird. So by having the instruments without any resonance whatsoever, then you could add your own. That was the concept of these studios. And there was a period there, when David Rubinson—I don't know—he fell into this thing where he didn't want the drums to have any resonance whatsoever. And so you get this very, very dry, dead sound. But as producer, that's his choice.[68]

As the discussion focused more on his recording of Hart and Mason, Catero went on to explain the differences of approach in recording the two styles:

> Q: Forgetting for a second an actual recording but just placing yourself into those parallel situations. Do you think that you would have made an adjustment as far as what kind of microphone you would use?
>
> Catero: No. More the EQ, the balance of the drum, depending on the kind of music, as well. In other words, if, like with Tony Williams: he had a tremendous—I won't say "need"—he had a tremendous consciousness of tuning the drums. In fact, he was the first drummer that I became aware of that actually tuned his drums to the key that the song was in. So that when he did his fills, he actually played music, rather than just do

> beats. And there, it was important for me to try to get the tonality of the drum. Whereas [with] other drummers, it was more important that the beat be right, and that the beat not interfere with the bass, for instance. So that you could hear them, you could hear them as separate. If they had to blend—depending on what the pattern was. If the kick [bass drum] and the [electric] bass are playing the identical thing, then you don't want them to sound like two different things. Because one reinforces the other. So you treat it one way. But if the kick is playing one pattern and the bass is playing between the beats there, then it's a different story. And so each setup, I always treated it differently.[69]

From my own playing experience as a rock drummer, I well remember the frustration of trying to capture a jazz "touch" on my bass drum as I began learning to play jazz. My foot was too heavy, the bass drum too "thuddy." I gradually learned that I could sound like "jazz" by returning the resonating head to the drum, removing the pillow, and tuning the drumheads tighter. These alterations improved my "jazzness" considerably—at least as much as learning to control my foot. As these experiences suggest, and as the interviews confirm, the differences between a "jazz" and a "non-jazz" recording are at least as tied to timbre as to playing style.

Choosing the Personnel for HEAD HUNTERS

With the adjustments to the sound just described, as well as the attention to post-production and the incorporation of new instruments, one might think that Hancock would also hire musicians in ways that would further his control. As it turned out, this was both true and untrue. As Patrick Gleeson's description of Hancock's leadership style in a rehearsal attests, Hancock was anything but dictatorial when it came to playing an arrangement, because he would come armed with only the sketchiest of charts. Yet he was painstaking in the editing process for the *Head Hunters* album. If he was painstaking after the recording was committed to tape, why did he not dictate what notes would be played, at least by having a detailed arrangement in advance?

The answer lies in Hancock's approach to personnel. In a manner reminiscent of Miles Davis's approach, Hancock cast his groups according to the proclivities of the members to get the sound he wanted, rather than directing the play of each member.[70] Hancock explained:

> Q: I'm gathering that your style of leadership has taken some lessons from Miles as well. In the sense of who you collect into the same room together and the kinds of direction that you give.
>
> Hancock: Yeah, yeah. That too. Because we're talking about 1973. I had just left Miles five years earlier, and all the stuff I had done with the Mwandishi band was a follow-up to work I had done with Miles, [as well as] stuff I had done on my own recordings. Because I had other tunes on my own recordings that really didn't lend themselves to Miles's band. But they kind of converged with the Mwandishi band, and then we carried it further into the more avant-garde playing, that is, a more empathetic kind of playing. Depends on the empathy between musicians.
>
> Q: Yeah, the collective improvisation that you brought to another level.
>
> Hancock: Exactly. And then, with the Headhunters, the core of the spirit of constantly trying to find a new way of doing things was still there. And I hope always remains there. That's a part of what I got from Miles's band that I want to keep [laughs].[71]

The part that Hancock wanted to keep is summed up by Bennie Maupin's experience, which was typical. Davis was known for keeping informed about up-and-coming musicians through a network of associates and then prowling the clubs, staying a short while to listen to a musician, and leaving—only to surprise the object of his brief stay later with an invitation to record. In this way, he had located many, if not most, of his sidemen during the sixties.[72] Once in the band, the members were expected to produce their own ideas:

> Because [Davis's] whole thing was, "Well, I hired you." You know? "I didn't hire you to tell you what to do" [laughs]. "You're the one playing the bass clarinet, not me." So he would tell the guys. But some guys get really uptight. Because they wanted more specific information. He was not the guy to get it from. I mean, when it came to some of the harmonic structures and some of the textures that the keyboards are playing [on *Bitches Brew*], he was very involved with them on that. But even so, there was something that he wanted, but he was never so overly specific that it took away from what the guys themselves might be thinking about.[73]

Rather than dictate notes, Davis would often use his role as leader to prod his sidemen beyond what they believed they were capable of: "Many, many times—he just would turn to me and say, 'You play, I can't think of anything.' I would just be taken by all this and say 'Man, what?' I'm in here with him, and he's saying that he can't think of anything and that I should play. Consequently, I'm playing all over the place. He loved it. He loved it. So he would talk to me and say, 'What *is* that you're playing?' That was from *Miles*. . . . [Later,] I just looked at him, and I realized he was just saying something to evoke something, for me."[74] Similarly, Hancock's style of choosing personnel was to surround himself with musicians whose tastes and inclinations he could estimate and identify with but whose precise artistic choices moment to moment would be unpredictably fresh.[75] Patrick Gleeson noted:

> He was relying on the fact that Harvey [Mason] was playing as a groove player and then, live, Mike Clark was a groove player and that Paul [Jackson] was basically a rhythm-and-blues guy. And that they would therefore have that. And I think Herbie always felt about the music that he made, rather than here were the guys making the music and now he would tell them how to make it, that *Herbie would have in mind the kind of music he wanted to make, and then he would—just like you cast parts—he would cast the guys that would do that.* And therefore [he would] never have to [correct them]. . . . But it was kind of like, there are two different worlds. There's the rock world, where the leader tells the people what to play, and there's the jazz world where basically you do what you're going to do, and that's it.[76]

The notion of *fusion jazz*, then, works most accurately not as a syncretic blend of parent styles, because the parentage is always slippery; and not exclusively through its personnel. Fusion jazz musicians do not cooperate with the classification, being drawn into myriad other styles. Instead, the style of production provides the most prominent unifying thread: an orientation of how to produce a recording, influenced by pop, rock, funk, and jazz recording techniques.

If, as Benjamin Brinner has said, "interactive competence is a multifaceted structure linking many domains of competence," the truth of this is clear not only with regard to live interaction but in the studio as well.[77] The competencies in demand for fusion jazz musicians in the mid-seventies were manifold: under the large umbrella of jazz; within the myriad idioms of bebop and post-bebop styles; among other musical traditions, such as funk and rock; with the explosion of amplification, effects, and synthesis equipment; and within the multitrack studio recording process.

Jazz improvisation generally and interaction specifically were entwined with notions of personal competence. With the rise of fusion, the standards of evaluation were *changed*, not lessened. As musician, producer, journalist, and educator Ben Sidran told me, "The question has always been: how do you apply the spirit of jazz to the technology at hand."[78] Despite the death pronouncements, jazz was alive and well, although transformed, in the studio.

CHAPTER 6

Selling Herbie

Marketing and HEAD HUNTERS

> My generation found all music, but particularly all the different aspects of black music, as being one. . . . That's really been the foundation of my life, that it's all one music. And there's really one word that describes that whole area, and that's the word *fusion*.
>
> —*Vernon Slaughter, Columbia Records promotion man*

Most observers seem to find it impossible to consider an album like *Head Hunters* without centering on its sales success, despite its artistic and production-oriented innovations. Jazz historians who mention the album tend to grant more space to the album's sales than to its sounds and artistic impact.[1] To these observers, the album seems as much "product" as "music." Both the critical response at the time of the album's release and its subsequent historical treatment dwell obsessively on this success, almost as if its sales performance *were* its significance. Stuart Nicholson's assessment is typical:

> *Head Hunters* was an instant hit, with the single "Chameleon" appearing on DJ play lists alongside Stevie Wonder's "Living for the City" and Marvin Gaye's "Let's Get It On." The album rocketed to 13 on the *Billboard* pop chart, and by the end of the year [1974] it sold 750,000 units, making it one of the biggest-selling jazz albums of all time and the first to be certified gold, later going on to platinum status. . . . Overnight Hancock became a major attraction on the rock and jazz circuits, per-

> haps explaining his subsequent reluctance to stray far from the funk field, despite occasional acoustic excursions, until the mid-nineties.[2]

If, in fact, the album was primarily a commercial enterprise, the early sales results must have been a deep disappointment, both to Hancock and to Columbia Records. Far from an "instant hit" or a "rocketing" success, the album sold slowly in its first days on the market. Released on October 13, 1973, it took over three months to appear on the *Billboard* Top 200 chart, on January 12, 1974. Lack of a clear marketing path for this music, even four years after the landmark *Bitches Brew*, hurt the initial sales of the album. Jazz radio stations were not inclined to play such funk-oriented fare, nor were jazz-oriented record stores likely to feature the album prominently. Radio play was slim at first, and the album sold relatively little. Yet, by the close of 1974, as Nicholson rightly points out, *Head Hunters* had become certified gold; and, as it simultaneously went to number 13 on *Billboard* magazine's Top LPs chart, it became the best-selling jazz album that year, amassing a record that would not be eclipsed until the aggregated sales of Miles Davis's *Kind of Blue* (1959) finally exceeded it.[3]

The critical reception was, to say the least, mixed. The European jazz aficionado magazine *Jazz Forum* devoted an entire issue to the problem of marketing's effect on jazz, with Hancock as its poster boy. Reacting to Hancock's post-release tour appearance at the 1974 Berlin Jazz Days festival, *Forum* editor Joachim Berendt fulminated: "The question here is obvious: what has been the effect of Hancock's success with *Head Hunters* on his music—and on his personality? I believe that only a few critics do not think that this effect has been a bad one." Elsewhere in the article, while assessing Hancock's fusion work in general, he was even blunter: "It is unbelievable that a man with Hancock's level of achievement and musical wealth should make such music."[4] Lee Underwood's review of a Headhunters performance in Los Angeles shortly after was just short of vicious: "Mr. Communicate-With-A-Wider-Audience, Herbie Hancock, opened to a full house recently, again pleasing the funkers while disappointing the more cerebrally oriented connoisseurs. At its worst, Hancock's music is commercial trash; at its best, it is almost as schizoid as Frank Zappa's offerings."[5] Clearly, the album demonstrated that a jazz figure of Hancock's stature had the power to capture an unprecedented crossover market, a point that critics used as evidence of Hancock's pandering. Further, a number of critics stood ready to point to Hancock's commercialization as proof of fusion's grab for the gold generally.

The critics' position gained credibility from the fact that the album first gained success in rhythm-and-blues, not jazz, markets. That said, the album began its life as a jazz release; its expansion of the jazz market had a profound impact on the music scene, with far-reaching repercussions. Among these repercussions were expanded commercial opportunities for jazz musicians generally—even jazz musicians not identified with fusion. *Head Hunters* and other fusion jazz projects led to an opening up of music categories, even if only temporarily.

Yet there was, and remains, a cost. Jazz musicians often bemoan their penury while at the same time expressing suspicion over those musicians whose projects have become too successful.[6] The reception of *Head Hunters* among musicians and critics demonstrates what I call the "commercial" problem. Jazz writing, especially since the late forties, had increasingly portrayed the music either in quasi-classical terms (and therefore for collectors and aficionados) or as a black avant-gardist realpolitik.[7] In any case, though, writers tagged jazz as unfathomable and unattractive to the hoi polloi. By the mid-sixties at least, when *Down Beat* and *Billboard* threatened jazz's cultural prestige by expanding their coverage to embrace rock music, arcane esotericism had become part of jazz's appeal.[8] As jazz became more irrelevant commercially, devotees embraced its lack of commercial value, all the while trumpeting its cultural value as America's classical music. In commercial terms, the association of jazz with Western art music was understandable. Jazz's listenership had been as small (and partisan) as classical music's. Venues for jazz performance included concert halls and college campuses as well as clubs, and jazz fans, like their classical music counterparts, most likely heard the music on noncommercial radio. Musical discourse about jazz had taken on "classical" characteristics: jazz theory texts, now in use in dozens of college campuses, invariably meant "harmonic theory" as a parallel to texts on harmonic theory and counterpoint in their more mainstream sister classes.[9]

Because jazz generally suffered, as it continues to suffer, from a lack of commercial viability, *Head Hunters'* very success sowed the seeds of doubt about the album's artistic value. Critics who assumed *Head Hunters* (and fusion generally) to be motivated by the Big Cash Register used Hancock's turning his back on the Miles Davis years, as well as on the avant-garde Mwandishi septet, as proof. These assessments centered on the questions of whether Hancock pandered to crossover tastes at the expense of jazz integrity and whether the lure of crossover success was becoming a visible symptom of a large-scale artistic slide within the jazz tradition—a slide, in Nicholson's words, "away from the traditional aspirations of artistic endeavor towards a somewhat less elevated goal of art-as-a-means-of-communication."[10] The idea that "art-as-a-means-of-communication" is less elevated than "traditional aspirations of artistic endeavor" (read: "autonomous art") is a core value—expressed here as a truism—that this chapter addresses.[11]

Head Hunters' sales were materially aided, maybe even rescued, by the decision of one record promoter ("promo man") to ignore the trend toward genre petrifaction that had begun in the late fifties, when "the music got separated," as Andrew Hill and David Rosenthal recall.[12] By following promo man Vernon Slaughter's impact on the marketing effort, this chapter recounts how the album, somewhat accidentally, became a major crossover hit. Music merchandising was and is an important and integral element of jazz music's cultural signature—despite the reluctance of many musicians and music scholars to come to terms with this "unseemly" side of jazz.

Popular culture scholarship that documents the music industry's changes from the late forties through the sixties has tended to focus on rock 'n' roll and, to a lesser degree, rhythm-and-blues. Jazz records throughout this period, however, were not merely produced: they were also sold, in a robust but narrow marketplace. Yet the potential always existed for the jazz venture to reach other, larger publics, in particular the rhythm-and-blues and rock markets. Notably, two albums, *Bitches Brew* and *Head Hunters*, stretched jazz's mercantile boundaries and by doing so called into question the notion of the music's generic boundaries. Miles Davis's album demonstrated that jazz's high-art claim could attract young, hip (white) consumers, and *Head Hunters* demonstrated, first, that jazz improvisation could gain vitality by reconnecting with black youth culture and, second, that this new populism could translate not only to unprecedented market gains but also to a marriage between "art-as-personal-expression" and "art-as-communication." Along the way, *Head Hunters* hastened already building changes in the music industry infrastructure.

Production and marketing wings of the music industry fed each other—as they would in launching any commercially released music—creating *Head Hunters* the music, *Head Hunters* the product, and *Head Hunters* the sales juggernaut. The two arms of the music industry always operate in interaction, a fact made plain when we look at the album's marketing from several points of view: of the label, the radio, and retail.

Creating the Product

In 1972, Hancock was under contract with Warner Brothers but was unhappy because he experienced a lack of financial support for production and promotion and, even worse, disaffection with his music. The trouble at Warner had started with the beginning of the contract. The label expected a different Hancock from the one they got. Bob Blumenthal, in his liner notes for Hancock's *Complete Warner Bros. Recordings* reissue, quotes Hancock's explanation from a 1971 interview: "I did the music for the *Fat Albert* cartoon show Bill Cosby did on TV. Bill had the soundtrack tape, which he played for the executives at Warner Bros., and they flipped over it; they just loved it."[13] Hancock's next two phrases tell the whole story. The first of these, "So I chose to record *Fat Albert Rotunda* as my first album for the label—," recounts a decision that delighted the label executives. Projecting a cheerful funkiness, with broad appeal that reflected Cosby's lovable animated inner-city characters, the album sold briskly. To the label, all would have been well if Hancock's sentence, truncated earlier, had ended there. But another shoe was ready to drop, as the rest of the sentence makes plain: "*which gave me the freedom to do Mwandishi next.*"[14] The trouble was, *Mwandishi* was the last thing the label execs expected or wanted.

On the heels of the sales excitement generated by *Fat Albert Rotunda*, Warner Brothers in late 1971 put Hancock in touch with David Rubinson. Rubinson recalled that "the Iron Butterfly's manager fell in love with Herbie's music, and he's really the key. He is the one who brought Herbie . . . the Warner's deal" and with it Rubinson.[15] Rubinson previously had worked for Columbia Records but had struck off on his own as an independent producer. His experience in hit-making, and his close association with the enormously popular San Francisco sound and Bill Graham, made him an obvious choice, to Warner's, for the Hancock project. Rubinson was charged with the specific task of producing albums with Hancock that would develop the crossover youth appeal that they felt was possible with Hancock's music, a mission Rubinson largely ignored.[16] Instead, his working relationship with Hancock would soon expand, and Rubinson would become Hancock's manager and producer for many years.

Rubinson's directorial and editing role is detailed earlier (see chap. 5). His duties included those typical for an independent producer: hiring musicians, recording engineers, and studio time, as well as overseeing the recording and post-production processes. An independent producer is powerless to do these things, however, without developing a contractual relationship with the record label that includes enough financial backing to get the job done.[17] I quote historian Michael Fink:

> Hiring recording studios and musicians requires both artistic and business judgment on the part of the producer. His relationship with the record company, however, is pure business. Initially, the independent producer will work out a budget for the recording. If he obtains record company support, he will receive an advance payment before the recording is made. This is partly to help defray initial costs and partly a production fee for the producer himself. This and other advances may or may not be recoupable by the record company from royalties, depending upon how valuable (or risky) the producer and his product are to the company. If the independent producer finances his recording from a source other than the record company, an advance against royalties is usually paid upon delivery of the master tape to the company and the signing of the master purchase agreement.[18]

The producer has a focal role, in the eyes of both the musicians and the label. The musicians may or may not keep the final marketing plan in mind, but the label must keep its focus on creating a profit, even when label executives have entered into the business through an attraction to the music. Often the two sides have distinctly nonparallel, or even opposing, goals. The producer must navigate these currents. The skills he or she brings to bear on the project—getting production and promotion funding from the label, as well as influencing song selection, musical arrangements, and style choices, hiring musicians, securing access to the studio, and so on—materially affect both the musical outcome and the marketing endgame.

Rubinson was a proven hit-maker. As he told me:

> I was brought in by Warner's to make a Santana kind of record. You see, that was my thing right then, it was that kind of music I was making. I was making hits with Tower of Power, Cold Blood, Santana, that kind of stuff. So they brought me in to be the Commercial Guy. And I went and made them *Mwandishi*. Which was *not* a commercial record, in their view. And they went crazy. They were really upset. I mean, [Warner president] Joe Smith loved Herbie, but this was not the record he had been looking for. And I got called on the carpet. So we had a sales meeting down in LA. And I was supposed to play the record. And I brought in two tapes. The first tape I played was the B side of *Bitches Brew*. Because they'd never heard that, either. And I told them it was Herbie's new record. And they sat there, and after about ten minutes they said, "Oh man." They said, "This is great, but it's never going to sell." And I said, "It's number 6 right now [on the *Billboard* Jazz Album chart]." They said, "What do you mean?" I said, "I just played you [an unreleased tape of] *Bitches Brew*. *Bitches Brew* is over 350,000 [units in sales]. So you don't know what the fuck you're talking about." That's the kind of guy I was then. . . . [Shortly thereafter,] Warner Brothers dropped Herbie, La Belle, and Earth, Wind, and Fire.[19]

When Hancock was no longer under contract to Warner, in early 1973, Columbia's chief of artists and repertoire (A and R), Bruce Lundvall, suggested Hancock to president Clive Davis, who agreed to offer Hancock a contract. The first Columbia album was *Sextant*, which used the same personnel as (Warner's) *Crossings* and nearly the same as *Mwandishi* before it. According to Lundvall, *Sextant* sold at about the same rate as *Mwandishi*, in the tens of thousands. This was respectable enough for an acoustic jazz album but decidedly lackluster considering the performance of the rhythm-and-blues-oriented *Fat Albert Rotunda*, at over one hundred thousand units.[20] It was disappointing, considering the growing importance of other jazz artists who had taken a page from rock, producing such albums as the Mahavishnu Orchestra's *Inner Mounting Flame*, Weather Report's eponymous debut album, and of course *Bitches Brew*. Further, the Mwandishi-era albums, compared to a typical acoustic jazz album of the time, were major investments. The typical acoustic jazz album of the time, recorded on two or three tracks, cost as little as $12,000 to $40,000 to produce. In contrast, a typical rock album cost in excess of $100,000 and often over $150,000.[21] Considering the poor showing and spiraling costs of Hancock's projects, one might guess that the budget-planning meetings for the *Head Hunters* project at Columbia were tense affairs: the album cost $100,000 to produce.

Lundvall, though, recalls being sanguine about the expense at the time because of his attraction to Hancock as a musician.[22] Besides, he and Clive Davis could take comfort in the fact that Hancock was retooling his group, having disbanded the Mwandishi lineup of Julian Priester, Billy Hart, Buster Williams, Eddie Henderson, Pat Gleeson, and Bennie Maupin—all deeply invested in Mwandishi's avant-gardism—keeping only Maupin for the new group. Along with himself and Maupin, he added one of the leading R&B session groove-masters, drummer Harvey Mason. To these he added percussionist Bill Summers, virtually unknown outside a twenty-mile radius from the East Bay, and bassist Paul Jackson, whose career as a versatile sideman was flourishing and who was developing a local reputation as a Larry Graham–style funk stylist. The attractions for Hancock were that both men, although young, were highly accomplished and creative and that each was deeply involved with the young, hip Bay Area funk scene. Jackson in particular seemed poised for his leap to wider recognition, having recently recorded with the first-rate Latin-rock group Azteca.[23] Columbia recognized that Hancock's new lineup positioned him to tap a younger market, with potential sales as strong as those of the fusion recordings already mentioned.

Years later, Lundvall would step away from mainstream pop and return to his first musical love. In 1984, he reconstituted the defunct Blue Note Records, now a subsidiary of EMI Records, pinning the label's success on reissues of classic post-bebop jazz from the fifties and sixties. From this historical vantage point, Lundvall naturally might be seen as a keeper of the flame in bebop and post-bop jazz, but such a view misrepresents Lundvall's catholic tastes in music and his business acumen. Although he is a lover of post-bebop jazz, Lundvall avoids rigid, doctrinaire positions.[24] In the mid-seventies, Lundvall, as Columbia Records' president, would devise a contract with Hancock that called for both post-bebop ("acoustic") and fusion ("electric") albums, with separate budget structures for each. In retrospect, then, Lundvall embraced Hancock's new project (as did Clive Davis) primarily because of his overall confidence in Hancock's musicianship and secondarily because of his belief in the market potential for fusion jazz in general, as additional to "straight-ahead" post-bebop.

As the array of genre names encountered here demonstrates, however (see chap. 1), the market for fusion jazz was anything but unified. The same was true for the sound of fusion; *Head Hunters* bore little stylistic resemblance to other fusion recordings of the day. With such an album by a major jazz artist in hand, the question became not only how to promote it to a jazz listenership but also how to promote it to a crossover audience, how to cross the boundary framed by the record-store jazz section.

When I asked Hancock if the album first showed significant sales in a particular city or region, he pointed me to the Washington, D.C., area and to that area's local Columbia promo man, Vernon Slaughter. We may think of a jazz recording as having a particular style, sound, instrumentation, and so on, but part of a jazz record's identity also comes from the way it is promoted and distributed. At the time of *Head Hunters*' release, marketing a record included an interactive dance among the label, the media (broadcast and print), and retailers. Although the playbill often included the same dancers for jazz as for rhythm-and-blues recordings, the choreography differed. Slaughter, as one of these movers and shakers, found a way to play two roles at once.

Selling Styles: R&B versus Jazz

The art of promoting rock, pop, and rhythm-and-blues records developed with the emergence of AM radio in the fifties and sixties, begetting an infrastructure that largely held true to the turn of the twenty-first century.[25] From the label's point of view, promotion typically began with the promo man–sales rep partnership. Promo men have always had the job of generating excitement for their label's records. As radio formats shifted from dramas and variety shows to deejays spinning platters in the fifties, especially rock 'n' roll and rhythm-and-blues, the promo man targeted radio stations to play the songs in their precious daily rotations. This allowed the labels' sales representatives (sales reps) to go to the store buyers and pitch the song, based on the buzz from the airplay. The label's sales rep would contact the store buyer every week to work up an order. It was the sales rep's job to turn the listeners' response to radio airplay into sales dollars for the label.

Tim Clark, former promo man and eventually marketing director for Island Records until 1980, describes the promo man's job:

> The promotion manager . . . must know the right program producers and disk jockeys. . . . The promotion manager's most important task is to get enough airplay for singles to give them a chance of becoming a hit. . . . In fact, if a promotion manager knows his job and the right program directors, he may even make a significant contribution to the choice of the single from a band's album. The promotion manager has one of the hardest and most competitive jobs in the record industry, because vast quantities of singles are released every week, but only a handful get airplay.[26]

The cycle, as of the fifties, was this: multiple plays on the station, with appropriately enthusiastic patter by the deejay, generated requests for the song on the neighborhood jukebox and at the record store. To prevent being caught without the song in stock, the store buyer relied on the sales rep to feed him or her information on sales response to the song in similar stores within the same market or in similar markets. Without the promo man, the sales rep would have little to pitch, and thus the store buyer would be left without a key forecasting tool for placing the weekly order. Also, without the promo man, the disk jockey (or the deejay's boss, the radio station's programming manager) would be left to navigate through the hundreds of recordings released each week without a map.

Of course, the promotional model described here was based on single, rather than album, releases. The so-called battle of the speeds between RCA and Columbia from the late forties to the early fifties resulted in two distinct but complementary record formats, both on vinyl microgroove.[27] The AM-radio and jukebox industries were based on single tunes and so on seven-inch, 45-rpm disks. By the late sixties the model had shifted slightly. As LP sales grew in importance, labels could release an album, get a sense of customer response toward particular tracks, and decide which tracks to release as singles based on this response. In this business environment, the sales rep also had a reporting function—back to the promo man and the label's sales wing generally. By reporting on local sales trends in weekly conference calls, promo men and sales reps were able to decide which songs to emphasize. Promo men and sales reps filled a vital role in helping the label judge which tracks garnered the most response and should therefore be released as 45-rpm singles.

In the art of the promo, buzz became very important. Songs that "charted"—that is, that appeared on best-selling lists of the industry magazines *Record World*, *Cash Box*, and *Billboard*—drew the most attention. Using a technique similar to television's "Nielsen" ratings, *Billboard*, the most influential of these magazines, would survey a selection of stores (mostly of the independent "mom-and-pop" variety), chosen for their demographic characteristics, to build a weekly national sales profile. Stores simply reported their top sellers for the week. Chart compilation reflected who store owners (and by extension labels and *Billboard* itself) assumed their customers to be. Thus, a customer purchasing Little Richard's "Tutti Frutti" contributed to its R&B chart position when that customer bought it in a mom-and-pop store that specialized in R&B—the customer was at that moment an "R&B" customer. If he bought it the next day as a gift for his cousin from a more mainstream store, his purchase contributed to the pop chart. He was now a "pop" customer. Despite this demographic slipperiness, marketing strategies proceeded from the basic assumption that a "rock" customer (or a jazz, R&B, or country-and-western customer) was a different person from a "pop" customer and required different merchandising approaches.

The *Billboard* chart, reporting sales from the largest sample of stores and recordings, was the most prestigious, but the sales reps found other industry charts useful, as well. Promo buzz might sound something like this: "This record debuted in *Record World* two weeks ago, and it's growing fast—looks like it's going to hit *Billboard* next week, so you'd better double your order to handle the demand."

Upping the order would cause the store very little anxiety, because the sales rep could grant a return authorization for unsold records. In the meantime, label sales staff could "talk up" the quantities of product being ordered in similar markets or by competitors. This would build up the buzz, at the wholesale level, that a record was starting to move. Buzz-building was a delicate part of the "dance" for the label—buyer enthusiasm was wasted if a product wasn't in the bins when radio and chart excitement began to build buyer interest. The product pipeline, from labels ordering pressings of a particular product, to distribution through wholesalers, and eventually to retailers, was far from instantaneous. Timely delivery required many anticipatory and speculative decisions, which, to the degree possible, were tied to specific market plans.

By focusing attention on key musicians with proven histories of accomplishment and name recognition, it was easier to get a station to put a new release on the playlist—as long as the artist kept to an identifiable style. It was essential that the station maintain a coherent stylistic format—Top Forty, rhythm-and-blues, rock, whatever—and that the promo man keep the bulk of his efforts to the center of the format stylistically. The pitch to the store owner reflected the same logic, since, with the rising importance of radio and the decline of the jukebox as the fifties transited to the sixties, customers were likely to become aware of new songs through radio first. Underlying the effort was a constant attentiveness to a potential crossover hit that could generate sales in the rhythm-and-blues rack *and* the rock 'n' roll rack, or the neighborhood store that stocked rhythm-and-blues *and* the downtown department store.

Promo men often worked directly for a big label or for a group of indies or were sometimes hired as independent contractors to promote a targeted high-profile recording or artist. Often, though, the promo man for a label's jazz recordings and its popular records was the same person. But promoting jazz often took a different tack.

By the late fifties, most jazz releases began as twelve-inch, 33-rpm albums. Despite some conspicuous successes, like Miles Davis's "'Round Midnight" or Dave Brubeck's "Take Five," album tracks, rather than 45-rpm singles, dominated the jazz airwaves. The difference in format reflected basic differences in marketing. Whereas popular AM radio, including R&B stations, operated on song recognition through repetitive, rotating programming, jazz radio stations played songs from a broad range of recordings that had or portended historical importance, featured virtuosic musical personnel, and demonstrated the station's extensive library of both the mainstream and the arcane—generally reflecting "collector" aesthetics and desires. With few exceptions, jazz recordings failed to make the *Billboard* sales charts; the annual *Down Beat* and *Playboy* polls featured artists, not their records.

A given record, distributed by a small independent label, would likely sell only a smattering of copies. Additionally, the records rarely earned royalties for the artists, owing partially to the boilerplate recording contracts for jazz sessions. Knowing this, jazz musicians recorded as often as possible. Considering the small, collector-oriented jazz-buying public, issuing a steady stream of new recordings became a key survival strategy. Further, creating a deep discography gained artists name recognition and prestige, if not fat royalty checks. This suited independent labels, because indies desperately needed to come up with enough titles to be taken seriously in the marketplace. All of these factors contributed to relatively small sales for most records and encouraged collector-aficionados to buy ever more arcane titles.

From the vantage point of the early twenty-first century, it's easy to forget that such classic recordings as Sonny Rollins's "Blue 7" and Thelonious Monk's "Well, You Needn't" sold only a few thousand copies when they were initially released.[28] Yet even if particular tunes sold insignificantly, the steady stream of album releases widened the fame of a broad constellation of jazz musicians. Personality cults, growing out of the hipster reception of bebop (and Dixieland before it, as Bernard Gendron points out), sprang up, mostly in urban markets, across the country.[29]

Jazz labels, and their promo men and sales reps, discovered over time that niche marketing worked very well in this environment. Timed to coincide with an album's release, promotional tours and musician profiles in newspaper arts-and-entertainment sections proved valuable, although the question remained as to whether the main product was the tour (promoted by the recording) or the recording (promoted by the tour).[30] Endorsements of instruments, accessories, stereo equipment, and so on by prominent musicians kept their names and faces in advertisements, prominently placed in the music industry press.[31] Placing an ad to coincide with a magazine's feature article or interview was seen as especially effective, although the label itself probably benefited more than either the musician or the individual recording.[32] With the magazine article in place and the artist's face smiling from magazine ads and posters, the promo man's typical strategy would be to meet with deejays over lunch and "talk music." The pitch was low-key and directed primarily toward the label's "sound" and artistic direction.[33]

Small retailers counted on a long shelf life for their jazz titles to make up for their slow stock turnover. For a small store in an urban black neighborhood, for example, this meant that the R&B racks would feature the current hot sellers, often displayed according to chart position; the jazz racks in the back would be organized by artist, with as many as a dozen albums by a single artist, spanning several years, in the bin.

Hard bop, one of the emerging streams in jazz, found avid customers in urban, black neighborhoods. Hard bop developed in the fifties out of several wide-ranging styles, including rhythm-and-blues, gospel, jump swing, and bebop. But at the retail level in the mom-and-pop neighborhood stores, owners needed to make categorical choices about how to rack new product tangents such as this. Most used an approach that was perhaps suggested by the marketing slant(s) pushed by the label but also paid serious attention to the tastes and shopping habits of their main customers. Neighborhood stores often needed to carry a bit of everything to meet cultural preferences across age groups and sometimes ethnicities. Their genesis and economic vitality grew from serving a market whose tastes were sometimes grossly underrepresented or made geographically inconvenient in more mainstream stores and chains. This smaller-market strategy, of course, fit with the business dictum of "know your customers and sell what they want" but strayed slightly from the industry's overall trend to specialization. Yet for mom-

and-pop stores or national chains, radio formats strongly influenced in-store racking decisions, in obvious tandem with radio's strong ability to generate sales. And in this inescapable linkage, industry magazine sales charts certainly influenced radio-play choices, though less so with jazz.

Behind all this activity were two conflicting yet paradoxically complementary strategies: concentrate the effort on a core number of recordings and simultaneously provide customers with a broad enough assortment of titles to encourage them to make impulse add-on purchases.

At the same time, the larger single-unit stores and chain stores emerged and were generally dispensing much more product. To help customers find the records they wanted, as well as to aid in browsing for additional purchases, these stores tightened their stock organization even as they expanded their number of titles. The term *crossover* had its own industry-wide meaning, discussed later, but at the most local level "crossover" meant placing a recording in more than one kind of specialty store or more than one section in a larger store.

With *Billboard* introducing its Top Jazz Album chart in 1969, stores adapted the same method, creating two rack locations for jazz in the store—by chart position and/or hot sellers and traditional bins by artist. As David Rubinson explained it to me:

> The way they did it was, they'd monitor a group of stores. So *Billboard* would get on the phone on Thursdays and talk to the *Billboard*-reporting stores. Maybe 150 out of the whole country. So if they wanted to find out what was selling in jazz, they would call jazz stores. They had a hundred stores that sold a lot of jazz. That's how they'd know the "jazz consumer." . . . In order to make the R&B chart, they would have little mom-and-pop stores all over the country, and they would call in their sales. To have the jazz chart, they would have these little jazz stores around the country, and they would call in their sales. And that's not scientific, but that's the way you'd do it.[34]

There were two main reasons for charting these sales: to identify trends within the jazz market (both to maintain appropriate distribution levels and to identify emerging musical trends) and to identify the potential for a record to sell outside its primary market, to *cross over*.

Propped by the buzz created by the promo man's efforts, the sales rep would use the chart debut ranking or a chart position change to convince a store buyer to stock a title. In our model of the urban, black, mom-and-pop store, the presence of a title on the soul chart (as *Billboard* rechristened rhythm-and-blues in 1964) would make the decision easy for an R&B store buyer. After the jazz chart debuted in 1969, the sales rep could point to a record's rising position on the chart to convince an R&B or pop buyer to take a chance on stocking the record. With their own chart, jazz records now appeared on the buyers' radar screens. Dramatic upward movement on the jazz chart made it possible to argue that an album could also sell in the more visible pop (or R&B or rock) racks at the front of the store.

An intermediate goal would be to convince a chain outlet, like Tower Records, Sam Goody, or Music Land, to stock a record in the pop racks as well as the jazz aisle. "It starts to become a story you can tell to the buyers in the Towers and the Sam Goodys," Rubinson continued. "You had to start at the jazz bin and small retail, and say, 'You see, this thing's selling.' And then they'd buy it."[35]

Even with sales in more than one kind of store, or in more than one section of a chain of stores, few records stood a chance of selling a million copies by the early seventies. However, success in chain stores brought a record to the attention of the really big fish: rack-jobbers, wholesalers who lease space, supply product, and manage displays within department or mass-merchandise stores:

> It's not Tower. Tower is retail. That's [merely] the next step. You know it's a crossover when you start seeing sales from Heilicher Brothers. Or Schwartz Brothers in Washington, who are selling in mass-merchandise stores, like Kresge's and Kmart and those kinds of things. Woolworth's. So once it goes to big retail, like Sam Goody—Sam Goody had a jazz department. Tower had a jazz department. So it was good, but that wasn't really crossover. Crossover was when it hit the mass merchandisers, who were the rack-jobbers at that time.[36]

A jazz record might have a moderate chance to cross into R&B or pop territory at the intermediate chain-retailer level, but only a handful, like Dave Brubeck's "Take Five" or Vince Guaraldi's "Cast Your Fate to the

Wind," could aspire to make it to the rack-jobbers, and thence to crossover heaven, during the sixties.[37] It wasn't until *Bitches Brew* demonstrated the cross-market potential for jazz that major labels began actively to work toward crossover success. By the time *Head Hunters* was released, the rack-jobbers loomed tantalizingly closer.

The jazz industry as a whole, however, now had two decades of small, confined, but profitable operations under its belt. At the same time, the rock and R&B markets (which now contained Motown, soul, and funk trajectories) were growing explosively; promo men, and the labels that paid them, tended to concentrate their efforts on the sure thing.

"This Is the One"

With *Head Hunters* now recorded, edited, and packaged, Columbia sent advance copies of the record to its network of promo men. One of these, Vernon Slaughter, had recently started working the Washington-Baltimore slot.[38] Slaughter, during his college years at the University of Nebraska, had been a student representative for Columbia. There he had first become exposed to Hancock, through Hancock's association with Miles Davis: "So it was my job to turn on the college campus and the cities around there to new music. And I'm pretty sure the first album I heard Herbie on was the Miles Davis record right before *Bitches Brew*: *In a Silent Way*. Then getting into [*Filles de*] *Kilimanjaro* and the other ones prior to that with Herbie and Wayne Shorter on the records, I just fell in love with Herbie Hancock . . . so [by the time of *Head Hunters*] I was [already] a fan."[39] By 1973, Slaughter had joined the promotion staff at Columbia full-time, with the Washington-Baltimore market area as his territory. Receiving an advance copy of *Head Hunters*, "I immediately raised my hand and said, 'This is the one.'"[40] As a fan of Hancock's, Slaughter had already followed the developments of the *Fat Albert Rotunda* album and the Mwandishi projects. He recognized *Head Hunters* as an arrival point. To him, the album belonged on R&B radio, as well as jazz radio. Slaughter's worldview, as a young, idealistic, black man, made this a given: "In 1973, I was twenty-two years old for most of that year. And we were in an environment, in the sixties, throughout, where particularly music, if you want to use the term 'black music' or whatever, it was truly a 360-degree experience. *My generation found all music, but particularly all the different aspects of black music, as being one.* . . . That's really been the foundation of my life, that it's all one music. And there's really one word that describes that whole area, and that's the word *fusion*."[41] Slaughter found himself unique in thinking outside the normal marketing boundaries:

> Slaughter: And keep in mind, during those days, most of the promotion guys, even back then we called them "old school." Because they came out of traditional R&B and that type of thing, and they weren't into this type of music. I also started the first number-one record, that same year, with Earth, Wind, and Fire. So it was right up my alley. . . . And it wasn't easy. It really wasn't easy.
>
> Q: Because it didn't fit into a format?
>
> Slaughter: Yeah. Record companies, still today—my attitude has always been that the music dictates the marketing, not the other way around. . . . And so when people couldn't pigeonhole it, then they didn't want to deal with it. They just put it on the side.[42]

Buoyed by the success of *Earth, Wind, and Fire*, Slaughter took *Head Hunters* to a Washington FM station, WHUR, that played not jazz but R&B:

> Slaughter: But I took it over there, and they [understood] it. And they started playing it.
>
> Q: So they got response?
>
> Slaughter: They got response. But the record, I have to say, that it in effect crossed when I got to play it for a disk jockey on WOL. It was the number-one Urban station, or back then R&B station. Black station. AM. And back then, AM was still king. A midday guy, a guy who came on in the afternoon, went by

> the name Chuck McCool. And I took it to him, asked him to listen. He actually listened to it, and he started playing it on his show, in the afternoon show. From there, the record just took off. And Chuck McCool didn't say a thing. He would fade it a little bit when it got to the heavy improvisation. But after a while, he would just play it all the way through.[43]

The track Slaughter played for McCool was "Chameleon."

Gaining radio airplay, although a crucial component in marketing the album, was not the only strategy. Washington had a lively dance-club scene, with music supplied both by live bands and by deejays. It was a normal part of the promo man's job to expose dance-club deejays to the latest dance recordings: "I took it to clubs, and persuaded disk jockeys there. . . . And they would play it. I just suggested that they fade it when it got to the real heavy improvisation but just play the groove. And people got up on the floor, and they started dancing. So they started doing their own edits. And they would play ['Chameleon']."[44] By now the album was selling in the Washington-Baltimore area as well as a single might be expected to sell. The national sales management noticed the movement, gleaned Slaughter's approach, and channeled the efforts of other promotion men across the country to follow suit. This gave the first sales impetus to the album, and thus stores added *Head Hunters* to the R&B racks in addition to the jazz racks.

Immediately on the heels of this success, *Head Hunters* began to get airplay on free-format (free-form) FM stations in key markets. From the late sixties through the mid-seventies, FM stations began broadcasting high-fidelity signals at considerably lower wattage than their AM cousins did.[45] Programming at these stations was often left to the deejay, giving rise to the term *free-form*. With the advent of album-oriented rock (AOR), a product of a post–*Sgt. Pepper* afterglow in the rock recording industry, deejays played an eclectic mix of rock, funk, and R&B popular musics, as well as various styles of jazz, folk music, poetry, political satire—in short, nearly whatever they wanted. These free-form stations, and the deejays manning the turntables, appealed to an audience of disparate ethnic and class backgrounds, its members nonetheless allied in a loosely defined ideology based on cultural and social progressivism.

The underlying aesthetic highlighted eclecticism and alterity to a perceived mainstream.[46] On free-form radio, this aesthetic was reflected in a willingness to include a variety of emerging, self-consciously artistic musics outside mainstream rock and soul fare, while still retaining close ties to these musics.[47] *Head Hunters* fit this model entirely.

For their part, Top Forty AM stations viewed their smaller cousins with a mixture of condescension and interest. "Lower wattage" translated to "smaller audience," hence lower commercial importance. Thus, Top Forty stations were content to continue their existing format of narrow playlists, recycling current top 45-rpm singles. AM stations regarded free-form stations as an insignificant competitive threat, although they could be useful in identifying trends. Because of the FM stations' much lower broadcast-signal strength, then, the relationship of free-form radio to the AM giants was similar to that of indie record labels to the majors in the fifties.[48] Free-form radio began as a grassroots movement, but by the early seventies there was a growing number of such stations.[49] This development began to change perceptions of genre within the record industry. Not only were free-form stations identifying trends, but they were holding listeners: Top Forty stations began to lose listenership to the upstarts. This was the wave that Columbia, under Clive Davis and his successor, Bruce Lundvall, began to ride:

> In that whole era of fusion, when we had the *Head Hunters* album, or Mahavishnu or *Weather Report*, or *Birdland*, and things like that: they fit beautifully into the whole excitement of the rock industry in that period. So it was almost like one music—not one kind of music but one area where you could treat these people the same way you would treat a rock musician.
>
> I think those albums were advertised together, and they had radio [airplay], because you did have free-form radio then. They would play, you know, a rock album, and then they'd play something from a Weather Report record or a Herbie record. It wasn't quite so fragmented as it is now, not at all so.[50]

The free-form FM antiformat played a significant role in the popularity of *Head Hunters*.[51] The deejays based their programming on their own assessments of what was hip; often they looked to black popular music for inspiration, and R&B hits not yet on the mainstream radar often appeared on deejays' idiosyncratic playlists.[52] These deejays began to play *Head Hunters* for their ethnically blended, socially progressive audiences. Crossover sales momentum was now established for *Head Hunters* in several markets: jazz, R&B, and free-form. Thus anointed, the album went on to sell well over a million copies, an unprecedented achievement for a "jazz" album and likely an *impossible* achievement, had the album stayed within the marketing boundaries and apparatus of jazz.

Categorizing Black Music as "One"

In retrospect, such a move was much more possible then than now. In 1969, *Billboard* expanded its list of marketing categories to ten from the previous half dozen; by the mid-nineties, those categories had expanded to twenty-four.[53] Further, with the more recent advent of electronic sales tracking, buying trends have become increasingly predictable, and therefore marketing practices have become increasingly prescriptive.

Evidence of this lies in Hancock's experience with a more recent album, *Dis Is Da Drum* (1995). Although Hancock calls it some of his best work, it bombed in the market.[54] The album, made in close collaboration with Bill Summers, uses *bátà* drums, African percussion, sampling, multitimbral synthesizers, and a guest rapper. It is influenced by African, Afro-Caribbean, and hip-hop musics and includes a cover of "Butterfly," a new, slow interpretation, like "Watermelon Man," of a familiar Hancock standard. The album thus shares many characteristics with *Head Hunters*: it crosses genres; it is influenced by, but is not really *of*, the dominant black hip music of the time; and it juxtaposes "traditional" and "pop" instruments. But in the mid-nineties market setting, *Dis Is Da Drum* lacked the marketing wiggle room of earlier days. Marketing categories have become more numerous and, to maintain separation, definitions of differences more refined and entrenched. Black Adult Contemporary now abuts Black Urban, Quiet Storm/Contemporary Jazz, and Hip-Hop on the *Billboard* charts. With little overlap among the categories, although the songs on *Dis Is Da Drum* could conceivably be played on stations in any of these categories, they would not be an exact fit with any of their formats. In the current climate of strict categorization, there is far less possibility to transcend the expected. We might ask, where are Vernon Slaughter, Chuck McCool, and the free-form deejays now? The problem for *Dis Is Da Drum* is the same as it was for *Head Hunters*, but the earlier solutions are no longer available.[55] In the case of *Head Hunters*, Slaughter could reasonably turn to McCool, because it was still possible to act as if "it's all one music"; or, to revisit Andrew Hill's comment, Slaughter was able to conceive of black music as it was "before the music got separated."[56]

Categorizing Black Music as "Many"

The proliferation of broadcast, sales, and award categories through the seventies and later is open to more than one interpretation. Many proponents of black music sought this expansion, perceiving it as formal industry recognition of the music's importance and diversity. On a practical side, more categories provide more opportunities for awards recognition. It is axiomatic that winning a Grammy not only gives an enormous boost to the sales of a particular record or performer (as well as that performer's previous releases) but shines reflected glory on similar acts, as well as on the rest of the category.[57] Sometimes the addition of more narrowly defined awards categories generates more pointed marketing and more strategic, prominent positioning of the product in stores. This philosophy may backfire, however, if the product niche becomes insignificant in the public view and thus succeeds only in marginalizing the artist.

Conflicting forces are represented here—black music as a unified rubric versus black music as multivalent—in both ideology and marketing strategy. But as of the early seventies, the multivalent camp was clearly winning, and the expansion of marketing categories continues today.

The Effect of the Music on Marketing and Marketing on the Music

Conventional wisdom has it that jazz labels actively courted the youth market by suggesting to musicians that they "rock up" their sound.[58]

David Rubinson, from his vantage as a jazz and rock producer and as Herbie Hancock's manager for some two decades, advances a different view. From his perspective, the labels operated under an outmoded marketing concept, in which the expense-to-profit ratio had long before reached a comfortable balance point. Jazz recordings had for over two decades centered on small groups, efficiently and cheaply recorded. Not only were the production budgets small for these recordings, but the promotional budgets (typically equivalent to the recording budgets) ensured that promo men would spend little time pushing one particular recording.[59] Rather, they promoted the label as a "sound," an approach that suited jazz radio stations' broad, collector approach to programming (as opposed, say, to Top Forty's repetitive rotation). The net result to the musician in the old model was significantly lower contractual expectations than their more mainstream brethren:

> Jazz people don't get that kind of [top-tier performance] royalty; top people get that kind of royalty. Look at it from a record company point of view. If they can convince a group of people that they get a different deal because it's jazz, it's to their benefit. So if a rock 'n' roll band went into the studio with a $50,000 [production] budget in 1970, a jazz group went in with a $12,000 budget [for production and presumably another $12,000 for promotion]. So that's self-defeating. It keeps the horizons lower; it makes the potential market lower before the record ever comes out.[60]

Now, however, the pie was growing larger. Rubinson went on: "When *Head Hunters* came out and sold a million units, the sky became the limit. Everybody said, 'Well, if this can sell a million units, I'm not going in with a two-dollar budget and one day to record, because I can make a record that can sell a million copies.' And the musicians started demanding budgets, and time, and equipment, and control. And they got it."[61]

There is general agreement that fusion jazz enlarged the commercial boundaries of jazz and that greater sales coincided with bigger production and promotion budgets, greater rewards for the musicians, and bigger profits for the labels. Nevertheless, the crucial question of motivation—*was Herbie in it for the money or for the art?*—finds Rubinson fiercely on the side of musical expansion, made possible by musicians' increased control of production. Interviewing him, I suggested that "the cost of playing music suddenly skyrocketed. And in a way, playing fusion carried with it a commitment to kick your career up a notch in sales, etc. What I mean here has to do with infrastructure: to get a satisfying sound, as well as to offset the cost, it needed to be played in larger venues, right? So (1) the volume could make the most of the music, (2) more tickets could be sold to underwrite the investment."[62] Rubinson suggested I had it backward:

> It's all true, but you tied it to the sound improving to offset the cost, and needing to play in a larger venue. And that's really not the way it happened. Herbie was on the road, suffering for his music in a way that was really very mundane. He had to go buy a Ford Econoline. He drove the truck. He unpacked the gear. And I remember the first tour I booked him, it was like Baker's Keyboard Lounge in Detroit, and all that kind of stuff, the Jazz Showcase in Chicago. And the sound systems in these places were so shitty, because they were set up for piano, bass, drums, and saxophone. And he'd walk in there with all that [electronic] stuff. And so he basically had to do the sound himself, get a sound system himself, and so on. But they were still playing in small venues. *It was the commercial success of the records, and the changing of the quality of the music that reached out to more people, that made the venues bigger.*
>
> Musicians were inventing things creatively. And getting off that way. When they hear it back, just as in the studio, they go into a club, where they'd just come from the studio where they have control over the whole sound, with the first-run, top-quality equipment. They walk into a crap-hole . . . with two mikes that were left over from, you know, Illinois Jacquet's gig in 1947. And they say, "Man, I can't play on this shit." So their whole horizon increased. So what they do is, they start making those same demands in the clubs, live, as they are in the studio, which is wanting control and better quality. . . . To me the paradigm is: grab control; that leads to making your own music; that leads to becoming more popular, which leads to bigger venues, endorsements, getting more equipment because now you're becoming famous. So that dialectic is, *the more you have control over your music, the better the music is, no matter what direction it takes.* As it becomes more your own, the people react to it more. And therefore the money gets better

and everything else. And coincidentally, concomitantly, you get control of your business, and over the marketing, and everything else.[63]

By the early seventies, record companies had begun to seize the opportunity to trade comfortable profit margins for volume. Where their contracts had been usurious toward jazz musicians, they now began to fatten fusion jazz record budgets dramatically, to the disgruntlement of the musicians' more mainstream jazz counterparts. The discovery of a new, youthful market for fusion jazz had an impact on how the music would be produced and, inevitably, what it would sound like. The increase in production budgets for "electric" albums was not merely directed at the costs of producing an album that used amplified and electronic instruments. The multitrack recording process, not amplification, accounted for a threefold jump in production costs. It was a necessary leap. The recording aesthetics of the rock industry had so permeated the sensibilities of young listeners that it was imperative to replicate those aesthetics, even if the notes being recorded were not exactly rock.

Columbia became successful through its recognition of the importance of high production values in drawing in young audiences. Thus, they were ready to invest in projects, like *Head Hunters*, that required enormous outlays of money, compared to the jazz-industry practice of just a few years before. The benefit immediately to them, and soon to the jazz market itself, was that they now managed to attract the attention of a new crop of jazz listeners.

Clearly, record companies are in business to make a profit. A cynical view of the appeal to young audiences suggests that these companies, and the musicians associated with them, recognized an immediate need to expand their markets and "rocked up" the sound to appeal to the new target market. An idealist argument holds that jazz performers were trying to reconnect with their populist roots, from whence jazz originally sprang. Doubtless, elements of both interpretations were at work. Whatever the motivation, the solidification of a new market—despite or perhaps because of the fact that that market was never anointed as a category by name—served an ecumenical purpose. Overnight, people were listening to, and buying, more jazz.

Stuart Nicholson writes that, in the summer after the release of *Bitches Brew*, Miles Davis was to front a "supergroup" at a festival in New York, made up of members of his own band, along with Cream's Eric Clapton and Jack Bruce, and Tony Williams. (Davis later reneged on the commitment and played the festival with his own band.) Nicholson reports that Bruce, the festival organizer, explained to *Rolling Stone* that "Miles wants to be a pop star in the sense that he wants exposure in the pop world. [He] feels that he can turn on hip people if he has that exposure."[64] In a word, the strategy worked. *Bitches Brew* was soon to sell three hundred thousand copies, eventually becoming a gold record. Davis correctly perceived that his music could be appreciated by a young, hip crowd. His marriage of jazz with rock created in rock fans a space for attraction to jazz generally. Others saw the opportunity to participate with this new, expanded audience. Jazz has always been wedded to the blues, despite a trial separation or two, and several jazz musicians, less wedded to experimentalism than Davis, developed this core linkage further. Nicholson describes the impact on the market of fusing jazz with R&B: "In September 1971 [Creed] Taylor asked [Grover] Washington to deputize for Hank Crawford on a session, and, to everyone's surprise including Washington's, the resulting album, *Inner City Blues*, was a huge success. 'It happened so fast,' recalled Washington in 1973. 'One day people weren't listening to jazz . . . and the next thing jazz is selling.'"[65] This was the state of things as *Head Hunters* was released. There was a degree of precedent for a higher profile of jazz in the marketplace. And there had been significant hits by 1973. But the exposure of young listeners to jazz by way of *Head Hunters* was unprecedented.

Vernon Slaughter described the groundswell of enthusiasm among the new listeners. In the winter of 1974, the strong sales of *Head Hunters* was still only a regional phenomenon, Slaughter recalled. But the local momentum indicated that a shift in Hancock's listenership was occurring: "Herbie and Dave [Rubinson] first came to Washington on a promotional thing. They would come in and play. But it literally changed their audiencc. They had a bunch of young kids at their concerts. And I think it really changed Herbie's career. Where he was going—it was where he wanted to go."[66] A moment of epiphany came for Hancock shortly thereafter, when it became clear to him that his audience had not only changed but also expanded radically: "I remember one of the first concerts that I did after *Head Hunters*. We were working opposite a couple of other groups. . . . I walked in there, and one of the opening acts was on, and I looked at the audience. I said, 'Wow, that's a lot of people here. Who's the headliner? I thought I was one of the opening acts.' . . . And David Rubinson says, 'Don't you know what's happening here? You're headlining this show.'"[67]

There was no shortage of musicians and observers ready to decry this development as pandering. To this criticism, Bill Summers responded: "The people that were feeling that way were swallowed up by that great flood of people who were wanting to get on the Ark. That's how it was. There were so many people who were on the side of it and so many new people who got turned on to jazz. I mean, it was like having a bridge to heaven."[68] As sales climbed toward the million-unit mark, luster generated by Hancock reflected on jazz in general. This effect, at first seen as secondary, was to have a deepening impact on the jazz recording industry with the formation of V.S.O.P. In 1975, Hancock was still riding the crest of popularity from *Head Hunters*. George Wein, impresario of the prestigious Newport Jazz Festival, approached Hancock to appear in the 1976 festival. As Hancock related:

> My manager [David Rubinson], who was not so concerned about me participating in a jazz festival at that time . . . asked for something that he thought George would never do. He said, "Yeah, Herbie'll do it if you do a retrospective of Herbie's music." You know, thinking, "George ain't gonna do that; he hasn't done a retrospective on Miles's music yet. Or Duke [Ellington]. Why would he do Herbie Hancock?" you know. I was Miles's sideman. So George came back to him and said, "I think it's a great idea. Let's do it."
>
> So what wound up happening was we had a retrospective of my music at Town Hall in 1976, which was the year of the bicentennial. And I had three groups there [each representing a different part of Hancock's career]. . . . One of these was . . . the Miles Davis group [with the addition of Freddie Hubbard, who had also had a prominent place in Hancock's career]. . . . It was like a dream band because it contained a great part of the character of Miles's band from the sixties.

> And this was in 1976, and many people hadn't heard music in that direction since 1968, you know, or '69.[69]

Without the popularity of *Head Hunters*, the retrospective performance might never have happened. The event, and the subsequent tour and album, brought Hancock's newer audience into contact with post-bebop jazz—not as an object of nostalgia but as a vibrant alternate stream. Conrad Silvert, in the liner notes to *V.S.O.P.: The Quintet* (1977), proclaimed, "The fact that more than 100,000 people turned out in just one month to see the V.S.O.P. Quintet shows not only that jazz remains as vital as any American art form, but that five musicians, by playing (with their individual bands) music so many purists claim is destroying jazz, have actually helped broaden the 'pure jazz' audience."

While radio broadcast categories were expanding at this time—or kept amorphous, in the case of free-from radio—no distinction had been made between jazz and fusion jazz. In fact, as stated before, *Billboard* magazine had established the jazz sales category only as recently as 1969. There were no "fusion jazz" racks in record stores; rather, fusion jazz albums could be found in jazz racks, as well as in rock or R&B racks. With Vernon Slaughter leading, this is how Columbia marketed *Head Hunters*, resulting in a conflation of fusion jazz not only with R&B but also with jazz generally.

As evidenced by his present capacity as president of Blue Note Records, Bruce Lundvall is by all accounts someone with a deep love for jazz, particularly the post-bebop music of the fifties and sixties. In his role at Columbia during the early seventies, he was responsible for creating a marketing image for the label as a whole, including building a cohesive roster of artists. When I asked Lundvall if the success of *Head Hunters* had a direct effect on the way Columbia would treat fusion jazz (or jazz generally), he replied:

> It was one of those few records that allowed me, when I was later the general manager of Columbia and then the president of the label, to sign people like Dexter Gordon, as an example. Because we had around that time [i.e., in the aftermath of *Head Hunters*] Return to Forever, who had two albums that were, well, one was gold, and the other one was a little bit less. And we had Weather Report, who had gold

records. I mean, it was a time when essentially jazz musicians playing a fusion style of music were selling just a little less well than some of the major rock 'n' roll bands. So when I was there [as president], it opened the door for me to sign acoustic jazz players who I strongly believed in, as well. And they were able to sell more records. Because the sales force said, "Oh well, it's jazz. But that's OK: jazz sells."[70]

Although *Head Hunters* added important energy to resuscitating the jazz market, the market also had its effect on the creation of *Head Hunters*. Bennie Maupin, who had been with Hancock since *Mwandishi*, described the earlier group as having run its course:

> During that time, we pretty much had explored that way of playing [i.e., based on free improvisation] so that everything was very open-ended, in a sense. And we had explored probably as far as any band had up to that point. And we had gotten the amount of exposure that we had; even then, though, the exposure wasn't *that* great. So by the time the band ended, Herbie wanted to do some other things. And the music that I had been listening to—of course, I think we'd all been very attracted to—were James Brown and Sly. Because it was something that really felt good. And Stevie Wonder's music. So we wanted to incorporate some of those elements into the music. That was a conscious, creative decision, to make some music that could have some of those elements in it.[71]

In large part, this creative decision was rooted in a desire to come down from the rarefied improvisational atmosphere of the previous albums: "And we were still at the tail end of working through whatever we needed to work through. And then, of course, *Head Hunters* came. So it was an experiment; we did things that we felt had some groove potential. And we still wanted to maintain improvisation on top of those things but not make it so complicated rhythmically or harmonically that people wouldn't be able to have access to it."[72]

Maupin spoke from his point of view and from Hancock's, as the only two members of both bands. But the decision to regroup and to become more accessible, although an artistic one, was not merely so. Commercially, the Mwandishi band had run out of gas:

> We were working on group improvisation a lot. . . . And then we ran the course of that. This was made quite plain to us by Herbie's accountants. When we met in the Empire State Building with the entire band, we were told that we were basically going into his savings, just to have a band. And they said, "Not a good business decision." So we did a few more gigs and that was it.
>
> And so, at that point, Herbie asked me if I would be interested in staying and doing something with him in a different context. I knew exactly what it was, even though I hadn't spoken about it. Because intuitively we were both at a point where we knew we had to make some changes in what we were doing. In order to hopefully reach a wider audience and just create a different environment for ourselves.[73]

As the new group began to coalesce, its members began a process of improvising ideas on tape, listening to the results, and composing the songs by a process of refining and editing:

> Maupin: And at that point, we didn't know if it was going to fly or if it was going to flop.
>
> Q: Well, you probably had a clue from the audience reaction, right?
>
> Maupin: Well, it certainly felt good. But we got good audience reaction also from the sextet. But, you know, we didn't sell records from that.[74]

The process, then, to Hancock and Maupin, called for reconciling market demands with artistic and ideological attractions toward populism. Critics were largely unsympathetic. However, an anecdote related to me by Bill Summers sheds light on this intersection:

> Summers: The only times that I could feel any kind of problems was not during the early days [but] when Herbie tried to start singing in the vocorder. That's when I could visually see problems, like people throwing stuff at Herbie. In Europe, they were throwing apples and oranges, and tomatoes, and—

Q: You're serious?

Summers: Yeah. In every city, almost every city we went to. We'd do two sets. One was jazz, and then the second set, we started introducing this newfound toy, the vocoder. And that was on the *Sunlight* album [1977, issued 1978]. On "Feets Don't Fail Me Now," or something like that, was the name of it. I didn't like it. I thought certain people used the voice box or the vocoder—in the funk idiom, it was working. But for me, it didn't work for Herbie. For him to try to sing. And if he tried to sing a song without the vocorder, just him singing, he couldn't do it. So I don't think that's the way to go. You know, to manipulate the keys, I think that's a fantastic thing, because he's fascinated with stuff. So I think that it was more his fascination in new technology. I don't know, I can't speak for him. But I couldn't understand the move to that. And it was disastrous. I remember—and the thing that was really funny about it, they didn't throw . . . I mean, the things that were thrown were thrown directly at him and no one else.

Q: You *know* that's tough.

Summers: Oh yeah, and let me tell you something. Let me tell you what kind of fortitude this man has. He played right through that shit, Bro'. He'd play through it and go to the next gig and keep the show exactly the same. Knowing they were going to do it. He knew it.[75]

Summers was referring to the tour promoting the *Sunlight* album, the twilight of the Headhunters' cohesion as a group. He speculated that Hancock pressed on because "he did not want to be limited or confined or strapped down to doing what other people dictated he should do."[76] Whether Summers's assessment is correct or Hancock was simply committed to the concert dates, or to the music he had rehearsed in this form, or to promoting the album, is unknown. *Sunlight*, by most accounts, was not Hancock's best effort, and the musical tides were turning once again. Disco was ascendant, and Hancock's rhythm-and-blues-based music would wander briefly until he would again become molten, with "Rockit" (*Future Shock*, 1983). Meanwhile, he would give renewed attention to his acoustic jazz work, to acclaim.

The music industry ("the market") is often cast as a central, exploitive figure in the war of words surrounding fusion jazz and by extension as a denigrating force on jazz itself. The truth is, the market did have an effect: Herbie Hancock, in creating *Head Hunters*, actively sought to broaden his audience—for both artistic and commercial reasons.

The idea that somehow a mass-mediated music could exist that did *not* take into account the demands of marketing is specious. How could it be otherwise? Considering the inevitability of this music being placed in the marketplace, market considerations were intrinsically influential in *Head Hunters*, but not to the exclusion of other influences. More properly, market concerns were *points* of consideration, aspects of a web of affiliations. The balancing act for the musicians of *Head Hunters*, as well as for opera singers, rock musicians, and any other performers who offer their music for sale, concerned navigating between the muse and the market. Contention over the importance of the market's demands should not mask the deeper question of why, and to whom, the contention is important ideologically.

CHAPTER 7

Final Reflections

The Politics of Classification

In the first chapter, I mention Gary Carner's rephrasing of Scott DeVeaux's comment that jazz historical writing reflects a "near century-old eagerness to advance the music's respectability. In order to make jazz cohere as one majestic entity, jazz writers have habitually canonized their heroes, purchasing for their favorites a seat on the 'jazz tradition' train in which each conflicting style is assigned its evolutionary place no matter how different or wide-ranging."[1] In recent decades, jazz commentators have defended jazz's high-art trajectory. As one outcome of this, jazz performance and history courses have increasingly cropped up in college and university curricula across the nation. And yet jazz studies have not achieved anything resembling parity within musicological circles.

The desire to inscribe jazz as "one *majestic* entity" veils a fight for position and cultural prestige being waged on several fronts. Under the banner "America's classical music," jazz's momentum in the academy has improved black music's space there, as well. Until relatively recently, academic studies of African-based musics were primarily the province of anthropologists and ethnomusicologists, often, as Glenn Watkins and Samuel Floyd Jr. point out, with an inevitable undertone of the "exotic" or the "primitive."[2] Jazz, at least, has emerged as a legitimate topic for *musical* study, with many jazz history courses touting the high-art trajectory.

But this positioning has come at a price. Floyd pinpoints the early pitfall of academic acceptance as jazz developed:

> The zeal for jazz among some musicologists and musicologically oriented scholars and critics, who feel that they have to justify black music to the larger scholarly community, has been both fortunate and unfortunate for African-American music. It is fortunate that through their intense responsiveness to the music, they have helped pave the way for the eventual acceptance of the genre in the academy. These critics' need to have their writings published in mainline scholarly journals and books led them to shape their writings on jazz into academically acceptable form. The mannerisms, limitations, and traditions of academic form and substance help give the impression that the music is merely a species of European-derived music, causing both these critics and their listeners to miss the point of the music's real and essential aesthetic power. Explanations that result from their analyses are usually limited and aesthetically uninformative, for they presume cultural and artistic goals different from those of the tradition from which jazz springs. If the purpose of analysis is to explain and illuminate the aesthetic power of the music, the exclusive application of positivistic analysis to works and performances of black music is not only inadequate, but also a miscarriage of analytical purpose; such analysis reveals nothing about most of the culturally expressive features of the music.[3]

As part of the cost of admission to the academy, Floyd observes, too many jazz scholars have responded to an inherent pressure to portray the music in terms that resonate well within the walls of the traditional music department. The unintended effect of such a rhetorical move is clear: its ultimate result is the reinforcement of an academic point of view that limits the understanding of jazz in its richest context. Despite a growing, recent trend in jazz historical scholarship that integrates musical issues with cultural contexts, much work remains to be done to explore the many intersections that result in this profound music.

Jazz rises from and continues to tap an orientation in African conceptual approaches to music-making, in continual contact and realignment with other musical and cultural influences: a musical web. To understand jazz is to comprehend the interaction of musicians with other musicians and in the process to comprehend the multiple intersections of traditions, histories, and personalities, *as well as* the syntax of notes, rhythms, and timbres through which they interact.

During the past two decades, musicological scholars have taken a challenge laid on them by Joseph Kerman: "If the musicologists do not write the contextual history of Western art music, someone else will write it for them."[4] Kerman speculated that ethnomusicologists, rather than historians, would rise to the challenge. But instead, a body of scholarship has come from several disciplines in recent years, the trajectories of which are multiple and still developing.[5] Gone, or at least going, are the positivistic days of describing music as *merely* a text, score, or recording—an aesthetic object with no other associations. Opportunities abound to delve deeper into the context of music, to erase some of the conceptual boundaries closing off scholarly exchange and an open-eyed view of jazz—indeed, of any music—in the musical and cultural contexts unique to it.

To see just how removed jazz scholarship tends to be from a contextual approach, see the long history of solo transcriptions in jazz histories, analysis articles, and industry magazines such as *Down Beat* and *Keyboard*. These transcriptions give much attention to melody (and by extension formal plan), as well as harmony (given as chord symbols, sans voicings), but rarely if ever do they show the soloist's interaction with other instruments—a major omission in a genre so tied to interaction.[6] This pedagogical style dominates on campus; overwhelmingly, jazz's presence on campus is limited to performance and music education programs. Doctoral dissertations and master's theses still amount to a handful of works, especially compared with other topics in historical musicology and ethnomusicology, and the United States has yet to institute a Ph.D. program devoted to jazz studies.

We should direct our attention to jazz as a *practice*, rather than as a text. Whether the music is improvisational or arranged, subdivided in swing- or straight-eighths, funky, sophisticated, accessible, obtuse, modal, or rock-inflected, jazz happens as a process. Under this orientation, performance practice issues become as central as the notes being played. Miles Davis's ability to milk expression from every note he played is legendary. Louis Armstrong's electrifying playing style in the twenties relied on an extensive repertoire of expressive timbres and note attacks.[7] Similarly, Johnny Hodges's saxophone glissandi in his recordings with Duke Ellington, even when prescribed in the score, demonstrate his ability to shape a note as a personal statement. The examples go on and on, and they all exhibit the constellation of conceptual approaches outlined by Olly Wilson, prominently the *heterogeneous sound ideal.*

These missing perspectives are at the heart of my critique of strictly formalist descriptions of jazz. For example, in the 1989 *Musical Quarterly* article "Three Approaches to Defining Jazz," having a "sound" is not mentioned, nor is interacting, nor quoting.[8] Rather, such writing too often adopts the positivistic terms of an older musicology to explain the music, with the result that Hodges's glissandi, or "concert" material by a central figure like Duke Ellington, can be construed as not fitting a description—*any* description—of jazz.

Underlying the projection of jazz as high art is a perceptible anxiety that jazz might be vulnerable to being seen merely as "entertainment." At times, perhaps reluctantly and inadvertently, Herbie Hancock and Wynton Marsalis have come to represent these two opposing forces, entertainment and art. In one unguarded exchange between the two, the lines are drawn:

> Marsalis: I've had conversations with you, where you told me, "Man we're trying to get this kind of market." It's not like I don't know about pop musicians. It's not like I don't listen to music.
>
> Hancock: Then there's some things you don't understand about it. Because I *never* use the word *sell.*
>
> Marsalis: I don't know. Remember what you told me before? "Yeah, man, my record just went gold, man. I need to get me some more records like that." We had long conversations about that. We shouldn't be arguing about this in the press, man. We have to be cool. We've talked about this already.
>
> Hancock: Do you think I'd object if my records sold millions?

Marsalis: Don't say you don't think about that.
Hancock: Of course I would [think about that].
Marsalis: Because you do. You *do* think about that.
Interviewer: To think about it and have it as your aim are two different things.
Hancock: Thank you.
Marsalis: I'm getting tired. You said the opposite of what I wanted to hear.
Hancock: Look, I'd like to have a Rolls-Royce, too. But I'm not purposefully trying to set myself up to get a Rolls-Royce.[9]

In this 1999 exchange, Marsalis decries jazz's "entertainment" face, it seems, in order to position jazz as serious and transcendent. In this sense, Marsalis's concerns resonate with the general characterization of European art music, at least since the nineteenth century, as approaching the sublime, rather than being merely decorative.[10] Marsalis seems of two minds, though. He elsewhere describes jazz's essence as "swing[ing] and play[ing] some blues."[11] If his meaning is literal, he finds himself in the positivist camp of Mark Gridley, James Collier, et al. Marsalis has often argued for a "true art" identity for jazz. Yet if we interpret his statement more evocatively, we may understand that to play jazz is, figuratively, to revisit its cultural roots.

Certainly, a scholarly reception of jazz as artistically comparable to European art music would reflect a rise in jazz's cultural prestige. Ronald Radano calls attention to this neoclassical project:

> The revitalization of jazz as a new traditionalism or "neoclassicism" has been welcomed by many observers at a time of great cultural ferment. For some, it suggests that white America has now finally begun to recognize the achievements of black musicians, not simply as entertainers in the tradition of Sambo and Buckwheat, but as artists of real merit, and arguably of equal importance to the innovators of European high culture. . . . [The "young lions"] suggest that jazz is perhaps the lone certainty in an uncertain artistic era, a "true art" innovated by blacks. As it transcends difference, it reaches the height of cultural achievement, becoming once again, "America's classical art form."[12]

Jazz's recent acceptance in scholarly circles has come about through the reinforcement of certain high-culture values. Aesthetic values contained *within* jazz that coincide with European high-art values already in place are used in this context to *represent* jazz: emotional depth; melodic, harmonic, and formal complexities—values reified by a European-styled conservatory pedagogy. While these are laudable in many ways, they maintain European art aesthetics as the standard of measurement and efface rich divergences of approach. Unfortunately, entering a curriculum framed in this manner, jazz scholars and musicians may find themselves pushing jazz along an illusory and limiting path in pursuit of cultural stature.

While a new scholarship trend emphasizing cultural context is a growing presence, it still is anything but the dominant view on campus. This should, and I believe will, change.

Rethinking Classification

I began this book by problematizing the classification of fusion jazz and suggesting that we might open perspectives of jazz by considering *Head Hunters* in light of its many intersections and influences. Throughout, I have attempted to disrupt the rigidity of the classifications by which we understand the album. I am not arguing that we throw away the notion of classification out of hand. We will classify; it is in the human condition. The question is, how *should* we?

Notions of genre and classification can be helpful, in that they can help us to direct our attention to elements within a larger picture. If we know that fusion jazz recordings tend to make use of new timbres, for example, our attention will be more easily drawn to them in *Head Hunters*. But once we've gained some kind of entry into an album, song, person, instrument, whatever, we should discard the idea of genre. Rather, we should discover what elements come into the frame and what places them there. Like a massive series of hyperlinks on an Internet site (not what I was thinking of originally, when I chose the metaphor "web of affiliations"), each link, central or peripheral, adds explanation and context.

Eventually, we gain a critical mass, enabling us to organize our impressions into cohesion. But in considering the broad array of affiliations, the musical "folder" we construct may be surprising and not necessarily audible on the surface. In the case of *Head Hunters*, the folder includes Ravel, along with Stockhausen, Sly and the Family Stone, Afro-Cuban music, black nationalism, rhythm-and-blues, the Dozens, James Brown, the master marketing plan at Columbia Records, Miles Davis, the development of the synthesizer, and Grinnell College. How could we have predicted these associations, given only the understanding of *Head Hunters* as belonging to a "fusion jazz" genre? Rather than "one majestic entity," jazz is a paradox: a whole made of disjuncture, an eclectic language. And that's the beauty of it.

Appendix: Billboard Chart Categories

This appendix outlines changes in *Billboard*'s chart categories from 1969 through 1995, noting the issue dates when the categories first appeared.

January 4, 1969

- Best-Selling Classical LPs
- Best-Selling Folios
- Best-Selling Jazz LPs
- Best-Selling R&B Albums
- Best-Selling R&B Singles
- Breakout Albums
- Hot Country Albums
- Hot Country Singles
- Hot 100
- Top 40 Easy Listening
- Top LPs

January 3, 1970

- Best-Selling Classical LPs
- Best-Selling Folios
- Best-Selling Jazz LPs
- Best-Selling Soul Albums
- Best-Selling Soul Singles
- Breakout Albums
- Breakout Singles
- Hot Country Albums
- Hot Country Singles
- Hot 100
- Top 40 Easy Listening
- Top LPs

January 6, 1973

- Action Records
- Best-Selling Soul Albums
- Best-Selling Soul Singles
- FM Action
- Hot Country Albums
- Hot Country Singles
- Hot 100
- Top 40 Easy Listening
- Top LPs

January 7, 1995

Albums

- *Billboard* 200
- Contemporary Christian
- Country
- Gospel
- Heatseekers
- *Billboard* Latin 50
- New Age
- R&B
- Reggae
- World Music

Singles

- Hot 100
- Adult Contemporary
- Country
- Dance/Club Play
- Dance/Maxi-Singles
- Latin
- R&B
- Hot R&B Airplay
- Hot R&B Singles
- Rap
- Rock/Album Rock Tracks
- Rock/Modern Rock Tracks
- Top 40 Airplay/Rhythm-Crossover
- Hot 100 Airplay
- Hot 100 Singles Sales

Videos

- Top Video Sales
- Health and Fitness
- Kid Video
- Recreational Sports
- Rentals

Notes

Preface

1. Nicholson; Coryell and Friedman 1978.

2. In 1976, multiplatinum awards were added, for sales in multiples of a million copies. In 1999, the diamond category was added, for sales of ten million or more. Source: RIAA, http://www.riaa/gp/database (accessed Nov. 30, 2004).

3. Source: RIAA, http://www.riaa.com/gp/history/timeline.asp.

4. Hoffman and Albert 1998, 157.

5. Whitburn 2001, 361.

6. Michael Cuscuna, personal correspondence with the author, Feb. 12, 2003. (Note: hereafter, "personal correspondence" will be abbreviated "p.c." and may be assumed to be with the author unless otherwise indicated.)

Chapter 1

1. This is, of course, not the first time a new direction has been castigated as "not jazz at all." Imamu Amiri Baraka (LeRoi Jones) cites a similar bruising of bebop by the jazz critical press of the forties: "Far from a culmination of jazz, bebop is not jazz at all, but an ultimately degenerated form of swing, exploiting the most fantastic rhythms and unrelated harmonies that it would seem possible to conceive" (Rudi Blesh, qtd. in Baraka 1963, 190). See also Gendron 1995.

2. See, e.g., reviews by Don Heckman (1995), B. Houston (1967), and Valerie Wilmer (1967). Also see Miles Davis with Troupe 1989, 263.

3. The Mwandishi group is officially known as the Herbie Hancock Sextet, 1970–72, and the Herbie Hancock Septet, 1972–73. In this book, I refer to the two versions of the group as the Mwandishi group.

4. Throughout the book, I describe this music generically as *fusion jazz*.

5. See, e.g., Schuller 1979. Scott DeVeaux (1997, 273–436) provides a welcome exception to this omission.

6. For the "sellout," see Crouch 1996, 34–35; Feather 1970, 10. For the "new direction," see Nicholson 1998; Micallef 1995.

7. Miles Davis, *Bitches Brew* (1969, issued 1970); Mahavishnu Orchestra, *Birds of Fire* (1972, issued 1973); Weather Report, *I Sing the Body Electric* (1971–1972, issued 1972); Return To Forever, *Hymn of the Seventh Galaxy* (1973).

8. Sales 1992, 202.

9. See, e.g., Marsalis 1990 and Scherman 1995. For controversy surrounding these characterizations, see Pond 2002, 2003.

10. Marsalis and Stewart 1994.

11. Marsalis and Stewart 1994, 141. For a rare historical treatment of avant-garde and fusion jazz considered together, see "Avant-garde Jazz and Jazz-Rock Fusion: Two Opposites?" (Porter 1997, 219–44).

12. For Braxton and the A.E.C., see Radano 1993, 141 n. 6, 104. For Davis, see Miles Davis with Troupe 1989, 205.

13. Taylor 1999, 331–32, 328.

14. For more on "America's classical music" and its role in historiography, see Pond 2003.

15. Although a cluster of jazz topics have surfaced in musicology and ethnomusicology dissertations over the past couple of decades, their number remains disturbingly small. Rutgers-Newark University currently has the only master's program dedicated to jazz history and research, as opposed to performance or music education. For a discussion of jazz programs in the United States, see Pond 2003, 13–14. For a listing of jazz education programs in the United States, see the *Jazz Times* supplement, the *1999–2000 Jazz Education Guide* (1999). See also *Down Beat*'s annual education guide, e.g., "Where to Study Jazz: College and University Jazz Education Guide" (*Down Beat*, July 19, 2003, special pull-out section, 62 pp.).

16. Leonard Bernstein, qtd. in Sales 1992, 37.

17. Scherman 1995, 81.

18. Crawford 1983; Baraka 1963.

19. While the commentary on racial politics in jazz is too extensive to capture here, examples include the following. Robert Levin, describing avant-garde jazz, notes: "On its own terms, the New Jazz [i.e., avant-garde jazz] has been persistently unnegotiable. . . . Not the least of the reasons for this circumstance is the direct relationship, aesthetic and attitudinal, of the New Jazz and Black Nationalism. For one thing, fired by an unabashed 'pride in black,' the New Jazz is determinedly an Art Music" (Rivelli and Levin 1970, 2–3). In the introduction to *The Story of Jazz*, Marshall Stearns calls jazz a "separate and distinct art, to be judged by separate and distinct standards" and uses *jazz* as an umbrella term for "most of the music created, with the help of the American Negro, in the United States" (1972, 2, 3). Leonard Feather saw jazz as an effective tool in the fight against Jim Crow racism (1999, 157).

20. Monson 1996.

21. Roberts 1979.

22. Sales 1992, 37.

23. See DeVeaux 1995.

24. Gendron 1995, 2. Use of the term "moldy fig," meaning "clinging to an outmoded idea," first surfaced, to the best of my knowledge, in the political rhetoric during the years preceding the Civil War, between members of the Whig and the Democrat parties. The *Random House Historical Dictionary of American Slang*,

however, gives more recent provenance. In that reference, the phrase surfaces specifically related to jazz, in a 1945 invective against jazz conservatives, as Gendron summarizes (1995). Elsewhere, Robert F. Gold cites a similar castigation: "The moldy figs . . . are certain the greatest jazz ever played . . . was played in New Orleans in 1915" (1964).

25. Gendron 1995, 32.

26. Examples of the assertions of a classicist jazz aesthetic are enumerated by Ronald Radano (1993, 52–53 nn. 67–69). Amiri Baraka makes explicit the white-black polarization: "Except for individuals like Miles Davis, who is always cited as the innovator of the post-bop cool approach, most of the musicians readily associated with the style were white musicians who abandoned (or didn't properly understand) Parker's rhythmic innovations, and put to dubious use his melodic and harmonic examples" (1963, 209). Davis's prominence in the movement's beginnings makes Baraka's assertions problematic, but Baraka does elucidate a commonly held opinion of the time.

David Rosenthal elaborates on the notion of jazz's rootedness in African American expressivity in *Hard Bop* (1992), especially in chap. 2, "Hard Bop Begins." Citing a variety of musicians' viewpoints, Horace Silver's "meaningful simplicity" is particularly apt—Rosenthal points out that the target audience and the aesthetic goals were centered on African Americans: "As a result, jazz regained a measure of acceptance in black neighborhoods and reaffirmed its connections with its terpsichorean rhythms" (39–40). Set against this backdrop was the West Coast "cool school," which was "overwhelmingly a white phenomenon, both in its protagonists and its audience" (23).

27. Kamin 1975, 280. Kamin addresses rock 'n' roll, as opposed to rhythm-and-blues.

28. Nicholson 1998, xiii.

29. Gridley, Maxham, and Hoff 1989, 531, 518. See also Wittgenstein 1953, 32a.

30. Patrick Gleeson, interview with the author, Feb. 27, 1997. (Subsequent interviews may be assumed to be with the author, unless otherwise indicated.) Gleeson officially joined the Mwandishi group in 1972, expanding it to a septet on *Sextant* (1972) and on tour. Prior to this, he had operated ex officio, adding synthesizer tracks to *Crossings* (1971).

31. Gleeson, interview, Feb. 27, 1997 (vocal stress emphasized).

32. There is disagreement on what to call the category (genre? style? trend?). Dictionary definitions culled from *Webster's Seventh New Collegiate Dictionary* (Springfield, Mass.: Merriam-Webster, 1976) may assist us here. *Category:* A general class to which a logical predicate or that which it predicates belongs; *genre:* a distinctive type or category of [music]; *style:* a mode of expression; *trend:* a current style or preference, *also* a line of development, approach. The approaches to categorization that I cite in this section treat fusion jazz primarily as a genre, according to these definitions.

33. The only book-length treatments of jazz-rock fusion are the collection of interviews by Julie Coryell and Laura Friedman (1978), which does not provide

an academic analysis, and the more recent history by Stuart Nicholson (1998), which does.

34. One of the serious problems with the "rock" component of the generic name is that "rock" is as subject to multiple meanings as "jazz" is. Thus, "jazz-rock" glosses over the very important contribution of rhythm-and-blues of the forties, as a progenitor of "rock."

35. This is the basis of Grover Sales's comment about "bored" rock musicians and pandering jazz musicians. Sales's comment does not account for a similar distancing of rock from pop in the late sixties, parallel to an art-versus-commerce dialectic discussed in this section.

36. See Kamin 1975, especially 280. Kamin compares white, middle-aged, middle-class resistance to rock 'n' roll with resistance to jazz generally a generation before. In the case of rock 'n' roll, resistance partly arose from racist associations of black popular music (rhythm-and-blues) with low moral character. Bebop's bohemian associations had assured similar resistance in the forties. By the mid-fifties, however, bebop had begun to outlive the low-haunt stereotype associating it with bohemianism, earning cachet as high art. With bebop now endorsed by their parents (even though not completely), middle-class teens found rhythm-and-blues more relevant to their own tastes, a relevancy soon transferred to rock 'n' roll.

37. With regard to audiences, Bill Milkowski describes an early band with bassist Jaco Pastorius, saying that audiences, even though they liked what they heard, had a hard time deciding what to call it: "As [band leader Ira Sullivan] remembers, 'They'd sit there during the first set and say, "Man, it sounds like Miles." Second set they'd say, "No, it sounds more like what Herbie's doing with the Headhunters." Then, after the third set, they'd tell us, "Man, we never heard no music like this before." And that's why I decided not to record it. I figured anything that good, just let it lay'" (1995, 53).

38. Bob James, interview, Oct. 9, 1996.

39. Collier 1988, 557.

40. Although the *New Grove Dictionary of Jazz*'s second edition keeps a slightly updated version of Collier's article, a separate jazz-rock article written by Mark Gilbert includes more influences than simply jazz and rock. Gilbert calls jazz-rock "a style of music, initiated in the sixties, which combined the harmonic resources and improvising techniques of modern jazz with the instrumentation, rhythms, and idioms of rock music and funk. . . . By the late seventies 'jazz-rock' had largely been replaced by the term 'fusion,' which was also used to describe the blending of jazz with any other type of music, including folk, ethnic, and classical." Still, Gilbert's bibliography features a jazz history text by Joachim Berendt (whose 1975 article "I Wanna Make It: The Problem of Success in Jazz" leaves no doubt of his sympathies), as well as Mark Gridley's jazz style history, which limits the influences in fusion to jazz and funk (2003). See Gilbert 2002.

41. Garofalo 2005, 207 (emphasis added).

42. "Fundamentally, it is an *ideological* divide that carries more weight:

'rock' is considered more 'authentic' and closer to 'art,' while 'pop' is regarded as more 'commercial,' more obviously 'entertainment'" (Middleton 2004).

43. Kamin 1975, 282.

44. For the movement of audiences from jazz to rock, see Kamin 1975, 283.

45. Crouch 1996, 34, 35.

46. Nicholson 1998, xiii.

47. Sales 1992, 207–8.

48. Nicholson 1998, viii and throughout.

49. See Baraka 1963; DeVeaux 1997; Crawford 1983. LeRoi Jones changed his name in the 1960s to Imamu Amiri Baraka (most commonly Amiri Baraka). To avoid the confusion of constantly pointing out that Jones and Baraka are the same person, I consistently refer to him as Amiri Baraka.

50. Gleeson, interview, Feb. 27, 1997.

51. David Rubinson, interview, Jan. 11, 1998.

52. Patrick Gleeson, interview, Mar. 5, 1997.

53. Crouch 1996, 35.

54. Gridley 1983, 29. Gridley reiterates his point in *Jazz Styles* (2003), chaps. 15 and 16.

55. See Gridley, Maxham, and Hoff 1989.

56. Samuel Floyd Jr. points out that not only the sounds but the myths and rituals associated with the concert-hall Western art tradition were attractive to Renaissance philosophy. He writes: "These values of high culture were embraced by turn-of-the-century black modernists and the thinkers of the Negro Renaissance. . . . [A journal of the time, the *Negro Music Journal*,] promoted the propaganda of the 'elevating influence' of concert-hall organizations. . . . [In contrast,] the journal rejected the popular music of the black heritage . . . [as] 'vulgar' and 'degrading'" (1995, 150–51). For Crouch, jazz had entered the concert hall, and the view from that seat was a good one.

57. While rock-associated players who joined the movement—Brian Eno, Jeff Beck, Bill Bruford, and others—gained in artistic stature, jazz players were thought to have "married down."

58. Nicholson 1998.

59. Simmel 1955; Slobin 1992.

60. Most, but not all, musical historians avoid talking about the market. Donald Grout and Claude Palisca note matter-of-factly in their textbook *A History of Western Music*, "Most of Mozart's music was composed either on commission or for a particular occasion; even in those works that do not seem to have been intended for an immediate performance, he had in mind a definite type of potential performer or audience and took their preferences into consideration" (1988, 608). They note that Haydn spent nearly thirty years in the service of a succession of Esterházy princes, "obligated to compose whatever music the prince demanded, to conduct the performances, to train and supervise all the musical personnel, and to keep the instruments in repair," a situation they characterize as "well-nigh ideal for his development as a composer" (1988, 585). In contrast, Carl Dahlhaus points in unflattering terms to a web of influences on composers' out-

put in the nineteenth century, occasioned by the rise of the bourgeoisie. See "The Music Culture of the Bourgeoisie" in the introductory chapter of *Nineteenth Century Music* (1989, 41–51). See also Henrich Schenker's "The Masterwork in Music" (1994).

61. Carner 1996, 21. Carner cites Scott DeVeaux's "Constructing the Jazz Tradition: Jazz Historiography" (1991), which in turn amplifies a section of DeVeaux's dissertation (1985), "Jazz in Transition: Coleman Hawkins and Howard McGhee, 1935–1945." In the dissertation, DeVeaux discusses the fact that, although historians seem loath to admit it, artistic and economic factors were typically balanced by jazz performers as a matter of course: "For the musician, if not the scholar, the boundary between the two concerns is fluid" (44). DeVeaux amplifies the point in *The Birth of Bebop* (1997). The political aspect of genre-building is also raised in explorations of the establishment of various canons in musicology and ethnomusicology by Bergeron and Bohlman (1992) and with regard to African American culture generally by Gates (1988).

62. These writers include Stuart Nicholson, Mark Gridley, Stanley Crouch, and James Lincoln Collier.

63. Rubinson, interview, Jan. 11, 1998.

64. Sales 1992, 208. Sales, similar to Nicholson and others, makes a distinction between artistic "jazz-rock fusion" and commercialized "crossover."

65. See Corea 1971, 16. According to Davis: "Critics always like to pigeonhole everybody, put you in a certain place in their heads so they can get to you. They don't like a lot of changing because that makes them have to work to understand what you're doing" (1990, 311). Zawinul has remarked: "Number one, I never felt like that was 'fusion' what we did. I think we were coming out of the jazz tradition and using other instruments. And that music is still very alive, I'm telling you, man. You can listen to old Weather Report things. Especially things coming out now on Legacy [Columbia Records' Jazz Reissue label]. Unissued stuff from concerts, with different bands. I would never think we were either rock, jazz, or anything. We just played great music" (Josef Zawinul, interview, Aug. 30, 1997).

66. Herbie Hancock, interview, May 27, 1998.

67. Rubinson, interview, Jan. 11, 1998 (vocal stress emphasized).

68. Zabor and Garbarini 1999.

69. Silvert 1977.

70. Hancock, in Sidran 1995, 269.

71. The straight-eighth orientation also dominated rock, soul, and funk.

72. Sidran 1995, 267–68.

73. Rubinson, interview, Jan. 11, 1998.

74. Bill Summers, interview, Apr. 15, 1998.

75. Carner 1996, 21.

76. A tempting alternative is to search for musicians' assertion of fusion jazz as postmodern, a broad "sampling," or bricolage process, along lines describing punk and dub musicians' gleefully improvised recontextualizing of musical "found objects" (Hebdige 1979, 1987).

77. Rubinson, interview, Jan. 11, 1998.

78. Akiko Jackson, p.c.

79. Rubinson, interview, Jan. 11, 1998.

80. For DeVeaux's image, see Carner 1996, 21.

81. Rosenthal 1992, 68–69; emphasis added.

82. See the appendix.

83. *Rhythm-and-blues* is as similarly vague and contested a term as *jazz*, and I cannot fully address it here.

84. Rosenthal's use of the jukebox reflects the jukebox industry's importance to the record industry generally in the forties and fifties. Although the jukebox had waned in importance by 1960, historian Kerry Segrave cites estimates that as late as 1953, jukeboxes accounted for "15 percent of total label [production] and 30 percent of singles output, excluding albums and children's material" (2002, 246).

85. Rubinson, interview, Jan. 11, 1998.

86. Arjun Appadurai (1990, 7), qtd. in Slobin 1992, 5.

87. Slobin 1992, 32.

88. By the mid-sixties, jazz had become a paradox: music of resistance to the mainstream, at least since the rise of bebop, it had now become identified with the generation who had been young during the forties but who were, in the eyes of youth, now the mainstream.

89. Corea 1971, 16.

90. Marsalis and Hancock, in Zabor and Garbarini 1999, 343.

91. Gaer 1973.

92. Herbie Hancock, interview, June 4, 1999.

93. The relationship of funk to these albums is open to some interpretation. Drummer Ndugu Leon Chancler's presence on *Crossings*, for example, argues for a funk connection, as does the recent attraction of hip-hop samplers to such pieces as "Rain Dance" (*Sextant*). But these connections are not explicit. Further, they were never mentioned in my interviews with the players (although philosophical connections to Black Nationalism peppered many discussions of the albums). However, the climate of the times makes the interpretation plausible. Lewis Porter (1997, 233; p.c.) suggests a broad move in avant-garde circles toward more "accessible" forms that bowed to funk, R&B, and rock in varying proportions.

94. For record jackets, see the illustrations. "Sleeping Giant"—whose title refers to Africa (Gleeson, interview, Mar. 5, 1997)—is on *Crossings*. "Rain Dance" is on *Sextant*.

95. See also Radano 1993; Stuckey 1987; and Floyd 1995, 185. Regarding his name, Hancock said: "My purpose in having this name is firstly I like the sound of it, and secondly I want to recognize my African Ancestry. . . . We [African Americans] are taking a look at ourselves and recognizing our heritage" (1971, 8).

96. Gaer 1973.

97. For "rapaciously commercial," see Crouch 1996, 35.

Chapter 2

1. See Mercer 1990, 247–64, for a discussion of the politics of black hairstyles.

2. Steven Feld (1996) also calls attention to the discursive qualities of this album art.

3. David Rubinson, p.c., Dec. 5, 2003. I was asking about the disparity between the commonly used name *Headhunters* and the album's official title, *Head Hunters*. See the preface.

4. See illustrations. The cover photograph for the anthology *The Best of Herbie Hancock: The Blue Note Years* (1988) reinforces these impressions, lending them historical importance.

5. Covers for *Crossings* (1971), *Sextant* (1972), and *Thrust* (1974) all feature illustrations by Rob Springett.

6. "African diaspora" in this book means the broad sphere of cultural influence emanating from the slave-exporting area of sub-Saharan West Africa to points across the Atlantic in which the economy relied heavily on slave labor. This diaspora includes the United States, various European colonial powers, various Caribbean islands, and the Atlantic shores of Central and South America, particularly Brazil (Bohannon and Curtin 1995, 185–88; Gilroy 1991, 1993). "African diaspora" is a shorthand term for this cultural geography. The dangers here are (1) using a term that names a continent but more specifically meaning a region within that continent and (2) glossing over cultural differences within a region. Regarding the first point, since the term has found its way into general use, it will also be used here, with the cautionary that the meaning of "African" in the term refers to the sub-Saharan, Western region that fed the slave trade. Regarding the second point, see Gilroy 1991; Wilson 1974, 4; Monson 2000; and Mintz 1989.

7. Hancock, interview, June 4, 1999.

8. Hancock, qtd. in Palmer 1974, 17 (emphasis added).

9. Vincent 1996, 31.

10. Agawu 2003.

11. Gilroy 1993.

12. Cross-cultural contact within sub-Saharan West Africa and across the Sahara goes back centuries, even before European contact. Groups in the slave-exporting region of West Africa, despite being distinct, encountered each other routinely through trade, conquest, empire, and intermarriage across the region, dating from at least the fourteenth century and likely well before (Roland Oliver and Fage 1962, 110). It is not accurate, historically or culturally, to think of Africa as a single, homogenous entity, but it is also a mistake to conceive of any particular African culture, even in earlier times, as isolated.

13. See Gilroy 1991 (126), reprinted in Gilroy's book *The Black Atlantic* (1993) as "Jewels Brought from Bondage: Black Music and the Politics of Authenticity" (72–110). Gilroy's reference (1993, 101) is to Baraka's 1966 article "The Changing Same (R&B and New Black Music)," in Baraka's *Black Music* (1967, 180–211). Although Gilroy puts Baraka's term to new use, he extends Baraka's landmark

exploration of a diasporic connection between African legacies and African American cultural realities in *Blues People* (1963).

14. See, e.g., Roberts 1979, 1998, 1999; Baraka 1963, 1967; Gates 1988; and Nketia 1962.

15. Nketia 1962, 11, cited in Wilson 1974, 4.

16. Agawu concurs with this last point. See his section "Inventing Traditional Music" (17–20) in chap. 1 ("Colonialism's Impact") of *Representing African Music* (2003).

17. Summers, interview, Apr. 15, 1998.

18. Wilson 1974 (20), 1983, 1992.

19. These are introduced throughout Wilson's work and are recapped in Wilson 1992 (328–29).

20. *Ostinato*—"a musical figure which recurs unchanged and at the same pitch"—and other common musical terms are used as defined in the *Oxford English Dictionary (OED)*, unless otherwise noted. "Ostinato, *a.* and *n*": *OED*, 2d ed., ed. J. A. Simpson and E. S. C. Weiner (Oxford: Clarendon Press, 1989); *OED Online* (Oxford: Oxford University Press, 2000), http://dictionary.oed.com (accessed Dec. 26, 2003).

21. Wilson 1974, 12–15. For an extended engagement with Wilson's analysis, see Bracket 2000, 108–56. For a similar approach to analysis, this time regarding hip-hop, see Walser 1995. For a similar point about earlier African American music, see Southern 1997, 352–54.

22. See *The Signifying Monkey: A Theory of African American Literary Criticism* (Gates 1988). See especially chap. 1, "A Myth of Origins: Esu-Elegbara and the Signifying Monkey" (3–43).

23. Locations include such widely dispersed areas as Nigeria and Benin (*lucumi*), Brazil (*candomblé*), Cuba (*santería* and *lucumí*), Haiti (*vodou*), and adaptations in the United States. Other authors have commented on this; see, e.g., Jahn 1961, Amira and Cornelius 1992, and Olmos and Paravisini-Gebert 2003.

24. Gates conflates the deity's various names.

25. Although *trope*, according to the *OED*, originally refers to scriptural interpretation, Gates's use refers to the more common "figure of speech." Gates also uses a related word, *tropology*, which refers to a particular kind of moral discourse, "a secondary sense or interpretation of Scripture relating to morals," to describe an interpretive act that both builds upon a traditional moral lesson and stands in for it.

26. Gates considers the trope a guiding principle. Metaphor, allusion, and other forms of indirection hold center stage, since the "black tradition is double-voiced," an oblique reference to W. E. B. DuBois's concept of "double-consciousness" (Gates 1988). But where DuBoisian double-consciousness may be read as a survival strategy for a people constantly appraised by a hostile mainstream, Gates's double-voiced discourse lives in the dual realms of rhetoric and aesthetics. In Signifyin(g), tropes (figures of speech) are used tropologically (i.e., to give instruction by revising and reinterpreting a discourse's commonly understood meaning).

27. "Your momma's so fat that..." "Oh yeah? Well, *your* momma is so poor that . . . ," also known as "capping" or "dissing." See also Samuel Floyd Jr.'s commentary on Signifyin(g). As does Gates, Floyd ties the tradition to sub-Saharan African roots: "Recall the tale in which Esu wears a suit of black and red in order to trick two friends and destroy their relationship" (1995, 94). Gates's version (1988, 32–35) has Esu wearing a hat of black and white halves. In both versions, Esu's troublemaking is motivated by the friends' not seeking Esu's interpretive grace. Esu delivers the moral: "He who does not put Esu first in all his doings has himself to blame if things misfire" (Floyd 1995, 35).

28. See the *Merriam-Webster Online Dictionary* (2004), http://www.m-w.com (accessed Nov. 9, 2004). See also the *OED*. For a useful discussion of facticity in musical interaction, see Brinner 1995, especially his chapter "Towards a Theory of Musical Interaction" 167–207.

29. Floyd 1995, 95.

30. See Ladzekpo's "Foundation Course in African Dance-Drumming." The online course supports his courses on the topic at the University of California, Berkeley, where he is on the faculty.

31. Ladzekpo 1995.

32. Summers, interview, Apr. 15, 1998.

33. Ladzekpo 1995.

34. Summers, interview, Apr. 15, 1998.

35. This is true for reasons of both musical aesthetics and ritual life. Numerous studies have pointed out the syncretic connections in ritual, cosmology, and beliefs among many African and Afro-Caribbean peoples.

36. See, e.g., Dudley 1996, Crook 1982, Roberts 1998, and Maultsby 1990.

37. Figure 4 illustrates two main versions of son clave, one of the most basic patterns in Afro-Cuban musics.

38. Bill Summers, interview, May 17, 1998 (vocal stress emphasized).

39. Summers, interview, Apr. 15, 1988.

40. The bass line was prerecorded, of course. See chap. 5 for an investigation of sound production and recording as a compositional technique on *Head Hunters*.

41. "Groove" is as open to multiple definitions as "swing." For an extensive treatment of jazz musicians' descriptions of groove, see Monson 1996, chap. 2. Monson, foregrounding the collective aspect of groove, discusses it both as a shared sense of the beat, in interaction among players, and as a shared idealization of the beat (a "collectively produced sense of time"), which players may either reinforce or play against (67–68). For our purposes, "groove" refers to a metronomic, regular, (but) internal sense of the beat, reinforced through playing patterns. Under this meaning, it is possible for an individual to play a groove in reference to an understood metronomic pulse. However, in practice, the sense of groove is more strongly felt when two or more musicians are reinforcing each other's sense of that pulse. Hence, Monson's ethnographic research about groove yields descriptions from musicians that highlight musical agreement, interaction, and a sense of mutual well-being (93).

42. Herbie Hancock replicates this guitar-as-percussion sound via clavinet synthesizer keyboard: "I thought maybe if I played the clavinet in a rhythmic way like a guitar, I wouldn't have to use a guitar player" (qtd. in Scott H. Thompson 1992, 4).

43. The instrumental lines enter in the following order: "bass" (00:00), drums (00:10), "guitar" (00:31), synthesizer 1 (00:50), synthesizer 2 (01:09), and the saxophone melody (01:29).

44. Herbie Hancock, qtd. in Scott H. Thompson 1992, 4. Gary Larson's *Down Beat* performance review (1973) notes the percussive orientation to nominally nonpercussion instruments: "Hancock has become an increasingly percussive player since restricting himself to electronic keyboards, offering slapping left-hand chords and short, repetitive right-hand runs."

45. In the slow numbers, "Watermelon Man" and "Vein Melter," Mason's role becomes quite fixed. I discuss this further later.

46. Transcription note: The basic groove cell motive, which Harvey Mason plays in the first measure, is labeled "drum groove cell."

47. By "merely" the timekeeper, I mean the popularly understood role of drummers. Drummers assume the timekeeping role in many cases (Elvin Jones called it the "drummer's primary function" in an interview [Nolan 1977, cited in Porter 1982b]), but not to the exclusion of an embellishing, commentary, or soloistic role.

48. So much so that Hancock composed "Maiden Voyage" with an asymmetrical pattern—based on a clave rhythm—in which he strove to disrupt the backbeat as a given (Hancock, in Sidran 1995, 268).

49. The Hughes poem here is also cited by Samuel Floyd Jr. (1995, 100) as an epigraph to his chapter "The Negro Renaissance: Harlem and Chicago Flowerings" (100–135).

50. See Morgan 1975: "'About 3 years ago 30 to 40 percent of the acts (on Billboard's Top 100 chart) were English acts,' pointed out Barry Griff from A&M records. 'Last year, 30 to 40 percent were Black acts—soul and jazz' (heavily weighted toward soul)" (20). The year before *Head Hunters*, by Morgan's account, English (rock) acts still predominated. Had Hancock been prescient enough to jump on the new "Black acts" bandwagon, he still would have done better, financially, to focus on a pathway to a larger, mainstream segment of the market.

51. The acts whose records Rubinson produced include Cold Blood, Moby Grape, Malo, the Pointer Sisters, and others. See chap. 6.

52. This was coupled with Hancock's attraction to Brown's and Sly's musical vitality and audience popularity.

53. Agawu 2003; Gilroy 1993.

54. SNCC was known after 1967 as the Student National Coordinating Committee.

55. This is actually a sobriquet. Hancock did not legally change his name. This also became the title of his 1970 Warner Brothers album. The group members for this and the next two albums (*Crossings*, 1971, and *Sextant*, 1972) also took on Swahili names: Mchezaji (Buster Williams), Mwile (Bennie Maupin), Pepo

Mtoto (Julian Priester), Mganga (Eddie Henderson), and Jibali (Billy Hart). The exception was Patrick Gleeson, who joined the group in 1972.

56. Atia 2001b. See also Atia 2001a.

57. Gleeson, interview, Mar. 5, 1997 (emphasis added).

58. For discussions of intersections of exoticism-Orientalism-primitivism-Africa as a multifaceted construction of the Other, see Watkins 1994. See Monson 1995 and Floyd 1995 for discussions of these intersections pertaining more specifically to African Americans; see Agawu 2003 directed to representations of Africans.

59. Despite jazz's deep associations with African American musicians and cultural life, jazz's audience demographics were now headed resolutely toward the (predominantly white) upper middle class, as its numbers simultaneously dwindled. The trend has solidified over time; see DeVeaux 1995. For recent, published demographic information on a representative jazz radio station, see the Web site of Radio KUVO (Denver): http://www.kuvo.org/jzdemos.htm.

60. Regardless of who actually listened to funk, it provided a source of black pride and self-identity: "The idea and the importance of funk comes from the depths of black American life, particularly that aspect of black America which never got around to integrating" (Vincent 1996, 6–7).

61. See Palmer 1974.

62. Summers, interview, Apr. 15, 1998.

63. Monson 1994, 303.

Chapter 3

1. "Watermelon Man," on Herbie Hancock's *Takin' Off.*

2. "Watermelon Man," on Mongo Santamaria's *Watermelon Man.*

3. *Populist* here as distinguished from *popular.* In this chapter, *populist* means "seeking to [address or] represent the views of the mass of ordinary people" (*OED*, "populist" a. [n.] 4); *popular* means "designating [aspects of] art and culture whose forms appeal to or are favored by people generally; esp. in popular art, music, song, etc." (*OED*, "popular" a. 5a). *Populist* (populism) refers to a perceived affinity with the masses, and *popular* (popularity) refers to acceptance by them (often measured in sales).

4. Rosenthal 1992, 23.

5. See for example Gioia 1998, 360–69.

6. Gioia 1998, 362.

7. Rosenthal 1992, 10–14. For the notion of hard bop as a reaction against cool jazz, see, e.g., Baraka 1963, 217–22.

8. Porter and Ullman 1993, 257.

9. These recordings have been reissued on compact disk in recent years. "Opus de Funk" (1954) can be heard on Horace Silver, *Horace Silver Trio & Art Blakely & Sabu*, 2004; "The Preacher" (1960) appears on Silver, *The Best of Horace*

Silver, 2004; and "Dis Heah" (respelled as "Dis Here") can be heard on Cannonball Adderley, *The Cannonball Adderley Quintet: Paris, 1960*, 1997.

10. Ake 2002.

11. See DeVeaux 1997; Pond 2003.

12. Baraka 1963, 188, 217 (emphasis in original).

13. Baraka 1963, 217.

14. Baraka 1963, 217, 222.

15. In "The Fetish Character in Music and the Regression of Listening," Adorno takes aim at popular ("light") music in similar ways: "The delight in the moment and the gay façade becomes an excuse for absolving the listener" from contemplation and, ultimately, revolutionary social action. "The listener is converted . . . into the acquiescent purchaser" (1997, 273). Acquiescence resurfaces, as Adorno turns his gaze to the popular ("light") music listener: "The research finding, that among radio listeners, the friends of light music reveal themselves to be depoliticized, is not accidental" (1997, 294).

16. Rosenthal 1992, 43. Rosenthal remarks: "As with Dance's Mainstream, hard bop was wedged in between two styles (bebop and the 'free jazz' of Ornette Coleman, Cecil Taylor, and others) that were easier to define [conceptually, even if they could not be encapsulated aurally] in a few sentences" (1992, 42). The "mainstream" here refers to Depression-era jazz, encompassing but not limited to big band swing. Dance chooses " 'mainstream' for jazz of a 'central' kind, a music not inhibited by any particular instrumental combination, but emphasizing the twin virtues of communicable emotional expression and swing" (qtd. in Rosenthal 1992, 41, from Dance-produced records of the fifties).

17. These factors often get short shrift in jazz histories. Rosenthal's welcome exception surfaces most clearly in his description of Gene Ammons's varied career (1992, 25–77) and in his tracing the stylistic divergences and intersections among Thelonious Monk, Charles Mingus, Miles Davis, and John Coltrane (1992, 132–50).

18. Rosenthal 1992. Baraka argues that by the early sixties, "hard bop, sagging under its own weight, had just about destroyed itself as the means toward a moving form of expression. But there were a few musicians, like saxophonists John Coltrane and Sonny Rollins and drummer Elvin Jones, who had been identified closely with the style, who emerged in the sixties working in new areas, though their way had been prepared to a great extent by the 'funky' style" (1963, 223).

19. Rosenthal 1992, 44–45.

20. Several writers have investigated the attraction of white performers to jazz as a black music (see, e.g., Baraka 1963; Panish 1997, xii–xiv; Roediger 1994, 1–17; Radano 1993, 65–67; Monson 1995; and Kofsky 1970, 104–6). Although they concur about the attraction, they disagree about its motivation. Paraphrasing Roediger, Panish notes that the attraction is both an expression of racist domination and "a paradoxical longing for and rejection of the cultures of other racialized groups"—pointedly African American culture (1997, xiv). Their work interpreted as both homage and appropriation, many white jazz perform-

ers have made lasting contributions to the idiom. It defies logic, however, to suppose either that such performers as Gerry Mulligan, John McLaughlin, Dave Holland, Chick Corea, Joe Pass, Marian McPartland, and many others would enter into the stream of jazz in disregard of jazz's black history or merely to appropriate a successful black musical tradition or that Cal Tjader, for example, would exploit Afro-Cuban styles merely for their exoticism. If that were the case, one might expect to see these performers play with other appropriators, rather than in racially or ethnically mixed ensembles. Indeed, all of these performers are on record identifying jazz as, first, a black music. While the oppositions of longing/rejection have yet to be untangled, they are both present, like faces of Janus.

21. See, e.g., Tirro 1993, 345; Szwed 2000, 195; Radano 1993, 66; Rosenthal 1992, 38–39; Gridley 2003, 186. Gospel and rhythm-and-blues are likewise consistently linked to each other. See Floyd 1995, 175.

22. For the music's relationship to gospel, see Rosenthal 1992, 38–39.

23. Rosenthal 1992, 39.

24. Loza 2002, 203–4.

25. Roberts 1999, 255–56.

26. See Wilson 1974, 1992. In son-based music, the soloists' phrases are called *inspiraciones*.

27. Both of these songs are included on the anthology *Dizzy Gillespie and His Orchestra: 1947–1949*.

28. Gillespie 1979, 484. Gillespie notes: "Africa's children in the Western Hemisphere used different means of expressing their closeness to Mama [rhythm]. The Brazilian Africans created the samba, the West Indians created the calypso, the Cubans created the rhumba and various other rhythms, and my own is blues, spirituals. . . . The spirituals, gospels, and the blues walk side by side; they are married. The blues came before jazz" (Gillespie 1979, 483–84).

29. Art Blakey, qtd. in Hentoff 1956, 10.

30. Compare, e.g., Sonny Rollins's "St. Thomas" (heard on *Saxophone Colossus*), Horace Silver's "Song for My Father" (*Song For My Father*), and Bud Powell's "Un Poco Loco" (*The Amazing Bud Powell, vol. 1*).

31. Hancock, interview, May 27, 1998.

32. Hancock, interview, May 27, 1998 (emphasis added). See also Hancock's interview with Ben Sidran, in Sidran 1995, 261–63.

33. Roberts 1999. Roberts's book title *The Latin Tinge* (1979) adapts Morton's term.

34. Transcription note: The note heads of the habanera rhythmic pattern—corresponding to the "secondary rag" rhythm in ragtime—are indicated with accents.

35. Hancock, interview, May 27, 1998.

36. Hancock, interview, May 27, 1998.

37. With time, Hancock did become attracted to Afro-Caribbean and Brazilian musics of various sorts.

38. Vincent 1996, 5 (emphasis in original). Signifyin(g), in Henry Louis Gates Jr.'s formulation, taps the same "aesthetic of deliberate confusion."

39. Vincent is talking about a shared cultural identity—a "changing same"—rather than inherited, genetic traits.

40. Vincent 1996, 5–6. Vincent refers to Baraka's argument not only that rock 'n' roll emerged as a white appropriation of rhythm-and-blues but also that rock 'n' roll depends on rhythm-and-blues' aesthetics to drive its own. The argument is enlarged by Charles Keil (1966) as an "appropriation-revitalization" cycle and is embodied in the title of Lawrence N. Redd's book *Rock Is Rhythm-and-Blues* (1974). Also see Baraka 1963, 222, 223.

41. Tower of Power's "What Is Hip?" can be heard on *Tower of Power* and "You've Got to Funkifize" can be heard on *Bump City*. The Average White Band's "Pick Up the Pieces" appears on *AWB*, and Wild Cherry's "Play that Funky Music" appears on *Wild Cherry*.

42. Monson 1995, 413. These associations date from at least the twelfth century, according to historian Sander Gilman, whom Monson cites. Such associations intensified, of course, in the post-Reconstruction South. European perceptions of blackness exhibited similar associations, although more approvingly. For a discussion of a related primitive-Oriental-African identity conflation in pre–World War II Europe, see Watkins 1994.

43. Monson 1995, 398.

44. Vincent 1996, 24.

45. Vincent 1996, 24.

46. Vincent 1996, 174–75, (emphasis in original).

47. This refusal evokes fifties hard bop, despite Baraka's claims to the contrary, and it helps to explain Herbie Hancock's attraction to funk over rock.

48. Rock in the seventies has been often and needlessly maligned, especially the streams of glam, progressive, and "stadium" rock that flowered then. Regardless of whether the over-sophistication criticism of rock portrays the music accurately, the attitude was widespread.

49. Vincent 1996, 8 (emphasis in original).

50. Vincent 1996, 8.

51. Vincent 1996, 8.

52. Vincent 1996, 34–36.

53. Vincent 1996, 31.

54. James Brown, qtd. in Vincent 1996, 81–82.

55. The lyrics reinforce the point, not "funky" but "make it funky." See later discussion.

56. Brown writes in his autobiography that "Make It Funky" was particularly important in that it was one of the first recordings arranged by Fred Wesley, who consolidated the funk feeling in Brown's band. See James Brown 1986, 224. "Make It Funky" can be heard on *James Brown: Twenty All Time Greatest Hits*; "Thank You (Fallentinme Be Mice Elf Agin)" can be heard on *Sly and the Family Stone: Greatest Hits*.

57. Counting conventions here and throughout the chapter adhere to those used in Duckworth (2003). Subdivisions are counted as

58. The bass in this song is played by Bootsy Collins's replacement, Fred Thomas.

59. Significantly, such moments of rhythmic clash and resolution are at the heart of Anlo-Ewe music construction (C. K. Ladzekpo, p.c.).

60. Sly and the Family Stone, "Thank You (Falletinme Be Mice Elf Agin)" (1969), on *Sly and the Family Stone: Greatest Hits.*

61. Vincent 1996, 95.

62. Hancock, interview, May 27, 1998 (vocal stress emphasized).

63. Vincent 1996, 95.

64. Transcription note: The *x*-shaped note heads in the bass line indicate a sharply percussive attack ("thumb slap" or "pop").

65. That is, the lowered seventh scale degree (*te*, as opposed to *ti*) to the tonic note (*do*).

66. Berliner 1994; Monson 1996.

67. Hancock, qtd. in Vincent 1996, 144–45.

68. Hancock did not tell me that his interest in funk music only related to dance. Rather, funk also interested him for musical and cultural reasons.

69. Bennie Maupin, interview, Mar. 12, 1998. Vincent (1996, 160–61) describes the August 1972 Wattstax concert as a grand gesture by the Stax label, newly relocated to Los Angeles, "to give back to the community." Eight hours long, it "featured the entire label's entourage," including Isaac Hayes, the Staples Singers, and the newly formed funk group the Bar-Kays.

70. Transcription note: Harvey Mason plays accented hi-hat notes on the main beats of the measure. The eighth-note stems without note heads represent touches, not always audible. They are audible often enough to lead me to place them in the transcription. As a drummer, I often use such "ghost" strokes as timekeeping devices, rather than as expressive notes. Because of the ambiguity of their purpose, again, I include them.

71. In *samba-enredo*, or carnival samba, for example, the sixteenth-note pickup note before each main beat is reinforced across several instruments. On the *repinique* (parade drum), played with a stick (right hand) and open hand (left hand), it's the left-hand dampened hit before the strong, sticked downbeat. In the older *samba de roda*, the *pandeiro* (related to the tambourine) plays the pickup as a brush with the fingers just before landing on the downbeat with the heel of

the hand. Most telling of all, the pickup note coincides in all cases with the dance step; it's the moment of shifting from one foot to another, just before landing solidly on the ground at the downbeat.

72. Dancers in the seventies typically danced at half speed, relative to the music's tempo.

73. Transcription note: To show the interaction among the different tracks performed by Summers, I have aligned them according to the order of each line's entrance. Also, the blown notes on the bottles are all approximate pitches, but close to the pitches indicated. The one exception is the low bottle note (no. 4), which is approximately a quarter-tone sharp of the low C indicated.

74. For comparison with a transcription of the original hindewhu recording, see Wilson 1983. On Summers's introduction to "Watermelon Man" on *Head Hunters*, the tracks begin at 00:00 (first bottle/voice), 00:14 (second bottle/voice), 00:27 (pennywhistle), 00:33 (low bottle), and 00:33 (claps).

75. Summers, interview, Apr. 15, 1998. The recording is Simha Arom and Geneviève Taurelle's *The Music of the Ba-Benzélé Pygmies*.

76. Summers, interview, Apr. 15, 1998. Frequently sampled and reused in recent years in myriad contexts (Feld 1996), the section represents Africa, both evoking and Signifyin(g) on its exotic image. The treatments of Africa as an image of the homeland, in the Africanicity movements of the sixties and later, and of the exotic, in both the modernist idealizations and the ideologies of post-Reconstruction radical racism, are dealt with in Floyd 1995; Watkins 1994; Baraka 1963; and Feld 1996; among many others.

77. The tempos for the prototypical funk tunes described in this chapter also are within this tempo range. Sly and the Family Stone's "Thank You (Falletin Me Be Mice Elf Agin)" is 108 bpm, and James Brown's "Make it Funky" is 99 bpm.

78. An informal perusal from my collection places ballads in this range. Examples include jazz ballads (John Coltrane's "Naima" [60 bpm], Bill Evans's "Blue In Green" [55 bpm]) and fusion jazz ballads (Weather Report's "A Remark You Made" [53 bpm]). Finally, the tempo instruction "ballad" on a lead sheet will cue the musician to play in this same tempo range.

Chapter 4

1. Davis biographer Jack Chambers chronicles the changes: "[Davis] had been a member of the bebop revolution, the leader of the cool reaction to bebop and also, paradoxically, of the neo-bop reaction to cool, and then the leader in the modal reorganization of jazz structure" (1985, 24). After a three-year rejection of Ornette Coleman's "new thing," Davis embraced its freer form and emphasis on collective improvisation, beginning with E.S.P. (1965). The new

approach, in which "the band plays mostly his old repertoire, taking it sometimes to the point of disintegration" (Carr 1998, 204), is beautifully audible in *Complete Live at the Plugged Nickel* (recorded in 1965; issued as a seven-CD boxed set in 1995).

2. Hancock spoke to me of his interest in these composers (interview, June 4, 1999).

3. Radano 1993, 5.

4. Szwed 2000, 80.

5. For historians acknowledging "slipperiness," see, e.g., Szwed 2000; Waksman 2000; DeVeaux 1997.

6. Lewis Porter and Michael Ullman have called the notion of hard bop as a reaction to cool jazz into question (1993, 257). Gioia (1998) argues convincingly against the conflation of cool and West Coast jazz.

7. Baraka 1963, 222.

8. Baraka 1963, 224.

9. Rosenthal 1992, 44–45. See also chap. 3.

10. Baraka 1963, 223.

11. See also Baraka, 43, 45, 63.

12. For the traditional materials of melody, see Powers 1986, 482.

13. Wilson 1992.

14. Tapping directly into expression is a long-standing goal in Western music, codified as early as the "Doctrine of the Affections" in the early seventeenth century and theorized in the nineteenth century in terms of the sublime. By *expression* I mean the artistic manifestation of a personally felt but culturally inflected complex of emotion, idea, and identity.

15. An analogy to abstract expressionism is relevant here. Not only are the means and goals of the expressive modes similar, but if Ornette Coleman's *Free Jazz* can be heard as an extension of these techniques—as I will demonstrate later—then the reproduction of Jackson Pollack's abstract expressionist painting on the album's cover makes perfect sense.

16. I stress here that rhythm in jazz is necessarily combined with timbral heterogeneity. A rhythm could certainly be played on a single instrument with a single "sound"; what makes it interesting is the range of timbres to which these rhythms are assigned and juxtaposed.

17. Miles Davis, qtd. in Hentoff 1961a, 208 (emphasis added).

18. "My Favorite Things" is available on the anthology *The Best of John Coltrane: His Greatest Years*. See Budds 1990, 49; Porter 1998, 181–84.

19. Coltrane acknowledged Eric Dolphy as a strong influence in this change (DeMichael 1962).

20. Both quotations are Coltrane, qtd. in Quersin 1963, cited in Woideck 1998, 12. For an extended discussion of Coltrane's approach to modal jazz playing, see Porter 1998, 158–70.

21. The title of "Alabama" is assumed to be a veiled reference to the general resistance to integration in this southern state. Although the song is generally assumed to be a reaction to a racially motivated bombing in a black Selma,

Alabama, church in which three girls were killed, Coltrane demurred when asked about it (Williams 1997, 85). Lewis Porter (1997, 331 n. 11) casts doubt on the connection. "Alabama" is available on *The Best of John Coltrane: His Greatest Years.*

22. With this came a freer concept of meter: in many cases, the music was nonmetrical. Although the trend gained importance during the sixties, the trend to modalism had surfaced earlier and had been theorized by George Russell (1959).

23. See, e.g., Jost 1981; Budds 1990; Litweiler 1984; and Radano 1993. All make references to the interplay among the elements described herein and their adoption by Davis and Coltrane.

24. Jost 1981, 23.

25. To this list of techniques should be added the Davis and Coltrane groups' use of quartal harmonies: "The use of quartal harmony is, perhaps, most evident in the accompaniments and solos of jazz pianists, for example, McCoy Tyner, Bill Evans, and Herbie Hancock" (Budds 1990, 53).

26. Jost 1981, 48, 59–60, 59.

27. The smallest melodic component could most appropriately be called a "gesture," as opposed to a motive. "Motive" in melody is inescapably tied to the notion of identifiable, discrete tones. Elsewhere, John Litweiler (1984, 38) refers to small melodic components as "cell motives," recalling serial compositional technique during the same period. I prefer "gesture" because of its applicability to the myriad forms such cells might take, including such things as nonmelodic squeals, rhythmic mottoes, register shifts, and many more; and these materials transcend motive. Also, while aspects of free jazz are related to developments in Western experimental music of the time (as well as earlier), using the terms of academic music ("cell motive") to discuss developments in free jazz tends to limit discussion of the latter as *merely* a response to the former, which is not the case.

28. Baraka 1997, 228.

29. "Ornette Coleman claimed to base his improvisations on his 'impression' of a piece of music, not on the details of its harmonic or metric structure" (Budds 1990, 82).

30. Chambers 1985, 68. Jack Chambers's book *Milestones: The Music and Times of Miles Davis* was published in two volumes. Volume 1, published by Beech Tree Books in 1983, is *Milestones 1: The Music and Times of Miles Davis to 1960*; volume 2, published in 1985 by Beech Tree, is *Milestones 2: The Music and Times of Miles Davis since 1960*. The two volumes have been republished as a single volume by Quill (1989), with the two volumes' original page numbers intact. To avoid confusion, references in the text to *Milestones* point to the two original copyright dates.

31. Gridley 2003, 291. See also Carr 1998, 134–36 and Chambers 1985, 68, 70.

32. Chambers 1985, 70; Hancock, interview, June 4, 1999.

33. Chambers 1985, 70.

34. Sidran 1995, 264–66.
35. Hancock, in Sidran 1995, 265.
36. Hancock, in Sidran 1995, 265.
37. Hancock, in Sidran 1995, 265–66.
38. Miles Davis with Troupe 1989, 275.
39. Chambers 1985, 88–89.
40. McCoy Tyner, in Sidran 1995, 234 (emphasis in original).
41. Here, Porter (1998) refers to Barry Kernfeld's 1981 doctoral dissertation.
42. Porter 1998, 159–62, 222–23.
43. Tyner in Sidran 1995, 233.
44. Hancock, interview, June 4, 1999.
45. For an extended discussion of the role of post-production techniques in *Head Hunters*, see chap. 5.
46. Miles Davis with Troupe 1989, 277 (emphasis added). Davis's comment that he was really playing "about four" notes is unexplained, but I take it to mean that Williams had told Davis of Coleman's penchant for multiple tone centers, with the attendant expansion of destinations for resolution of any particular note.
47. See Floyd 1995; Gilroy 1993.
48. Indeed, the close similarities of much white rock 'n' roll to black rhythm-and-blues suggest appropriation of the black form, a frequent subject of commentary and critique, to say the least.
49. On this point, references abound. There are many differing accounts of how racial and class separations have occurred and what they mean, but there is unity in identifying these separations. See, e.g., George Lipsitz's appraisal of Simon Frith, Lawrence Grossberg, and E. Ann Kaplan (1990, 105–7). See also Kamin 1975.
50. Chambers 1985, 128 (emphasis added). The song "Stuff" is from *Miles in the Sky* (1968).
51. See, e.g., Stanley Crouch's critique "Play the Right Thing" (1996).
52. Chambers 1985, 173.
53. This is one of the bases of my argument for the term *fusion jazz*, outlined in chap. 1. Because of the multiple interpretations available for the many elements of the album, the label *jazz-rock* is not appropriate.
54. Hall 1974, 13. *Musique concrète* (lit. concrete music) developed as an avant-garde compositional technique in the fifties and sixties. The technique involves splicing snippets of recordings—any recordings, as "found" objects—and recontextualizing them, to create a new aural statement.
55. Chambers 1985, 151.
56. See, e.g., Crouch 1996.
57. Griffiths 1983a, 1750–51.
58. The song was released in 1974 on the *Big Fun* album. In 1998, Columbia/Legacy released *Complete Bitches Brew Sessions (August 1969–February 1970)*, which does include "Great Expectations."
59. Nicholson 1998, 184.

60. In fact, Hancock continued to record as a sideman, including albums by Ron Carter, Phil Woods, Paul Desmond, Luis Gasca, Milton Nascimento, Joni Mitchell, and many others. The thrust of his career, though, had now changed to leadership. As he told Julie Coryell, his album *Speak Like a Child* (1968) made up his mind: "When I did that record I knew that was the sound I wanted for my own band. That's when I knew I was going to switch from Miles" (Coryell and Friedman 1978, 148).

61. See the preface.

62. A side note: Henderson's stepfather at one time was one of Miles Davis's physicians.

63. Gleeson, interview, Mar. 5, 1997.

64. Appleton 1986, 186.

65. Gleeson, interview, Mar. 5, 1997. Hancock often praised Gleeson's contribution. Typical is his interview in Coryell and Friedman 1978, in which Hancock recalls this first encounter with Gleeson and Gleeson's subsequent adjustment to playing the synthesizer in real-time improvisation: "It just killed me. It just blew me away. Right after that I hired him. It was so funny because the synthesizer was still such a new instrument. It was only used on recordings; there was no precedent for him to follow. . . . He was like a pioneer playing the live synthesizer, and after that, when I broke up the band, and I was doing the *Head Hunters* album, I decided I was going to try a synthesizer myself" (162).

66. Gleeson, interview, Mar. 5, 1997.

67. Gleeson, interview, Mar. 5, 1997.

68. Summers, interview, Apr. 15, 1998.

69. Hancock had studied at Grinnell College, majoring first in engineering before switching to music.

70. David Rubinson (p.c., Nov. 4, 1997) characterizes the reconciliation of production with post-production even more explicitly: "If the musician is splicing, then it is simply a continuation of the creative process. Composing is, as Wayne [Shorter] says, just improvisation slowed down. So—who does it is crucial too."

71. Gleeson, interview, Mar. 5, 1997 (vocal stress emphasized). Gleeson had evidently listened to one of the two suites that Ravel extracted from his largest score, an enormous ballet work that occupied him for the better part of three years. He did not yet realize that Ravel had composed two suites (1911 and 1913) that included reorchestrations of his ballet symphony in three parts, of the same name (1909–12). Hancock's "complete" refers to the ballet symphony. The second suite, the one Gleeson was originally listening to, can be heard on Geoffrey Simon, *Maurice Ravel, vol. 2*; the ballet symphony (the "Complete" version Hancock referred to) can be heard on Kent Nagano, *Daphnis et Chloë.*

72. Patrick Gleeson, p.c., Oct. 18, 2004.

73. Hancock, interview, June 4, 1999.

74. Gleeson, interview, Mar. 5, 1997.

75. Gleeson, interview, Mar. 5, 1997.

76. Gleeson, interview, Mar. 5, 1997.

77. See the illustrations.

78. The insistence of the drum cadence is enhanced by the dry sound of the drums themselves. See chap. 5.

79. This is slightly varied in "Vein Melter." The tonic pedal becomes an oscillation do-te-do which is not cadential but sound as an articulation of the tonic. This oscillation could be thought of as a radically slowed trill. There is an absence of harmonic weight taking us away from *do*, implying a tonic pedal throughout.

80. Maupin, interview, Mar. 12, 1998; Hancock, interview, May 27, 1998.

81. Maupin appears with Brown on *Afternoon of a Georgia Faun* (ECM 1004).

82. Horace Silver: *Serenade to a Soul Sister* and *You Gotta Take a Little Love;* Lee Morgan: *Caramba* and *Live At the Lighthouse;* Woody Shaw: *Blackstone Legacy.*

83. Maupin, qtd. in Townley 1975, 18.

84. Miles Davis at first eyed the rise of Ornette Coleman (as well as Don Cherry) somewhat suspiciously: "I didn't like what they were playing, especially Don Cherry on that little horn he had. It just looked to me like he was playing a lot of notes and looking real serious, and people went for that because people will go for anything they don't understand if it's got enough hype" (Miles Davis with Troupe 1989, 251). Davis's view was changeable, however. Elsewhere he says, "What was good about Ornette Coleman was that his musical ideas and his melodies were independent of styles, and being independent like that would make you appear to be creating spontaneously" (Miles Davis with Troupe 1989, 277).

85. Baraka 1997, 224 (emphasis in original).

86. According to Maupin: "Miles was considering hiring me [at the time of *Bitches Brew*] but that never happened. However, I did make *Bitches Brew* and I'm sure that exposure helped me" (qtd. in Meadow 1973, 16).

87. Chambers 1985, 173.

88. "Right Off," recorded shortly after the *Bitches Brew* sessions and released on *A Tribute to Jack Johnson* (1970), exemplifies Davis's attention to free, collective improvisation. The legendary track began as a between-takes jam, captured on tape (Nicholson 1998, 117).

89. Gleason 1970.

90. The solo is the first of the piece, beginning at 2:17.

91. Wilson came to Berkeley in 1970, Ladzekpo in 1972.

92. Summers, interview, Apr. 15, 1998.

93. Summers, interview, Apr. 15, 1998. "T.A." stands for "teaching assistant." Summers was filling the teaching assistant role, although he was an undergraduate.

94. Summers, interview, Apr. 15, 1998.

95. Others contributed as well, such as David Rubinson and Billy Hart. Hancock recalled that Rubinson, his manager at the time, located Jackson, presenting him as an intelligent, quick-reflexed bass player, primarily playing funk yet with jazz sensibilities as well (Hancock, interview, June 4, 1999). I later discuss Billy Hart's contribution along these lines.

96. For the association of drummers with the exotic, see Watkins 1994.

97. By the next album, *Thrust*, this was no longer the case. Summers's percussion interaction with drummer Mike Clark and Jackson was far more integral to the musical structure.

98. "The guitar was extremely popular back then, but I had heard about the clavinet. It had a guitar-like sound, like a cross between a guitar and a harpsichord. I thought maybe if I played the clavinet in a rhythmic way like a guitar, I wouldn't have to use a guitar player" (Hancock, qtd. in Scott Thompson 1992).

99. Nicholson 1998, 195–96.

100. His abilities in capturing an R&B groove would contribute greatly to the success not only of *Head Hunters* but also of George Benson's "This Masquerade" (*Breezin'*) two years later.

101. Hancock, qtd. in Scott Thompson 1992.

102. Hancock, interview, June 4, 1999.

Chapter 5

1. For concise but helpful glossaries of common effects terms, see Zak 2001, 221–24, and George Martin 1983, 333–40.

2. Early music scholar John Hsu told me a perhaps apocryphal anecdote along these lines, involving concert pianist Glenn Gould. Gould, upon releasing a heavily edited piano concerto recording, was asked rhetorically by a conductor if he would like to be able to play as well as his record (John Hsu, p.c.).

3. In addition to the techniques of recording, producers were adept at enhancing a less than experienced featured artist's efforts by contracting accomplished studio musicians and arrangers who brought with them proven and recognizable styling.

4. Frith 1983, 35.

5. One "meter" exception here is the string "solo" section of "Within You, Without You," in which the metric pattern is a six-beat *tala*.

6. The lyrical content of the songs is another point of sweeping change. I omit a full discussion of lyrics here.

7. For an illuminating discussion of these techniques and the aesthetics of timbre in rock, see Lowenthal 1983, 196–204. The "Special Combinations" section of Lowenthal's essay (202–3) is particularly instructive. One example of the attention to timbre Lowenthal discusses is Paul McCartney's insistence, in "Yesterday," that the string quartet play *senza vibrato*. For a book description of the Beatles' attention to timbre in *Sgt. Pepper*, see George Martin with William Pearson 1995.

8. I mention the Beatles here to illustrate a general explosion of investigations of timbre at the time, but other equally strong examples spring to mind, prominently including Jimi Hendrix.

9. A typical structure is twelve-bar blues, which of course is shared with jazz, rhythm-and-blues, gospel, and country music. Another is AABA form (known as thirty-two-bar song form); examples abound in every historical peri-

od, and I cite for illustration the Beatles' "All My Loving," the Rolling Stones' "Sympathy for the Devil," and the Miracles' "(You'd Better) Shop Around." To be sure, traditional song structures are not exclusively a rock feature; the extensive use of "standard" tunes in jazz indicates a reverence for traditional forms. However, jazz pieces composed since the fifties are more likely to diverge from traditional forms than are rock pieces of the same vintage.

10. This mismatch is paralleled in an analogy once related to me concerning the humor in early Hollywood films. In many of the Mack Sennett films of the twenties, humor is tied to the element of surprise: the pratfall is an excellent example of this. In contrast, the comic success of the Laurel and Hardy films of the thirties depends upon the buildup to the inevitable: we *know* Hardy's blow is coming, and we likewise *know* Laurel will innocently and serendipitously cause the blow to backfire. Just so, playing to satisfy the expectation (rhythm-and-blues) instead of going for the surprise (bebop and later styles) should not be considered a flaw so much as an aesthetic choice.

11. Kamin 1975, 286.

12. The soloist was also recorded simultaneously, but often on a separate track. I will explain this development later.

13. *Sel-sync* is the industrial term for the process many musicians call *overdubbing*, which will be discussed later in the chapter.

14. Although Ben Sidran has not laid claim to identifying this dialectic, I became aware of it through him (Sidran 1995).

15. Regarding recording changes, cf. Keepnews 1988 and Zak 2001.

16. My ability to discuss the current point is due in large part to a series of illuminating conversations and correspondence with Rubinson, to whom I am grateful.

17. Rubinson, interview, Jan. 11, 1998. Rudy Van Gelder was the engineer and owner of Van Gelder Studio. Rubinson is talking about a hypothetical case, rather than a specific occurrence.

18. Rubinson, p.c., Nov. 4, 1997.

19. Gleeson introduced Hancock to the synthesizer (see chap. 4).

20. Gleeson, interview, Mar. 5, 1997.

21. Gleeson, interview, Mar. 5, 1997.

22. Gleeson, interview, Feb. 27, 1997.

23. Gleeson, interview, Mar. 5, 1997 (emphasis added).

24. Maupin, interview, Mar. 12, 1998.

25. Maupin, interview, Mar. 12, 1998.

26. Gleeson, interview, Mar. 5, 1997.

27. Summers, interview, Apr. 15, 1998.

28. "EQ" stands for emphasizing or deemphasizing frequency ranges, a fine-control version of the "tone" knob on a radio or amplifier.

29. Today's synthesizers are mainly digital, driven through interpretive computer software and connected directly to the recording engineer's soundboard. At the time of *Head Hunters*, synthesizers were exclusively analog. In both cases, because they have no acoustic properties of their own and cannot be

miked, they are plugged directly into the sound board, and this component of the sound is therefore largely under the control of the synthesist.

30. Rubinson, p.c., Nov. 4, 1997. See also Avalon 1998 and Lowenthal 1983. Lowenthal provides an excellent overview of this process, in more detail than can be provided here. Avalon discusses "tricks of the trade" beyond the array of technological tools.

31. My thanks to Lewis Porter (p.c., Oct. 13, 2004), who tells me that stereophonic sound had a predecessor: binaural sound, which was released to the public in 1933 but failed to catch on "due to complicated playback requirements."

32. Rubinson, p.c., Nov. 4, 1997. Rubinson's fastidious use of the term is correct. Despite this, many musicians and industry people continue to refer to the sel-sync process as overdubbing. Rubinson also refers here to Les Paul's tape-based innovations, which became highly influential in the recording industry. See Zak 2001 and Waksman 2000. Earlier, in 1941, Sidney Bechet had experimented with a similar multitrack technique, "except that he was recording himself back on a third 78 r.p.m. cutting turntable" used for creating record masters (Porter, p.c., Oct. 13, 2004). Regarding Rubinson's mention of the three-track machine, Ampex Corporation introduced its commercial three-track tape recorder in 1960.

33. Some of the work for *Head Hunters* was done this way, in a home studio called Funky Jack's.

34. Fink 1996, 58–59.

35. Perhaps the classic example from the rock repertoire of this shared control is the characterization of producer George Martin as the "fifth Beatle." An example of the integration of production techniques as part of the creative process is retold by Martin regarding the recording of "Being for the Benefit of Mr. Kite" from the Beatles' *Sgt. Pepper* album. According to him, the sound collage of calliope music on the recording was made from various old recordings of steam organs, cut into fifteen-inch strips, thrown into the air, and respliced in the random order in which they were gathered. Further exemplifying this was Paul McCartney's intention to electronically alter nearly every sound on the album (1983, 270).

36. Cole 1971. David Rubinson, later in this chapter, contradicts Cole.

37. Rubinson, p.c., Nov. 4, 1997.

38. Macero, qtd. in Hall 1974, 15.

39. Maupin, interview, Mar. 12, 1998.

40. Maupin, interview, Mar. 12, 1998.

41. Maupin, interview, Mar. 12, 1998.

42. Rubinson, p.c., Nov. 4, 1997.

43. Gleeson, interview, Mar. 5, 1997 (emphasis added).

44. Rubinson, p.c., Nov. 4, 1997 (original emphasis).

45. Zawinul, interview, Aug. 30, 1997. "Pharoah's Dance" is heard on the *Bitches Brew* album. A longer version of the piece can be heard on *The Complete Bitches Brew Sessions*. The seventy-minute reissue Zawinul mentions is still unreleased.

46. Chambers 1985, 171.

47. Rubinson, p.c., Nov. 4, 1997.

48. Rubinson, p.c., Nov. 4, 1997.

49. Alfonso 1992.

50. Hancock, interview, May 27, 1998. Regarding Hancock's mention of a click track, he may have misremembered this. The tempo increases nearly 20 percent over the course of the recording, which would not have happened if he had played to a click track.

51. Summers, interview, Apr. 15, 1998.

52. Maupin, interview, Mar. 12, 1998. By now the group was shuttling between rehearsals in Los Angeles and recording in San Francisco. The tape recordings Maupin refers to here are tapes of rehearsals, used for capturing improvised ideas.

53. Maupin, interview, Mar. 12, 1998. Maupin's reference is to Marin County, the county immediately north of the Golden Gate Bridge, comprised of an upscale collection of towns and unincorporated neighborhoods. The club Maupin mentions, now defunct, was in the Marin County town of San Anselmo. I thank Terry Frazier for this information. David Rubinson recalls the club as the Inn of the Beginning, in the nearby town of Cotati (p.c., May 12, 2000).

54. Hancock, interview, May 27, 1998 (emphasis added). The exception to his last statement, as he mentioned a beat later, was the bass clavinet groove on "Chameleon."

55. Maupin, interview, Mar. 12, 1998 (emphasis added).

56. Maupin, interview, Mar. 12, 1998; Fred Catero, interview, Apr. 7, 1998; Bill Summers, interview, Apr. 15, 1998.

57. Wilson 1992, 331; Monson 1996, 89.

58. Catero, interview, Apr. 7, 1998.

59. Maupin, interview, Mar. 12, 1998 (vocal stress emphasized).

60. Maupin, interview, Mar. 12, 1998 (emphasis added).

61. Carr 1998, 238–39.

62. Carr 1998, 237.

63. For a fuller description of Signifyin(g) in jazz, see chap. 2.

64. The sound is known alternatively as "dead" or "dry."

65. Catero, interview, Apr. 7, 1998.

66. See chap. 3 for a discussion of funk aesthetics.

67. Rubinson, interview, Jan. 11, 1998 (emphasis added). The context of the conversation centered on how fusion jazz required musicians to negotiate white and black identity.

68. Catero, interview, Apr. 7, 1998.

69. Catero, interview, Apr. 7, 1998. Note that Williams *could* tune his drums to be played melodically, because, as a jazz drummer, he tuned his drums to incorporate resonance—"ring." By "EQ," Catero refers to the degree of relative emphasis placed on the bass and treble frequencies of the sound the microphone picks up.

70. Gleeson, interview, Feb. 28, 1997.

71. Hancock, interview, May 27, 1998.

72. "Miles is the kind of guy who knows about everything. He knows who's doing it, because he'll go out and listen. I had a gig . . . in a place called Sugar Ray's . . . and it just happened that one night we were in there and in walked Miles. . . . I don't think my playing made any kind of impression on him. But later, when I used to work with McCoy Tyner a lot, doing Slug's, he used to come down a lot and listen. I can remember seeing Miles as many as two or three times in one week" (Maupin, in Townley 1975, 18).

73. Maupin, interview, Mar. 12, 1998.

74. Maupin, interview, Mar. 12, 1998 (vocal stress emphasized).

75. Hancock was aided in his search for personnel by Bill Summers and David Rubinson (see chap. 4).

76. Gleeson, interview, Mar. 5, 1997. In a separate interview (June 4, 1999), Hancock confirmed this to me. Harvey Mason was the drummer on the *Head Hunters* album, but due to his career as a recording sideman in Los Angeles, he did not remain with the group. Mike Clark joined for the album's promotional tour and remained in the Headhunters group for nearly ten years. When the Headhunters re-formed for a reunion album and tour in 1998, Clark was the drummer.

77. Brinner 1995, 311–12.

78. Ben Sidran, p.c.

Chapter 6

1. See Frank Tirro (1993, 416); Mervyn Cooke (1999, 174); and Mark Gridley (2003, 293), to name only a few. An exception is Henry Martin's *Jazz: The First 100 Years* (2001, 304–9), which acknowledges the album's sales success but treats it primarily in terms of style history.

2. Nicholson 1998, 191–92. Those "occasional acoustic excursions" included the 1977 *V.S.O.P.: The Quintet*. For the sales history of *Head Hunters*, see the preface.

3. Whitburn 2001, 361.

4. Berendt 1975, 39, 40.

5. Underwood 1975, 30.

6. This is not mere complaining. A recent survey by the National Education Association establishes factually what has long been known intuitively, that jazz musicians are chronically underpaid as a body (Heckathorn and Jeffri 2001).

7. For examples of the first, see Schuller 1979; Baraka 1963, 206. For the second, see Baraka 1963, 225–27; Radano 1993, 180–237.

8. DeVeaux 1991; Ake 2002, 48–49. Cf. Gridley 2003, 7–8.

9. Despite jazz's much lauded rhythmic vitality, rhythmic approaches to jazz gained barely a mention. Other important aspects of jazz playing suffered exclusion: despite the importance of "quoting," developing a stock of melodic

figures, and developing one's own timbral signature (one's "sound")—all considered essential to the improvisational art—theory texts relentlessly ignored these components. This orientation persists; the chapter titles in Kenneth Stanton's promisingly titled *Jazz Theory: A Creative Approach* (1982) are typical: "Minor Keys in Jazz," "Adding Color to the Chords: Unresolved Tensions," "New Ways to Go to the Tonic," "Substitute Chords," "Generalization of Cadence," "Diatonic Jazz Harmony," and "All about Diminished Seventh Chords," along with three chapters on practical uses of these harmonic topics. A more recent, but typical, example is Bert Ligon's *Jazz Theory Resources: Tonal, Harmonic, Melodic, and Rhythmic Organization of Jazz* (2001).

10. Nicholson 1998, 198.

11. Among other causes for fusionists' shift from "high art" to populist accessibility, Nicholson points to the rising impact of "pop" religion—for example, Chick Corea's conversion to the Church of Scientology and John McLaughlin's discipleship to Sri Chinmoy. Regarding Hancock, Nicholson says: "It's interesting to note a parallel to Herbie Hancock's career here. Hancock was playing an esoteric kind of music but when he became involved in an alternative philosophy—in his case Nichiren Shoshu Buddhism—he suddenly began playing a more accessible, commercial type of music" (1998, 205 n. 45).

12. David Rosenthal, in his book on hard bop of the fifties and sixties, recalls from his youth "those glorious jukeboxes where Jimmy Smith, Miles Davis, and Cannonball Adderley rubbed shoulders with Martha Reeves, the Impressions, Muddy Waters, and Howlin' Wolf." He continues, "All this occurred before, as Andrew Hill put it, 'the music got separated'" (1992, 68). Confirmation comes from the *Billboard* rhythm-and-blues sales charts of the fifties, which included recordings by such diverse artists as Louis Jordan, Don Byas, Sarah Vaughan, Charlie Parker, Howlin' Wolf, the Platters, Jimmy Smith, Miles Davis, and Stan Kenton.

13. Blumenthal 1994, 4–5. *Hey, Hey, Hey, It's Fat Albert*, animated film, dir. Ken Mundie, prod. Lou Scheimer (Los Angeles: Filmation Assoc., 1969); original broadcast (NBC) Nov. 12, 1969.

14. Blumenthal 1994, 4–5 (emphasis added).

15. Rubinson, interview, Jan. 11, 1998.

16. Rubinson, interview, Jan. 11, 1998; Bruce Lundvall, interview, Feb. 4, 2000.

17. I describe the role of the *independent* producer here because the formalized role set out in such a producer's contract makes his or her duties more clearly defined, and therefore more easily described, than the role of an in-house producer, which may be less easily articulated. Also, *Head Hunters* was produced by an independent producer, David Rubinson.

18. Fink 1996, 59. See also descriptions of these roles in Keepnews 1988, especially his chapter "What I Do for a Living" (156–87), and Avalon 1998.

19. Rubinson, interview, Jan. 11, 1998. Rubinson's projects immediately previous included best sellers at the time as well as others that have since come to be regarded as classics. Among these were eponymous first albums by Cold

Blood (1969; number 23 on the *Billboard* Pop Album chart) and Moby Grape (1967; number 24), as well as Tower of Power's *East Bay Grease* (1970; number 106), Taj Mahal's *Giant Step/De Old Folks At Home* (1969; number 85), and the Chambers Brothers' *Time Has Come* (1967; number 4). Rubinson produced other hit albums during the early seventies, including debut albums by Malo (1972; number 14) and the Pointer Sisters (1973; number 13). He recorded *Santana Live at the Fillmore* in 1968, but this was not released until 1998. Rubinson produced his hit commercial Santana production *Amigos* (number 10) in 1976.

Mwandishi, released Dec. 16, 1970, rose to number 16 on the *Billboard* Jazz Album chart but did not make the Pop Album chart at all. Neither had the earlier *Fat Albert Rotunda*, which crested at number 14 on the Jazz Album chart. The executives' disappointment in *Mwandishi* evidently rested on their assumption that, with *Fat Albert Rotunda*, Hancock's commercial appeal was aborning, not yet realized. *Mwandishi* seemed to prove them wrong.

Bitches Brew eventually went on to claim the number 1 Jazz Album chart position and number 35 on the Pop Album chart. Rubinson did not claim that Hancock's playing was on the tape, but the album did capture significant aspects of Hancock's music at the time and was clearly selling well. Hancock *did* record with the *Bitches Brew* personnel on material that was released later (*Big Fun*, 1969; issued 1974). He played with Davis, Steve Grossman, Maupin, John McLaughlin, Chick Corea, Harvey Brooks, Billy Cobham, and Airto Moreira—who all played on *Bitches Brew*—and with Khalil Balakrishna and Bihari Sharma, on sitar and tamboura. The recording was done in Nov. 1969, while *Bitches Brew* was still being edited, and, not surprisingly, is strikingly similar to *Bitches Brew* (Chambers 1985, 194).

20. Throughout my interview with Lundvall (Feb. 4, 2000), he characterized Hancock's (and others') post-bebop recordings as "acoustic jazz," a standard term in the recording industry. This industry designation is thus tied to the means of production—"acoustic" or "electric"—rather than to musical characteristics. I will point to the significance of this later.

Sextant, which rose to number 3 on the Jazz Album chart and number 176 on the Top LPs chart, outperformed both *Mwandishi* and *Crossings*, neither of which "charted" as a pop album at all. However, Lundvall's recollection suggests the label's anxiety over the shortfall between *Sextant*'s production costs and its sales.

21. Lundvall, interview, Feb. 4, 2000.

22. Lundvall, interview, Feb. 4, 2000.

23. Azteca, *Azteca* (1972). The group included members of Santana and featured Neal Schon (soon of Journey fame); Coke Escovedo; locally famous saxophonist Mel Martin; and Lenny White, whose drumming grounded both *Bitches Brew* and Chick Corea's band, Return to Forever. The album included the hit song "Suavacito."

24. By way of illustration, Blue Note's fourteen-disk retrospective anthology, *The Blue Note Years: Sixtieth Anniversary Box Set: 1939–1999*, which pointedly includes its "best" recordings (rather than its "best-selling"), includes the US-3 acid jazz hit "Cantaloop/Flip Fantasia." Jazz "purists" beware.

25. This infrastructure shifted at the twentieth century's end, with the increasing importance of the Internet, which is outside the scope of this book.

26. Clark 1983, 302–5.

27. For a discussion of the "battle of the speeds," see Garofalo 2005.

28. "Blue 7" can be heard on Sonny Rollins, *Jazz Colossus*, reissued 2000; "Well, You Needn't" can be heard on Thelonious Monk, *Genius of Modern Music, vol. 1*, reissued 2004.

29. See Gendron 1996. See also Monson 1995 and Mailer 1999.

30. Tours and recordings were often more or less equal money makers, each adding to the other. Commenting on trade journal ads, jazz historian Chris Albertson, who worked as a disk jockey in the early sixties, told me, "I expect these ads helped artists get booking that, in turn, sold records, but I don't know how one would have determined sales sparked by them" (p.c., Aug. 5, 2003).

31. See, e.g., ads published in *Down Beat:* for Fender Rhodes electric pianos on Nov. 8, 1973 (25–28), and Jan. 17, 1974 (39), and for Bose speakers on May 9, 1974 (7). The ads featured Herbie Hancock around the time of the *Head Hunters* release without specifically mentioning the album. CBS owned both Fender Rhodes and Columbia Records at the time.

32. This is because labels tended to promote their "sound" personalities, hence a Blue Note, Prestige, Riverside, or CTI recording could be identified as much by its sound qualities and style direction as by the artists on a particular recording. The only *Down Beat* ad in the first half of 1974 specifically mentioning *Head Hunters* featured it as part of an overall grouping. The headline "Fourmidable" (*Down Beat*, May 9, 1974, 7) linked *Solar Wind* (Ramsey Lewis), *Big Fun* (Miles Davis), and *Mysterious Traveler* (Weather Report) with *Head Hunters.*

33. Chris Albertson pointedly rejects the notion of playlists in jazz radio, saying: "I was never given a playlist nor was I told what to play. The local record distributor would drop by the station and do his best to get us interested in certain albums, but no pressure . . . We were occasionally wined and dined. Still, we played what we wanted to play" (p.c., Aug. 5, 2003).

34. Rubinson, interview, Jan. 11, 1998.

35. Rubinson, interview, Jan. 11, 1998.

36. Rubinson, interview, Jan. 11, 1998. The *OED* dates the term *rack-jobbing* to a 1959 mention in the *Economist:* "The supplier takes responsibility for the stock and display from week to week, the retailer simply provides the space, and accepts a lower margin on the goods that are sold" (Dec. 12, 1959). Rack-jobbing is not specific to records; different types of mass-merchandized commodities are serviced by rack-jobbers who specialize in them.

37. The records that did attract the rack-jobbers' notice tended to be Cool- or West Coast–style jazz, exemplified in the Brubeck and Guaraldi examples. "Take Five" can be heard on Brubeck's *Time Out* album (1959, reissued 2004) and "Cast Your Fate to the Wind" can be heard on Guaraldi's *Jazz Impressions of Black Orfeus* (1962, reissued 1995).

38. Slaughter is profiled in George 1988, 133–35.

39. Vernon Slaughter, interview, Feb. 11, 2000.

40. Slaughter, interview, Feb. 11, 2000.

41. Slaughter, interview, Feb. 11, 2000 (emphasis added).

42. Slaughter, interview, Feb. 11, 2000.

43. Slaughter, interview, Feb. 11, 2000. "Fading" is a technique of segueing from the end of one song to the beginning of another by gradually turning down the volume of the former while turning up the volume of the latter.

44. Slaughter, interview, Feb. 11, 2000.

45. When stations broadcast at a lower wattage, their broadcast area was smaller, and the signal, although of high quality, was relatively weak.

46. In his memoir, *FM: The Rise and Fall of Rock Radio*, free-form deejay and program director Richard Neer recalls, "The new rock music had transcended the pop music of the past's sole purpose to entertain and had become important and culturally essential and influential" (2001, viii–ix).

47. In my hometown, Sacramento, California, the local free-form station at the time was KZAP. Regular programming included a news show, hosted by Carey "Captain Carrot" Nosler, devoted to unprocessed foods and a lifestyle that promoted holistic health, and the station also served as a clearinghouse of information and commentary promoting political activism against the Vietnam War. Playlists included entire albums, an innovation for the time. KZAP first exposed me to *Head Hunters*, as well as to the Allman Brothers' *Eat A Peach*, the Mahavishnu Orchestra's *Birds of Fire*, Phoebe Snow's debut album, War's *All Day Music*, Sly and the Family Stone's *Stand!* and music by Les McCann, Tower of Power, Linda Tillery, Marvin Gaye, Gil Scott-Heron, Howlin' Wolf, and Malo.

48. The relationship of the indies to the majors is succinctly summarized by Simon Frith: "In the fifties an increasing number of independent record companies . . . emerged to service the music markets ignored by the major companies as too small" (1983, 23).

49. KZAP, quite publicly, was forever one step ahead of insolvency.

50. Lundvall, interview, Feb. 4, 2000.

51. Interestingly, *Head Hunters*' success also had an impact on a subsequent revival of hard-bop jazz, which I discuss later.

52. For precedent, see Ingrid Monson's discussion of "white hipness" regarding receptions of jazz in the fifties (1995), as well as Jonathan Kamin's discussion of the coinciding receptions of jazz and rock at that time (1975). The turn of the decade that marked the rise of free-form FM was an equally sensitive time.

53. Source: Arbitron (cited in Fink 1996, 131). These are roughly equivalent to format categories within the broadcast industry. In contrast to the early-seventies formats I've described, by the mid-nineties the formats were much more finely tuned, and playlist adherence within each format was strictly enforced. For comparisons, see the charts in the appendix.

54. Hancock, interview, May 27, 1998.

55. In this case, hindsight is not "twenty-twenty." No one can say for certain why the album sold so poorly. I have discussed my interpretation with both

Hancock and Lundvall, and both accept it as plausible (Hancock, interview, June 4, 1999; Lundvall, interview, Feb. 4, 2000).

56. Rosenthal 1992, 68.

57. I refer here to the awards category. Although radio-airplay formats, sales categories, and awards categories are not directly linked, there are strong correspondences among them.

58. See, e.g., Crouch 1996.

59. Moses Avalon (1998, 49–62) clearly, if alarmingly, outlines the details of production and promotion budgets.

60. Rubinson, interview, Jan. 11, 1998. This is further reflected in the fact that a record label's promotion budget normally equals its production budget for an album (paid for, it should be noted, by the artist through recoupment from artist royalties). What Rubinson describes here was industry-wide, not specific to a particular label.

61. Rubinson, interview, Jan. 11, 1998.

62. Rubinson, interview, Jan. 11, 1998.

63. Rubinson, interview, Jan. 11, 1998 (emphasis added).

64. Nicholson 1988, 120. Nicholson is quoting Jack Bruce in *Rolling Stone*, June 25, 1970, 10.

65. Nicholson 1998, 210.

66. Slaughter, interview, Feb. 11, 2000.

67. Hancock, in Sidran 1995, 268–69.

68. Summers, interview, Apr. 17, 1998.

69. Hancock, in Sidran 1995, 269–70.

70. Lundvall, interview, Feb. 4, 2000.

71. Maupin, interview, Mar. 12, 1998 (vocal stress emphasized).

72. Maupin, interview, Mar. 12, 1998.

73. Maupin, interview, Mar. 12, 1998.

74. Maupin, interview, Mar. 12, 1998.

75. Summers, interview, Apr. 17, 1998.

76. Summers, interview, Apr. 17, 1998.

Chapter 7

1. Carner 1996, 21.

2. Watkins 1994; Floyd 1995.

3. Floyd 1995, 273.

4. Kerman 1983, 180.

5. Examples include a special issue of the *Journal of the American Musicological Society* ("Music Anthropologies and Music Histories" [1995]), as well as work by Philip Brett, Gary Thomas, and Elizabeth Wood (1994); Suzanne Cusick (1991, 1987 [with Richard Leppert]); Robert Walser (1995); David Ake (2002); Travis Jackson (2000); Bernard Gendron (1995, 2002); Lewis Porter

(1998); Angela Davis (1998); Sherrie Tucker (2000); and Krin Gabbard (1995), to name just a few.

6. By way of comparison, Paul Berliner's *Thinking in Jazz* (1994) and Ingrid Monson's *Saying Something* (1995b) underscore the conception of jazz as interactive.

7. Schuller 1968, 91.

8. Gridley, Maxham, and Hoff 1989.

9. Hancock and Marsalis, in Zabor and Gabarini 1999, 350 (emphasis added).

10. Levine 1988; Grout and Palisca 1988, 656–65.

11. Marsalis and Stewart 1994, 141.

12. Radano 1993, 270.

Bibliography

Abrahams, Roger D. 1973. "Playing the Dozens." In Alan Dundes, ed., *Mother Wit from the Laughing Barrel: Readings in the Interpretation of Afro-American Folklore.* Englewood Cliffs, N.J.: Prentice-Hall. 295–309.

Adorno, Theodor W. 1976. *Introduction to the Sociology of Music.* Trans. E. B. Ashton. New York: Seabury Press.

———. 1990. "On the Fetish-Character in Music and the Regression of Listening." In Andrew Arato and Eike Gebhardt, eds., *The Essential Frankfurt School Reader.* New York: Continuum.

Agawu, Kofi. 2003. *Representing African Music: Postcolonial Notes, Queries, Positions.* New York and London: Routledge.

Ake, David. 2002. *Jazz Cultures.* Berkeley: University of California Press.

Alfonso, Barry. 1992. Liner notes to *All Day Music.* CD reissue. Avenue/Rhino R2 71042.

Amira, John, and Steven Cornelius. 1992. *The Music of Santería: Traditional Rhythms of the Bàtá Drums.* Crown Point, Ind.: White Cliffs Media.

Appadurai, Arjun. 1990. "Disjuncture and Difference in the Global Cultural Economy." *Public Culture* 2, no. 2: 1–24.

Appleton, Jon H. 1986. "Electro-acoustic Music." In Don Randel, ed., *The New Harvard Dictionary of Music.* 2d ed. Cambridge: Belknap Press of the Harvard University Press. 280–82.

Arnold, Denis, ed. 1983. *The New Oxford Companion to Music.* 2 vols. New York/Oxford: Oxford University Press.

Asante, Molefi Kete. 1988. *Afrocentricity.* Rev. ed. Trenton, N.J.: African World Press. (Orig. pub. 1980.)

Atia, Tarek. 2001a. "Conversation with the Chameleon." *Al-Ahram Weekly On-line,* April 5–11. http://weekly.ahram.org.eg/2001/528/fr2.htm (accessed December 30, 2003).

———. 2001b. "Real Jazz Comes to Town." Interview with Herbie Hancock. http://www.cairolive.com/newcairolive/frontpic/herbie.html (accessed December 30, 2003).

Avalon, Moses. 1998. *Confessions of a Record Producer: How to Survive the Scams and Shams of the Music Business.* San Francisco: Miller Freeman Books.

Baraka, Imamu Amiri. [LeRoi Jones.] 1963. *Blues People.* New York: Morrow.

———. 1967. "The Changing Same." In *Black Music.* New York: Morrow. 180–212.

———. 1996. "Homage to Miles Davis." In Gary Carner, ed., *The Miles Davis Companion: Four Decades of Commentary*. New York: Schirmer. 41–51.

———. 1997. "The Jazz Avant Garde." In Lewis Porter, ed., *Jazz: A Century of Change*. New York: Schirmer. 220–29.

Baraka, Imamu Amiri, and Amina Baraka. 1987. *The Music: Reflections on Jazz and Blues*. New York: Morrow.

Bartle, Graham. 1996. "Index of Program Areas: Jazz and Popular Music Schools and Programs: United States of America." In *International Directory of Music and Music Education Institutions*. Nedlands, Australia: Callaway International Resource Centre for Music Education at the University of Western Australia. 589–91.

Bascom, William R., and Melville J. Herskovitz, eds. 1959. *Continuity and Change in African Cultures*. Chicago: University of Chicago Press.

Bebey, Francis. 1975. *African Music: A People's Art*. Trans. Josephine Bennett. New York: L. Hill.

Berendt, Joachim. 1975. "I Wanna Make It: The Problems of Success in Jazz." *Jazz Forum* 39 (April 1975): 39–41, 55.

Bergeron, Katherine, and Philip Bohlman, eds., 1992. *Discipling Music: Musicology and Its Canons*. Chicago: University of Chicago Press.

Berliner, Paul F. 1994. *Thinking in Jazz: The Infinite Art of Improvisation*. Chicago: University of Chicago Press.

Berrios-Miranda, Marisól. 2002. "Is Salsa a Musical Genre?" In Lise Waxer, ed., *Situating Salsa: Global Markets and Local Meanings in Latin Popular Music*. New York: Routledge.

Berry, Jason. 1988. "African Cultural Memory in New Orleans Music." *Black Music Research Journal* 8, no. 1: 3–12.

Blumenthal, Bob. 1994. Liner notes to *Mwandishi Herbie Hancock: The Complete Warner Bros. Recordings*. Warner Bros. Archives 2–45732.

Bohannon, Paul, and Phillip Curtin, eds. 1995. *Africa and Africans*. 4th ed. Prospect Heights, Ill.: Waveland Press. (Orig. pub. 1964.)

Brackett, David. 2000. *Interpreting Popular Music*. Berkeley: University of California Press. (Orig. pub. 1995.)

Brett, Philip, Gary Thomas, and Elizabeth Wood, eds. 1994. *Queering the Pitch: The New Gay and Lesbian Musicology*. New York: Routledge.

Brinner, Benjamin. 1995, *Knowing Music, Making Music: Javanese Gamelan and the Theory of Musical Competence and Interactions*. Chicago: University of Chicago Press.

Broome, John. 1945. "On the Feather in *Esquire's* Bonnet." *Jazz Record*, August, 4–5.

Brown, Anthony. 1990. "Modern Drumset Artistry." *Black Perspective in Music* 18, nos. 1–2: 38–58.

Brown, James, with Bruce Tucker. 1986. *James Brown: The Godfather of Soul*. New York: Macmillan.

Budds, Michael J. 1990. *Jazz in the Sixties*. Iowa City: University of Iowa Press. (Orig. pub. 1978.)

Carner, Gary, ed. 1996. *The Miles Davis Companion: Four Decades of Commentary*. New York: Schirmer.

Carr, Ian. 1998. *Miles Davis: The Definitive Biography*. New York: Thunder's Mouth Press. (Orig. pub. 1982.)

Chambers, Jack. 1983. *Milestones: The Music and Times of Miles Davis to 1960*. New York: Morrow.

———. 1985. *Milestones: The Music and Times of Miles Davis since 1960*. New York: Morrow.

Chernoff, John Miller. 1979. *African Rhythm and African Sensibility: Aesthetics and Social Action in African Musical Terms*. Chicago: University of Chicago Press.

Clark, Tim. 1983. "How a Record Company Works." In George Martin, ed., *Making Music: The Guide to Writing, Performing, and Recording*. New York: Quill. 298–306.

"Coarse Hancock." 1974. Performance review. *Melody Maker*, October 12, 15.

Cole, Bill. 1971. Review of *Mwandishi*, by Herbie Hancock. *Down Beat*, September 16, 31.

Collier, James Lincoln. 1988. "Jazz (i)." In Barry Kornfeld, ed., *The New Grove Dictionary of Jazz*. New York/London: Macmillan Press. 1: 580–606.

Coltrane, John, with Don DeMichael. 1960. "Coltrane on Coltrane." *Down Beat*, September 29, 26–27.

Cook, Susan C. 1999. "Watching Our Step: Embodying Research, Telling Stories." In Elaine Barkin and Lydia Hamessley, eds., *Audible Traces: Gender, Sexuality, and Music*. Zürich/Los Angeles: Carciofoli, 177–212.

Cooke, Mervyn. 1999. *Jazz*. New York: Thames and Hudson.

Corea, Chick (Armando). 1971. "The Function of the Artist." *Down Beat*, October, 16.

Coryell, Julie, and Laura Friedman. 1978. *Jazz-Rock Fusion: The People, The Music*. New York: Delacourt Press.

Crawford, Richard. 1983. *The American Musical Landscape: Ernest Bloch Lectures on American Music*. Berkeley: University of California Press.

Crook, Larry. 1982. "A Musical Analysis of the Cuban Rumba." *Latin American Music Review* 3, no. 1: 92–123.

Crouch, Stanley. 1996. "Play the Right Thing." In Gary Carner, ed., *The Miles Davis Companion: Four Decades of Commentary*. New York: Schirmer. 21–40.

Dahlhaus, Carl. 1989. *Nineteenth-Century Music*. Trans. J. Bradford Robinson. California Studies in Nineteenth-Century Music. Berkeley: University of California Press.

Davis, Angela. 1998. *Blues Legacies and Black Feminism: Gertrude "Ma" Rainey, Bessie Smith, and Billie Holiday*. New York: Pantheon.

Davis, Miles, with Quincy Troupe. 1989. *Miles: The Autobiography*. New York: Simon and Schuster.

DeMichael, Don. 1962. "John Coltrane and Eric Dolphy Answer the Critics." *Down Beat*, April 12, 20–23.

DeVeaux, Scott. 1985. "Jazz in Transition: Coleman Hawkins and Howard McGhee, 1935–1945." Ph.D. diss., University of California.

———. 1991. "Constructing the Jazz Tradition: Jazz Historiography." *Black American Literature Forum* 25, no. 3: 525–60.

———. 1995. *Jazz in America: Who's Listening?* Carson, Calif.: Seven Locks Press.

———. 1997. *The Birth of Bebop: A Social and Musical History*. Berkeley: University of California Press.

Dollard, John. 1973. "The Dozens: Dialectic of Insult." In Alan Dundes, ed., *Mother Wit from the Laughing Barrel: Readings in the Interpretation of Afro-American Folklore*. Englewood Cliffs, N.J.: Prentice-Hall. 277–94.

Duckworth, William. 2003. *A Creative Approach to Music Fundamentals*, 8th ed. Belmont, Calif.: Wadsworth.

Dudley, Shannon. 1996. "Judging 'By the Beat': Calypso versus Soca." *Ethnomusicology* 40, no. 2: 269–98.

Elworth, Steven B. 1995. "Jazz in Crisis, 1948–1958." In Krin Gabbard, ed., *Jazz among the Discourses*. Durham/London: Duke University Press. 57–75.

Fay, Robert. 1999. "Afrocentrism." In Kwame Anthony Appiah and Henry Louis Gates, Jr., eds., *Africana: The Encyclopedia of the African and African American Experience*. New York: Basic Civitas Books. 45.

Feather, Leonard. 1965. *The Book of Jazz, from Then till Now: A Guide to the Entire Field*. New York: Horizon Press. 79–88.

———. 1970. "A Year of Selling Out." In *Down Beat Music '71* [Yearbook]. Chicago: Maher Publications. 10.

———. 1999. "Jazz: Goodwill Ambassador Overseas; Fighter against Jim Crow in the U.S." In Robert Walser, ed., *Keeping Time: Readings in Jazz History*. New York/Oxford: Oxford University Press. 302–5.

Feld, Steven. 1996. "pygmy POP: A Genealogy of Schizophonic Mimesis." *Yearbook for Traditional Music* 28:1–35.

Fink, Michael. 1996. *Inside the Music Industry: Creativity, Process, and Business*. 2d ed. New York: Schirmer Books. (Orig. pub. 1989.)

Floyd, Samuel A., Jr. 1995. *The Power of Black Music: Interpreting Its History from Africa to the United States*. New York/Oxford: Oxford University Press.

Frith, Simon. 1983. "Popular Music, 1950–1980." In George Martin, ed., *Making Music: The Guide to Writing, Performing, and Recording*. New York: Quill. 18–49.

Gabbard, Krin, ed. 1995. *Jazz among the Discourses*. Durham/London: Duke University Press.

———. 2005. *Rockin' Out: Popular Music in the U.S.A.*, 3rd ed. Upper Saddle River, NJ: Pearson Prentice Hall.

Gaer, Eric. 1973. "Herbie Hancock Fires His Band." *Down Beat*, August 16, 12.

Garofalo, Reebee. 2002. "Crossing Over: From Black Rhythm and Blues to White Rock 'n' Roll." In Norman Kelley, ed. *Rhythm and Business: The Political Economy of Black Music*. New York: Akashic Books. 112–37.

Gates, Henry Louis, Jr. 1988. *The Signifying Monkey: A Theory of African-American Literary Criticism*. New York: Oxford University Press.

Geertz, Clifford. 1983. *Local Knowledge: Further Essays in Interpretive Anthropology*. New York: Basic Books.

Gendron, Bernard. 1995. "'Moldy Figs' and Modernists." In Krin Gabbard, ed., *Jazz among the Discourses*. Durham/London: Duke University Press. 31–56.

———. 2002. *Between Montmartre and the Mudd Club: Popular Music and the Avant-Garde*. Chicago: University of Chicago Press.

George, Nelson. 1988. *The Death of Rhythm and Blues*. New York: Pantheon.

Gerard, Charley. 1989. *Salsa: The Rhythm of Latin Music*. Crown Point, Ind.: White Cliffs Media.

Gilbert, Mark. 2002. "Jazz-rock." In Barry Kernfeld, ed., *Grove Dictionary of Jazz*. 2d ed. http://ezproxy.library.cornell.edu:2097 (accessed October 30, 2004).

Gillespie, John Birks "Dizzy," with Al Foster. 1979. *To Be or Not . . . To Bop!* New York: Doubleday.

Gilman, Sander L. 1985. *Difference and Pathology: Stereotypes of Sexuality, Race, and Madness*. Ithaca: Cornell University Press.

Gilroy, Paul. 1991. "Sounds Authentic: Black Music, Ethnicity, and the Challenge of a Changing Same." *Black Music Research Journal* 11, no. 2: 111–36.

———. 1993. *The Black Atlantic: Modernity and Double Consciousness*. Cambridge: Harvard University Press.

Gioia, Ted. 1998. *West Coast Jazz: Modern Jazz in California, 1945–1960*. New York: Oxford University Press.

Gleason, Ralph J. 1970. Liner notes to *Bitches Brew*. Columbia CS 9996.

Gold, Robert F. 1964. *A Jazz Lexicon*. New York: A. Knopf.

Gridley, Mark C. 1983. "Clarifying Labels: Jazz, Rock, Funk, and Jazz-Rock." *Popular Music and Society* 9, no. 2: 27–33.

———. 2003. *Jazz Styles: History and Analysis*. 8th ed. Upper Saddle River, N.J.: Prentice-Hall. (Orig. pub. 1978.)

Gridley, Mark C., Robert Maxham, and Robert Hoff. 1989. "Three Approaches to Defining Jazz." *Musical Quarterly* 73, no. 4: 513–31.

Griffiths, Paul. 1983a. "Karlheinz Stockhausen." In Denis Arnold, ed., *The New Oxford Companion to Music*. New York/Oxford: Oxford University Press. 2: 1750–51.

———. 1983b. "Kryztoff Penderecki." In Denis Arnold, ed., *The New Oxford Companion to Music*. New York/Oxford: Oxford University Press. 2: 1402.

———. 1983c. "Pierre Boulez." In Denis Arnold, ed., *The New Oxford Companion to Music*. New York/Oxford: Oxford University Press. 1: 246.

Grout, Donald J., and Claude V. Palisca. 1988. *A History of Western Music*. 4th ed. New York/London: W. W. Norton.

Guilbault, Jocelyne. 1993. *Zouk: World Music in the West Indies*. Chicago: University of Chicago Press.

Gushee, Lawrence. 1997. "The Nineteenth-Century Origins of Jazz." In Lewis Porter, ed., *Jazz: A Century of Change*. New York: Schirmer. 92–119.

Hall, Gregg. 1974. "Teo: The Man behind the Scene." *Down Beat*, July 18, 13–15.

Hancock, Herbie. 1971. Interview. *Melody Maker*, August 7, 8.

Hebdige, Dick. 1979. *Subculture: The Meaning of Style*. London: Methuen.

———. 1987. *Cut 'n' Mix: Culture, Identity, and Caribbean Music*. London: Methuen.

Heckathorn, Douglas D., and Joan Jeffri. 2001. "Finding the Beat: Using Respondent-Driven Sampling to Study Jazz Musicians." *Poetics* 28, no. 4: 307–29.

Heckman, Don. 1995. "Watermelon Man: Herbie Hancock." In Frank Alkyer, ed., *Down Beat: Sixty Years of Jazz*. Milwaukee: Hal Leonard Corp. 131–33.

Hentoff, Nat. 1956. "Jazz Messengers Blazing a Spirited Trail." *Down Beat*, February 22, 10.

———. 1961a. "An Afternoon with Miles Davis." In Martin Williams, ed., *Jazz Panorama*. New York: Cowell-Collier. 167–68.

———. 1961b. *The Jazz Life*. New York: Dial.

Hentoff, Nat, and Albert McCarthy. 1959. *Jazz*. New York: Rinehart.

Herskovitz, Melville. 1958. *Myth of the Negro Past*. Boston: Beacon Press. (Orig. pub. 1941.)

Hirsch, Paul. 1985. *The Structure of the Popular Music Industry: The Filtering Process by which Records Are Preselected for Public Consumption*. Ann Arbor: Institute for Social Research, University of Michigan.

Hoffman, Frank, and George Albert. 1998. *Cash Box Album Charts, 1955–1974*. Metuchen, N.J.: Scarecrow Press.

Houston, B. 1965. "Herbie Hancock." Review of *Empyrean Isles*. *Melody Maker*, February 13, 14.

———. 1967. "Michelangelo Antonioni's film *Blow Up*." *Melody Maker*, May 27, 10.

Jackson, Bruce. 1974. *"Get Your Ass Out of the Water and Swim Like Me": Narrative Poetry from the Black Oral Tradition*. Cambridge: Harvard University Press.

Jackson, Travis A. 2000. "Jazz Performance as Ritual: The Blues Aesthetic and the African Diaspora." In Ingrid Monson, ed., *The African Diaspora: A Musical Approach*. New York: Garland. 23–82.

Jahn, Janheinz. 1961. *Muntu: An Outline of the New African Culture*. Trans. Marjorie Grene. New York: Grove.

Jost, Ekkehard. 1981. *Free Jazz*. New York: Da Capo. (Orig. pub. 1974.)

Kamin, Jonathan. 1975. "Parallels in the Social Reactions to Jazz and Rock." *The Black Perspective in Music* 3, no. 3: 278–98.

Keepnews, Orrin. 1988. *The View from Within: Jazz Writings, 1948–1987*. New York: Oxford University Press.

Keil, Charles. 1966. *Urban Blues*. Chicago: University of Chicago Press.

———. 1987. "Participatory Discrepancies and the Power of Music." *Cultural Anthropology* 2, no. 3: 275–83.

———. 1995. "The Theory of Participatory Discrepancies: A Progress Report." *Ethnomusicology* 39, no. 1: 1–20.

Kerman, Joseph. 1983. *Contemplating Music: Challenges to Musicology*. Cambridge: Harvard University Press.

Kernfeld, Barry. 1981. "Adderley, Coltrane, and Davis at the Twilight of Bebop: The Search for Melodic Coherence (1958–1959)." Ph.D. diss., Cornell University.

Kmen, Henry A. 1966. *Music in New Orleans: The Formative Years, 1791–1841*. Baton Rouge: Louisiana State University Press.

Kofsky, Frank. 1970. *Black Nationalism and the Revolution in Music*. New York: Pathfinder.

———. 1998. *Black Music, White Business: Illuminating the History and Political Economy of Jazz*. New York: Pathfinder.

Ladzekpo, C. K. 1995. "Foundation Course in African Dance-Drumming." http://www.cnmat.berkeley.edu/~ladzekpo/Foundation.html (accessed December 8, 2003).

Larson, Gary. 1973. "Headhunters." Performance review. *Down Beat*, November 8: 36

Levine, Lawrence. *Highbrow/Lowbrow: The Emergence of Cultural Hierarchy in America*. Cambridge: Harvard University Press.

Ligon, Bert. 2001. *Jazz Theory Resources: Tonal, Harmonic, Melodic, and Rhythmic Organization of Jazz*. Milwaukee: Houston Publishing.

Lipsitz, George. 1990. *Time Passages: Collective Memory and American Popular Culture*. Minneapolis: University of Minnesota Press.

Litweiler, John. 1984. *The Freedom Principle: Jazz after 1958*. New York: Morrow.

Locke, David. 1987. *Drum Gahu: A Systematic Method for an African Percussion Piece*. Crown Point, Ind.: White Cliffs Media.

———. 1992. *Kpegisu: A War Drum of the Ewe*. Featuring Godwin Agbeli. Tempe, Ariz.: White Cliffs Media.

Lott, Eric. 1995. "Double V, Double-Time: Bebop's Politics of Style." In Krin Gabbard, ed., *Jazz Among the Discourses*. Durham: Duke University Press. 243–55.

Lowenthal, Sandy. 1983. "Instruments in Combination." In George Martin, ed., *Making Music: The Guide to Writing, Performing, and Recording*. New York: Quill. 196–204.

Loza, Steven. 2002. "Poncho Sánchez, Latin Jazz, and the Cuban *Son*: A Stylistic and Social Analysis." In Lise Waxer, ed., *Situating Salsa: Global Markets and Local Meanings in Latin Popular Music*. New York and London: Routledge, 201–15.

Mailer, Norman. 1999. "The White Negro: Superficial Reflections on the Hipster." In Robert Walser, ed., *Keeping Time: Readings in Jazz History*. New York/Oxford: Oxford University Press. 242–46.

Marsalis, Wynton. 1990. "Why We Must Preserve Our Jazz Heritage; Trumpet Virtuoso Says Rich Musical Legacy Is Crucial to Black Identity." *The Best of Ebony: 45th Anniversary Edition* (November 1990): 159–64.

Marsalis, Wynton, and Frank Stewart. 1994. *Sweet Swing Blues on the Road*. New York: W. W. Morrow.

Martin, George, ed. 1983. *Making Music: The Guide to Writing, Performing, and Recording*. New York: Quill.

———, with William Pearson. 1995. *With a Little Help From My Friends: The Making of Sgt. Pepper, vol. 1*. New York: Little, Brown.

Martin, Waldo E., Jr., and Patricia Sullivan, eds. 2000. *Civil Rights in the United States*. New York: Macmillan Reference.

Maultsby, Portia. 1990. "Africanisms in African-American Music." In Joseph Holloway, ed., *Africanisms in American Cultures*. Bloomington: Indiana University Press. 185–210.

McClary, Susan. 1991. *Feminine Endings: Music, Gender, and Sexuality*. Minneapolis: University of Minnesota Press.

McClary, Susan, and Richard Leppert, eds. 1987. *Music and Society: The Politics of Composition, Performance, and Reception.* New York: Cambridge University Press.

McDonough, Jack. 1985. *San Francisco Rock: The Illustrated History of San Francisco Rock Music, 1965–1985.* San Francisco: Chronicle Books.

Meadow, Eliot. 1973. "Meet Bennie Maupin." *Down Beat,* January 18, 15–17.

Mercer, Kobena. 1990. "Black Hair/Style Politics." In Russell Ferguson, Martha Gever, Trinh T. Minh-Ha, and Cornell West, eds., *Out There: Marginalization and Contemporary Cultures.* Cambridge: MIT Press. 247–64.

Merriam, Alan P. 1958. "African Music." In William Bascom and Melville Herskovitz, eds., *Continuity and Change in African Cultures.* Chicago: University of Chicago Press. 49–86.

Micallef, Ken. 1995. "Critical Mass: On the History of Fusion." *Jazzis* 12, no. 6: 73–77.

Middleton, Richard. 2004. "Pop." In L. Macy, ed., *Grove Music Online.* Oxford: Oxford University Press. http://www.grovemusic.com (accessed February 24, 2004).

Milkowski, Bill. 1995. *Jaco: The Extraordinary and Tragic Life of Jaco Pastorius, "The World's Greatest Bass Player."* San Francisco: Miller Freedman Books.

Mintz, Sidney W. 1989. *Caribbean Transformations.* New York: Columbia University Press.

Mitchell-Kernan, Claudia. 1973. "Signifying." In Alan Dundes, ed., *Mother Wit from the Laughing Barrel: Readings in the Interpretation of Afro-American Folklore.* Englewood Cliffs, N.J.: Prentice-Hall. 310–28.

Monson, Ingrid A. 1994. "Doubleness and Jazz Improvisation: Irony, Parody, and Ethnomusicology." *Critical Inquiry* 20:283–313.

———. 1995. "The Problem with White Hipness: Race, Gender, and Cultural Conceptions in Jazz Historical Discourse." *Journal of the American Musicological Society* 48, no. 3: 396–422.

———. 1996. *Saying Something: Jazz Improvisation and Interaction.* Chicago: University of Chicago Press.

———, ed. 2000. *The African Diaspora: A Musical Approach.* New York: Garland.

Morgan, A. J. 1975. "Jazzmen Play New Tune: 'Please Don't Call It Jazz.'" *Soul,* May 26, 18, 20.

Neer, Richard. 2001. *FM: The Rise and Fall of Rock Radio.* New York: Random House.

Nicholson, Stuart. 1995. *Jazz: The 1980s Resurgence.* New York: Da Capo Press. (Orig. pub. 1990.)

———. 1998. *Jazz-Rock: A History.* New York: Schirmer.

1999–2000 Jazz Education Guide. 1999. Special supplement to *Jazz Times.* Silver Spring, Md.: Jazz Times.

Nisensen, Eric. 1997. *Blue: The Murder of Jazz.* New York: St. Martin's Press.

Nketia, J. H. Kwabena. 1962. *Unity and Diversity in African Music: A Problem of Synthesis.* Accra: University of Ghana Press.

Nolan, Herb. 1977. "Elvin Jones—Rhythmic Pulsemaster." *Down Beat,* December 15, 14.

Oliver, Paul. 1970. *Savannah Syncopators: African Retentions in the Blues*. New York: Stein and Day.

Oliver, Roland, and J. D. Fage. 1962. *A Short History of Africa*. New York: Viking Penguin.

Olmos, Margarite Fernández, and Lizabeth Paravisini-Gebert. 2003. *Creole Religions of the Caribbean: An Introduction from Vodou and Santería to Obeah and Espiritismo*. New York: New York University Press.

Palmer, Bob. 1974. "Jazz/Rock '74: The Plain Funky Truth." *Rolling Stone*, August, 16–17.

Panish, Jon. 1997. *The Color of Jazz: Race and Representation in Postwar American Culture*. Jackson: University of Mississippi Press.

Pekar, Harvey. 1976. "Miles Davis 1964–1969 Recordings." *Coda* 147, no. 8 (May): 8–14.

Peterson, Richard A. 1972. "Market and Moralist Censors of a Black Art Form: Jazz." In R. Serge Denisoff and Richard A. Peterson, eds., *The Sound of Social Change*. New York: Rand McNally. 236–45.

Pond, Steven F. 1997. "Jazz/Rock Fusion in the Studio: Improvisation and Competence." Paper presented at the Annual Conference of the Society for Ethnomusicology, October 25.

———. 1998a. "Crossing Over: Bob James, the Record Industry, and the Question of Genre." Paper presented at the annual meeting of the Northern California Chapter, Society for Ethnomusicology, March 1.

———. 1998b. "The Boundaries of Genre: Bob James and the Master Narrative." Paper presented at the annual meeting of the International Association for the Study of Popular Music, October 16.

———. 2002. Review of *Jazz* (Ken Burns, dir.) *Ethnomusicology* 46 no. 3 (fall): 553–56.

———. 2003. "Jamming the Reception: Ken Burns, *Jazz*, and the Problem of 'America's Music.'" *Notes: Journal of the Music Library Association* (September 2003): 11–45.

Porter, Lewis. 1982a. "An Historical Survey of Jazz Drumming Styles, Part 1." *Percussive Notes* 4 (June): 42–43, 70–72.

———. 1982b. "An Historical Survey of Jazz Drumming Styles, Part 2." *Percussive Notes* 4 (October): 46–47, 77–78.

———, ed. 1997. *Jazz: A Century of Change*. New York: Schirmer.

———. 1998. *John Coltrane: His Life and Music*. Ann Arbor: University of Michigan Press.

Porter, Lewis, and Michael Ullman. 1993. *Jazz: From Its Origins to the Present*. Englewood Cliffs, N.J.: Prentice-Hall.

Powers, Harold S. 1986. "Melody." In Don Randel, ed., *The New Harvard Dictionary of Music*. Cambridge, Mass.: The Belknap Press of Harvard University Press, 481–84.

Quersin, Benoit. 1963. "An Uncommon Market for Jazz in Europe." *Down Beat*, April 25, 12.

Radano, Ronald M. 1993. *New Musical Figurations: Anthony Braxton's Cultural Critique*. Chicago/London: University of Chicago Press.

Ravel, Maurice. 1911. *Fragments symphoniques (Suite no. 1).* Nocturne, Interlude, Danse guerrière from *Daphnis et Chloé.*

———. 1912. *Daphnis et Chloé.* Symphonie chorégraphique, 3 parts. M. Fokine and Ravel, after Longus, 1909–12. Paris: Châtelet.

———. 1913. *Fragments symphoniques II (Suite no. 2).* Lever du jour, Pantomime, Danse générale from *Daphnis et Chloé.*

Redd, Lawrence N. 1974. *Rock Is Rhythm and Blues: The Impact of Mass Media.* East Lansing: Michigan State University Press.

Rivelli, Pauline, and Robert Levin, eds. 1970. *The Black Giants.* New York/Cleveland: The World Publishing.

Roberts, John Storm. 1979. *The Latin Tinge: The Impact of Latin American Music on the United States.* New York: Oxford University Press.

———. 1998. *Black Music of Two Worlds.* 2d ed. New York: Schirmer.

———. 1999. *Latin Jazz: The First of the Fusions, 1880s to Today.* New York: Schirmer.

Roediger, David R. 1994. *Towards the Abolition of Whiteness.* London: Verso.

Rosenthal, David H. 1992. *Hard Bop: Jazz and Black Music 1955–1965.* New York/Oxford: Oxford University Press.

Russell, George. 1959. *The Lydian Concept of Tonal Organization.* New York: Concept Publishing.

Sales, Grover. 1992. *Jazz: America's Classical Music.* New York: Da Capo Press. (Orig. pub. 1984.)

Santoro, Gene. 1997. *Stir It Up: Musical Mixes from Roots to Jazz.* New York: Oxford University Press.

Saussure, Ferdinand de. 1966. *Course in General Linguistics.* Ed. Charles Bally and Albert Sechbechaye. Trans. Waade Baskin. New York: McGraw-Hill.

Schenker, Heinrich. 1994. "The Masterwork in Music." Trans. William Drabkin, vol. 1 Cambridge/New York: Cambridge University Press. (Orig. publ. 1925.)

Scherman, Tony. 1995. "What Is Jazz?" Interview with Wynton Marsalis. *American Heritage* (October 1995): 66–85.

Schuller, Gunther. 1968. *Early Jazz: Its Roots and Musical Development.* New York: Oxford University Press.

———. 1979. "Sonny Rollins and Thematic Improvising." In Martin Williams, ed., *Jazz Panorama.* New York: Da Capo Press. 168.

———. 1989. *The Swing Era: The Development of Jazz, 1930–1945.* New York: Oxford University Press.

Segrave, Kerry. 2002. *Jukeboxes: An American Social History.* Jefferson, N.C./London: McFarland.

Sidran, Ben. 1995. *Talking Jazz: An Illustrated Oral History.* New York: Da Capo Press (Orig. pub. 1992.)

Silvert, Conrad. 1977. Liner notes to *V.S.O.P.: The Quintet.* Columbia 34976.

Simmel, Georg. 1955. *Conflict and the Web of Group-Affiliations.* Trans. K. Wolff and R. Bendix. New York: Free Press. (Orig. pub. 1922.)

Slobin, Mark. 1992. "Micromusics of the West: A Comparative Approach." *Ethnomusicology* 36, no. 1: 1–88.

Slonimsky, Nicholas. 1947. *Thesaurus of Scales and Melodic Patterns.* New York: Coleman-Ross.

Smitherman, Geneva. 1986. *Talkin and Testifyin: The Language of Black America.* Detroit: Wayne State University Press.

Southern, Eileen. 1997. *The Music of Black Americans: A History.* 3d ed. New York: W. W. Norton. (Orig. pub. 1971.)

Stanton, Kenneth. 1982. *Jazz Theory: A Creative Approach.* New York: Taplinger.

Stearns, Marshall W. 1972. *The Story of Jazz.* New York/Oxford: Oxford University Press. (Orig. pub. 1956.)

Stuckey, Sterling. 1987. *Slave Culture, Nationalist Theory, and the Foundations of Black America.* New York: Oxford University Press.

Szwed, John. 2000. *Jazz 101: A Complete Guide to Learning and Loving Jazz.* New York: Hyperion.

Taylor, William "Billy." 1999. "Jazz: America's Classical Music." In Robert Walser, ed., *Keeping Time: Readings in Jazz History.* New York/Oxford: Oxford University Press, 327–32.

Thompson, Robert Farris. 1983. *Flash of the Spirit: African and Afro-American Art and Philosophy.* New York: Random House.

Thompson, Scott H. 1992. Liner notes to *Head Hunters.* CD reissue. Columbia/Legacy CK47478.

Tirro, Frank. *Jazz: A History,* 2nd ed. New York: W. W. Norton.

Toll, Robert C. 1977. *Blacking Up: The Minstrel Show in Nineteenth Century America.* New York/London: Oxford University Press. (Orig. pub. 1974.)

Tomlinson, Gary. 1993. *Music in Renaissance Magic: Toward a Historiography of Others.* Chicago: University of Chicago Press.

Townley, Ray. 1974. "Muhal Richard Abrams." Interview. *Down Beat,* August 15, 34.

———. 1975. "Bennie Maupin: Not to Be Confused with Bernie Taupin." *Down Beat,* May 22, 17–19.

Tucker, Sherrie. 2000. *Swing Shift: "All-Girl" Bands of the 1940s.* Durham: Duke University Press.

Turner, Jonathan. 1988. *A Theory of Social Interaction.* Stanford: Stanford University Press.

Underwood, Lee. 1975. "Around the World: Los Angeles." *Coda* 143 (Nov.): 30.

Vincent, Rickey. 1996. *Funk: The Music, the People, and the Rhythm of the One.* New York: St. Martin's/Griffin.

Waksman, Steve. 2000. *Instruments of Desire: The Electric Guitar and the Shaping of Musical Experience.* Cambridge: Harvard University Press.

Walser, Robert. 1995. "Rhythm, Rhyme, and Rhetoric in the Music of Public Enemy." *Ethnomusicology* 39, no. 2: 193–217.

———, ed. 1999. *Keeping Time: Readings in Jazz History.* New York/Oxford: Oxford University Press.

Washington, Joseph R., Jr. 1964. *Black Religion: The Negro and Christianity in the United States.* Boston: Beacon Press.

Waterman, Christopher A. 1990. *Jùjú: A Social History and Ethnography of an African Popular Music.* Chicago: University of Chicago Press.

Watkins, Glenn. 1994. *Pyramids at the Louvre: Music, Culture, and Collage from Stravinsky to the Post-Modernists.* Cambridge: Belknap Press of Harvard University.

Welding, Pete, and John Tynan. 1962. "Double View of a Double Quartet." *Down Beat,* January 18, 18.

Whitburn, Joel. 2000. *Joel Whitburn's Top Pop Albums, 1955–2001.* Menomonee Falls, Wis.: Record Research.

Williams, Martin. 1961. *Jazz Panorama.* New York: Cowell-Collier.

———. 1970. *The Jazz Tradition.* New York: Oxford University Press.

———, ed. 1997. *The Smithsonian Collection of Classic Jazz.* Booklet. Smithsonian Collection of Recordings. Smithsonian A5 19477. (Orig. pub. 1973.)

Wilmer, Valerie. 1967. "Herbie—One of New York's Inner Circle." *Melody Maker,* September 23, 8.

Wilson, Olly O. 1974. "The Significance of the Relationship between Afro-American Music and the West." *Black Perspective in Music* 2, no. 1: 2–22.

———. 1983. "Black Music as an Art Form." *Black Music Research Journal* 3, 1–22.

———. 1992. "The Heterogeneous Sound Ideal in African-American Music." In Samuel A. Floyd Jr. and Josephine Wright, eds., *New Perspectives in Music: Essays in Honor of Eileen Southern.* Warren, Mich.: Harmonie Park Press. 326–37.

Wittgenstein, Ludwig. 1953. *Philosophical Investigations.* Trans. G. E. M. Anscombe. Oxford: Blackwell.

Woideck, Carl. 1998. *Charlie Parker Companion: Six Decades of Commentary.* New York: Schirmer.

Zabor, Rafi, and Vic Garbarini. 1999. "Wynton Marsalis vs. Herbie: The Purist and the Crossbreeder Duke It Out." In Robert Walser, ed. *Keeping Time: Readings in Jazz History.* New York/Oxford: Oxford University Press. 339–51.

Zak, Alban J., III. 2001. *The Poetics of Rock: Cutting Tracks, Making Records.* Berkeley: University of California Press.

Discography

Adderley, Cannonball. *The Cannonball Adderley Quintet: Paris, 1960*. Pablo 5303, 1997.

Allman Brothers. *Eat A Peach*. Capricorn 2CP 0102, 1972. CD reissue, Mercury 000234936, 2004.

Arom, Simha, and Geneviève Taurelle. *The Music of the Ba-Benzélé Pygmies*. Field recording with explanatory notes. Bärenreiter Musicaphon BM 30 L 2303, 1966.

Average White Band. *AWB*. Atlantic 7308. CD reissue, Rhino 71588, 1995.

Azteca. *Azteca*. Columbia 31776, 1972. CD reissue, GNP Crescendo 2237, 1995.

Basie, William "Count." *The Essential Count Basie, vol. 1*. Columbia CK 40608, 1936–39.

The Beatles. *Sgt. Pepper's Lonely Hearts Club Band*. Capitol/Parlophone CDP 7 46442-2, 1967. CD reissue, Capitol C2-46442, 1987.

Benson, George. *Breezin'*. Warner Bros. BS 2919, 1976. CD reissue, Rhino 76713, 2001.

Blakey, Art, and Horace Silver. *The Jazz Messengers*. Columbia C 897, 1956. CD reissue, Columbia/Legacy 65265, 1997.

The Blue Note Years: Sixtieth Anniversary Box Set: 1939–1999. Blue Note 4964272 14, 1998.

Brown, James. *James Brown: Twenty All Time Greatest Hits!* Polydor/Polygram 314-511-326-2, 1991.

———. *Papa's Got a Brand New Bag*. Polydor/Polygram 847 982, 1965. CD reissue, Special Music 847982, 1992.

Brubeck, Dave. *Time Out*. Columbia CL 1397, 1959. CD reissue, Sony 65122, 2004.

Coleman, Ornette. *Free Jazz: A Collective Improvisation*. Atlantic 1364, 1960. CD reissue, Rhino 75208, 1998.

Coltrane, John. *The Best of John Coltrane: His Greatest Years*. Impulse! AS-9200-2, 1970. CD reissue, Impulse! 549913, 2001.

Davis, Miles. *Big Fun*. Columbia: PG 32866, 1974. CD reissue, Columbia/Legacy 63973, 2000.

———. *Bitches Brew*. Columbia CS 9995-9996, 1970. CD reissue: Columbia/Legacy 65774, 1999.

———. *Complete Bitches Brew Sessions (August 1969–February 1970)*. Columbia/Legacy CD 65570, 1998.

———. *E.S.P.* Columbia 9150, 1965. CD reissue, Columbia/Legacy 65683, 1998.
———. *Filles de Kilimanjaro.* Columbia CS 9750, 1968. CD reissue, Columbia/Legacy 86555, 2002.
———. *In a Silent Way.* Columbia CS 9875, 1969. CD reissue, Columbia/Legacy 86556, 2002.
———. *Kind of Blue.* Columbia 8163, 1959. CD reissue, Columbia/Legacy 64935, 1997.
———. *Miles in the Sky.* Columbia CS 9628, 1968. CD reissue, Columbia/Legacy 65684, 1998.
———. *The Sorcerer.* Columbia 52947 [CL2732], 1967. CD reissue, Columbia/Legacy 65680, 1998.
Ellington, Duke. *Black, Brown, and Beige.* Columbia JCS 8015 (recorded 1944–46). CD reissue. Columbia/Legacy 65566, 1999.
Evans, Bill. *Bill Evans: The Complete Riverside Recordings.* Riverside R-018, 1984. CD reissue, Riverside 12RCD-018–2, n.d.
Gillespie, Dizzy. *Dizzy Gillespie and His Orchestra: 1947–1949.* Classics 1102, 2000.
Guaraldi, Vince. *Jazz Impressions of Black Orpheus.* Fantasy 8089, 1962. CD reissue, Fantasy/OJC 437, 1995.
Hancock, Herbie. *The Best of Herbie Hancock: The Blue Note Years.* Blue Note CDP 7 91142 2, 1988.
———. *Crossings.* Warner Bros. BS 2617, 1971. Included in CD anthology *Mwandishi Herbie Hancock: The Complete Warner Bros. Recordings.*
———. *Dis Is Da Drum.* Mercury 314 522 681–2, 1995.
———. *Fat Albert Rotunda.* Warner Bros. WS 1834, 1970. Included in CD anthology *Mwandishi Herbie Hancock: The Complete Warner Bros. Recordings.*
———. *Flood.* Columbia (Japan) 1835, 1977 (recorded 1975). CD reissue, Sony 35439, 1999.
———. *Future Shock.* Columbia 25540, 1983. CD reissue, Columbia CK-38814, 2000.
———. *Head Hunters.* Columbia 32731, 1973. CD reissue, Columbia/Legacy CK 47478, 1992.
———. *Maiden Voyage.* Blue Note 40020, 1966 (recorded 1965). CD reissue, Blue Note 46339, 1997.
———. *Man-Child.* Columbia 33812, 1975. CD reissue, Sony 9501, 1999.
———. *Mwandishi.* Warner Bros. WS 1898, 1971. Included in CD anthology *Mwandishi Herbie Hancock: The Complete Warner Bros. Recordings.*
———. *Mwandishi Herbie Hancock: The Complete Warner Bros. Recordings.* Warner Archives 9-45732–2, 1994.
———. *Sextant.* Columbia KC 32212, 1972. CD reissue, Columbia/Legacy 64983, 1998.
———. *Sunlight.* Columbia 34906, 1978 (recorded 1977). CD reissue, Sony 486570, 2001.
———. *Takin' Off.* Blue Note BST-84109, 1962. CD reissue, Blue Note B2–46506, 1987.
The Headhunters. *Evolution Revolution.* Basin St. 0601, 2003.

———. *Return of the Headhunters!* Verve/Forecast 314539028–2, 1998.
———. *Straight from the Gate.* Arista 4146, 1977. CD reissue, BMG Intl. 40953, 2001.
———. *Survival of the Fittest.* Arista 4038, 1975. CD reissue, BMG 140952, 2004.
James, Bob. *One.* CTI Records CTI 6043, 1974. CD reissue, Tappan Zee 45964, 1995.
Lewis, Ramsey. *Ramsey Lewis Trio: The In Crowd.* Cadet LPS 757, 1965.
Mahavishnu Orchestra. *Birds of Fire.* Columbia KC 31996, 1973 (recorded 1972). CD reissue, Columbia/Legacy 66081, 2000.
———. *The Inner Mounting Flame.* Columbia 31067, 1971. CD reissue, Columbia/Legacy 65523, 1998.
McCann, Les, and Eddie Harris. *Swiss Movement: Live at the Montreux Jazz Festival.* Atlantic: SD 1537, 1969. CD reissue, Rhino R2–72452, 1996.
Monk, Thelonious. *Genius of Modern Music, vol. 1.* Blue Note 81510, 1947.
Morgan, Lee. *Caramba.* Liberty 8946, 1970. CD reissue, Blue Note 56658B, 1996.
———. *Live at the Lighthouse.* Blue Note 2–89906, 1970. CD reissue, Blue Note 35228, 1996.
———. *The Sidewinder.* Blue Note BST-84157, 1964. CD reissue, Blue Note B2–84157, 1989.
Moreira, Airto. *Virgin Land.* Salvation SAL 701, 1974. CD reissue, King Japan 8115, 2001.
Nagano, Kent and the London Symphony Orchestra and Chorus. *Daphnis et Chloé, Ballet for Orchestra.* Erato 91712, 1992.
Powell, Bud. *The Amazing Bud Powell, vol. 1.* Blue Note B2–8153, 1989.
Return to Forever. *Hymn of the Seventh Galaxy.* Polydor 5536, 1973. CD reissue, Polydor 825336–2, 1991.
———. *Light as a Feather.* Polydor PD 5525, 1973. CD reissue, Polydor 827148–2, 1991.
Rollins, Sonny. *Saxophone Colossus.* Prestige/OJC 291, 1956. CD reissue, JVC 60158, 2000.
Santamaria, Mongo. *Watermelon Man.* Battle 6120, 1963. CD reissue, Milestone MCD-47075–2, 1998.
Scott, Tom. *Tom Scott and the LA Express.* Ode/A&M PET 34952, 1974. CD reissue, Sony 64959, 1996.
Shaw, Woody. *Blackstone Legacy.* Contemporary 7627/8, 1970. CD reissue, Contemporary 762728, 1999.
Silver, Horace. *The Best of Horace Silver.* Blue Note BST-84325, 1968. CD reissue Blue Note 66034, 2004.
———. *Horace Silver and the Jazz Messengers.* Blue Note BST-81518, 1955. CD reissue, Blue Note B2–46140, 1987.
———. *The Horace Silver Trio & Art Blakey & Sabu.* Blue Note 1520, 1952. CD reissue, Blue Note 9142, 2004.
———. *Serenade to a Soul Sister.* Blue Note 84277, 1968. CD reissue, Blue Note 94321, 2004.

———. *Song for My Father*. Blue Note 84185, 1963–64. CD reissue, Blue Note B2-85195, 1989.

———. *You Gotta Take a Little Love*. Blue Note BST-84309, 1969.

Simmo, Geoffrey and the Philharmonia Orchestra of London. *Maurice Ravel, vol. 2*. Cala 1005, 1991.

Sly and the Family Stone. *Sly and the Family Stone: Greatest Hits*. Epic EK 30325, 1971. CD reissue, CD 30325, 1990.

———. *Stand!* Epic BN 26456, 1969. CD reissue, Epic 64452, 1995.

Smithsonian Collection of Classic Jazz. Smithsonian Folkways A5 19477, 1973. CD reissue 1991.

Snow, Phoebe. *Phoebe Snow*. ABC/Shelter SRL 52017, 1974. CD reissue, The Right Stuff 31972, 1995.

Tower of Power. *Bump City*. Warner Brothers 2616, 1972. CD reissue, Warner Brothers 2616, 1993.

———. *Tower of Power*. Warner Brothers 2681, 1973. CD reissue, Warner Brothers 2-2681, 1990.

V.S.O.P. *Live under the Sky*. Sony 87165, 1979. CD reissue, 2004 (recorded 1979).

———. *V.S.O.P.: The Quintet*. Columbia 34976, 1977. CD reissue, Sony 9654, 2001.

———. *V.S.O.P., Vol. 1*. Columbia 34668, 1977 (recorded 1976).

———. *V.S.O.P., Vol. 2*. Columbia FC-40015, 1977.

———. *V.S.O.P.* CD reissue of V.S.O.P. vols. 1 and 2, Sony (Japan) SRCS 9195–6, 1997.

War. *All Day Music*. United Artists 5546, 1971. CD reissue, A Street 10605, 1995.

Washington, Grover, Jr. *Inner City Blues*. Kudu 03, 1972. CD reissue, Motown Jazz 530577, 1995.

Weather Report. *I Sing the Body Electric*. Columbia PC 31352, 1972. CD reissue, CK-46107, 1990.

———. *Mysterious Traveler*. Columbia CQ 32494, 1974. CD reissue, Sony 65112, 2002.

———. *Weather Report*. Columbia PCT-30661, 1971. CD reissue, Sony 9658, 2001.

Wild Cherry. *Wild Cherry*. Epic 81630, 1976. CD reissue, Columbia 34195, 1990.

Williams, Tony. *The Old Bum's Rush*. Polydor PD 5040, 1972. Included on *Spectrum: The Anthology*. Verve/Chronicles 314-537-075-2, 1997.

Credits

Interviews

(All dates indicate interviews with the author unless otherwise noted.)

Fred Catero, April 7, 1998.
Dr. Patrick Gleeson, February 28, 1997, March 5, 1997; email communication November 2, 1998.
Herbie Hancock, May 27, 1998, August 6, 1998, and June 4, 1999.
Bob James, October 9, 1996.
Bruce Lundvall, February 4, 2000.
Bennie Maupin, March 12, 1998.
David Rubinson, January 11, 1998; email communications November 4, 1997, January 2, 1998, and December 5, 2003.
Ben Sidran, August 12, 1997.
Bill Summers, April 15, 1998 and April 17, 1998.
Vernon Slaughter, February 11, 2000.

Printed Material

Jack Chambers. *Milestones.* (2 vols.) New York, HarperCollins, 1983, 1985. In the United States, the Philippines, and Open Market, used by permission of HarperCollins Publishers. In Canada, used by permission of the Bella Pomer Agency.

Miles Davis with Quincy Troupe. *Miles: The Autobiography.* New York: Simon & Schuster, 1990. In the United States, its territories, the Philippines and Canada and Open Market, used by permission from Simon & Schuster, New York. In areas outside the above, used by permission from Pan Macmillan, London.

Samuel A. Floyd, Jr. *The Power of Black Music: Interpreting Its History from Africa to the United States.* New York/Oxford: Oxford University Press, 1995. Used by permission from Oxford University Press, Inc.

Ben Sidran. *Talking Jazz: An Illustrated Oral History.* New York: Da Capo Press, 1995. Used by permission from Ben Sidran.

Vincent, Rickey. *Funk: The Music, the People, and the Rhythm of the One.* St. Martin's Griffin, 1996. Used by permission from St. Martin's Press.

CREDITS

Album Cover Images

Crossings. Reproduced courtesy of Warner Strategic Marketing, Inc.
Head Hunters. Reproduced courtesy of Columbia Records.
Sextant. Reproduced courtesy of Columbia Records.
Takin' Off. Reproduced courtesy of Blue Note Records.

Musical Transcriptions and Examples

"Chameleon" composed by Herbie Hancock, Paul Jackson, Harvey Mason, and Bennie Maupin. Copyright © 1973 by Hancock Music, renewed 2001. Used by permission.

"Make It Funky, Part II" composed by James Brown and Charles Fred Bobbit, copyright © 1971 by Dynatone Publishing Company, administered by Unichappell Music Inc. Used by permission of Warner Brothers Publications U.S. Inc.

"Sly" composed by Herbie Hancock. Copyright © 1973 by Hancock Music, renewed 2001. Used by permission.

"Vein Melter" composed by Herbie Hancock. Copyright © 1973 by Hancock Music, renewed 2001. Used by permission.

"Water Torture" composed by Bennie Maupin, copyright © 1973 by Benpin Music Co. Used by permission.

"Watermelon Man" composed by Herbie Hancock. Copyright © 1962, renewed 1990 by Hancock Music. Used by permission.

Index

INDEX

Index

Text design by Mary H. Sexton
Typesetting by Delmastype, Ann Arbor, Michigan

The text face is FFQuadraat, designed by Fred Smeijers,
and launched by FontShop International in 1992.
—Courtesy www.fontfont.com

The display font is Syntax, designed by Hans Eduard Meyer
for the Stempel foundry in 1968.
—Courtesy www.adobe.com